THE STORYTELLER

THE STORYTELLER

How Hard Can Teaching 8th Graders Be?

David L. Schapira

ISBN: 1523974370
ISBN 13: 9781523974375

ACKNOWLEDGEMENTS

I WANT TO thank the following: Rod, for walking every inch of the way through the fires with me, Dick, for your dedicated friendship during and after we retired, Karen, a more dedicated teacher I never met, Jane, Dean, Susan, Bill, Jay and Keith, all who have influenced the way I taught. I also want to thank all the other teachers and students whom I don't have the time to mention right now, for every lesson you taught me about what it takes to be a teacher of junior high children.

PROLOGUE

FINDING A JOB that DIDN'T turn into the four-letter word 'work' was the situation most adults sought in the early 1970's. As a 24-year-old man, fresh out of the army, I, Abraham Dicker Stein, had the same dream.

It seems I had three strikes against my achieving that goal when I began attending the University of Iowa in the fall of 1970. First, I have to tell you that my grades at the university had been less than stellar....poor, really....since I entered college in 1964. Secondly, the woman I married in 1968, told me, after we returned from our honeymoon and I received my draft notice, that she was anti-military. Our marital problems were compounded, upon my return from Vietnam, when she piled on by telling me that she had cheated on me with other men while I was in the war. That made for a VERY shaky start to our marriage. Finally, the only REAL physical skills I learned were taught to me while I was in the service. Somehow I didn't feel comfortable that 'I know how to blow things up,' or 'I am a guerilla war expert,' would be desirable attributes to put onto a job application.

Like many veterans, during that time in history, I felt confused and frustrated as to my future. I had tried pre-dentistry, pre-business, and just plain Liberal Arts, while at the University of Iowa....all of which came about in three different years.

In order to try and save my marriage, AND to get a fresh outlook on life, my wife and I moved to Phoenix, Arizona in the summer of 1971.

I enrolled at Arizona State University, and took an education class, trying to broaden my horizons and interests. I LOVED that class, consequently changing my entire school schedule. I wanted to become an educator.

It took me nine years after high school, but I FINALLY found my calling. I also knew I wanted to teach junior high kids. I felt younger children to be too clingy. High school kids were too set in their ways. Working with thirteen and fourteen-year-old kids, an age group trying to figure out, on a daily basis, if they were children or young adults, would prove to be a real challenge for me. From my first day working with those students, until well after I retired, (a total of 32 years of educational instruction) my life was rife with ups and downs, successes and failures, and interesting twists of fate.

Teaching is a time-honored profession, but the men and women who choose to join its ranks fight every day for the respect they so richly deserve. I offer this book as proof.

1

LET'S GET THIS STARTED

GETTING OUT OF the army, in 1970, was both a boon and a bane for me. Having survived twenty-two and a half months in the service, and ESPECIALLY having survived the war in Vietnam, I developed more confidence in myself. My new-found maturity made me feel like a more responsible person, too. I felt I could handle most any situation that came my way. I couldn't WAIT to become a student at the University of Iowa again.

My educational problem, however, was trying to decide what classes to study in order to graduate and get a good job. Before getting drafted, I had tried pre-dentistry, but didn't particularly like studying the sciences involved. I then tried to take classes in business, but found most of THOSE classes boring.

I did realize that I was no longer the platoon sergeant for a group of battle-tested veterans. Sadly, THAT was the only job I had known in quite some time. In fact, I didn't even want to TELL anyone that I had been in the army, (unless asked) because the war was so unpopular on most campuses. Soldiers were seen as scourges, and pretty much shunned….at least in Iowa City in the early seventies. I just wanted to be one of the masses of students, and move along with my life.

However, with no idea of any specific course of study to pursue, I found myself stuck taking P.E. classes, and Liberal Arts classes…. truly NOTHING to help me toward a worthwhile 40-year profession.

To make matters worse, I came home to a marriage situation that had turned tumultuous. My wife had been unfaithful to me, while I was gone, and was mostly anti-military like her peers. While she told me she had changed her infidelity-like tendencies, I only worked HARD trying to save my shaky relationship because my mother had asked me to give that cheating wench a second chance. I'm still a bit bitter as you can see.

I never really had time to experience PTSD, either. I was too busy trying to make decent grades in school, constantly worrying about who my wife was flirting with, AND I was trying my best to NOT think about my past two years.

THEN, one winter day, the missus and I got trapped in our trailer during a severe snowstorm. We had no substantial food in the home for TWO straight days. That was the last straw. I made the decision to NOT live in Iowa City, Iowa any longer. When spring-time came around, I took out a map, and my wife and I decided that we would move to the largest city in the desert that we could find. Jill saw the move as an interesting adventure. However, while I had told my wife that the weather was my reason for moving, (sleeping in the rain had been hard on me in Vietnam) and that I wanted to live in an area that had no rain or snow, I had a MUCH stronger reason to move. Jill, STILL seemed to have a strong support system (both men and women) wanting to be around her constantly. I came to realize that if I was EVER going to make my marriage work, I needed for Jill and me to find a completely different environment….a place where it would be just the two of us against the world. Phoenix looked like it would fill the bill. On a hot day in June, we packed our car and headed to the Southwestern part of America

My one regret was that I had to leave my mother in Iowa City, and that made me sad. She was aging rather poorly. Emphysema was ravaging her lungs, and I just hated leaving her while she was in such a poor state of health. I rationalized the move by realizing that I still had one brother and a sister still living in Iowa City, and a second brother, who didn't live far away.

My wife and I had a plan in place, too. We had taken ALL the money we had. First, we planned on staying in a Phoenix motel for just one week. During that week, however, Jill would have to find a teaching position for the following school year, I had to enroll into Arizona State University, we'd have to find a place to live for the next year, AND we would both have to find summer jobs.

The trip, from Iowa City to Phoenix was a pretty long journey, and might have been just fine. BUT, we had Jill's cat with us in the car, too. She had gotten the animal, against my wishes, (I wanted a dog) when I was in Vietnam. Catnip was NOT happy, EVER, and meowed most of the time we were traveling. The incessant noise caused my wife and me to have some rather heated discussions along the way. I won't get into THAT, but suffice to know that the cat, constantly making her cat noises, disturbed the hell out of me, and I could NOT stop telling Jill how much I hated riding in the car with that beast.

We had a car repair to make in Gallup, New Mexico, too, which delayed our arrival into Phoenix. Money was used that I had counted on to help us through the summer. I knew we REALLY needed to get decent jobs quickly in Phoenix, or the summer would be quite difficult for us to survive, financially.

Descending from the high country toward the desert made the inside car temperature increase drastically, and it became almost unbearable. Naturally, the stifling heat made the cat REALLY uncomfortable, which in turn, made the animal's meowing MUCH louder. At that point, even Jill was tired of the cat's racket.

But the 'fun' wasn't over for us yet. We had ANOTHER unexpected surprise develop as we headed down the mountains near Sunset Point....we hit a swarm of bees! The windshield was a mess INSTANTLY....but not as much of a mess as when Jill turned on the WINDSHIELD wipers. The smeared insect guts made vision of the road in front of us nearly impossible. By THAT time, however, Jill and I weren't even talking to one another. She didn't stop to clean the windshield, and I didn't ask her to.

FINALLY, we found a motel near downtown Phoenix. We were hot, sweaty, and disgustingly uncomfortable with one another, and I was very glad that we FINALLY could stop traveling. I really hoped the misery was over....it wasn't.

When I got out of the car, I took the cat out, too. I let her drop onto the parking lot. The drop was ONLY from about the distance of my knee, as I was bending over for the drop. I had NO idea just how hot tar could get during the blazing heat of a mid-June day in Phoenix. But the cat let me know. She landed on all fours at the same time, and catapulted, straight up into the air, to where I could reach straight out and catch her.....shoulder level. Another 'discussion' between Jill and me ensued.

The next day arrived, and we set out to get some things done. First on the list, Jill needed a teaching job. It wouldn't take too long for her to find one, but she didn't get the job she looked into, either. She was a bleeding-heart liberal, and felt compelled to work in the ghetto neighborhoods of Phoenix, which was called the Inner City. We headed to Phoenix Union High School, located in the heart of downtown Phoenix.

Jill was dressed the part of a school teacher, looking prim and proper, but the principal took one look at her, and decided the students would tear her apart. At five-foot-two, and one hundred pounds, she would have been smaller than 90% of the students in that high school. Plus, she was very attractive, and would be one of only a few White people in the school, so he feared for her safety.

He liked MY size, though, and indicated he would hire me. I told him I wasn't finished with school yet, and had no degree in education. The principal suggested the elementary school across the street, and said he would call and set up a quick interview for Jill.

I was actually surprised when the PUHS principal told me he would hire me as a teacher. I think it was because he was looking to hire men for his school. I certainly wasn't dressed for a teacher interview, that is for sure. I was wearing stove-pipe, multi-colored pants, which tapered severely at the ankles. My shirt was made of velvet, and had a deep 'V' in front, where my large 'peace medallion' necklace was hanging. I also wore blue-colored shoes, with three-inch-high, white soles. Looked like I was wearing marshmallows on my feet. Also, my hair grew, reaching below my shoulders. I wore bangs, cut straight across, which made me look like Prince Valiant. (I cut my own hair....couldn't afford haircuts) Actually, I looked like the protestors that I detested.

The elementary school across the street from Phoenix Union hired Jill that very day!

We went to Arizona State University, and I enrolled for the up-coming school year. I decided to just take Liberal Arts classes, but at least I was going to school.

Finding summer jobs didn't happen until our second day in Phoenix. I got a job driving a van for a dance school, and Jill got one in a department store, selling cosmetics.

Since we only had one car, we found an apartment, for the summer, next door to the department store. Jill could walk to work, and I would drive the four miles to my job. We would find a more permanent place to live before the start of the next school year. We moved OUT of the motel after only three days, saving us money, which we would need in order to meet our summer expenses.

Things went WELL for less than three weeks. That is when Jill got fired from her cosmetic sales job for arguing with her boss.... SEVERAL times. We were on our last financial legs, in September, when we moved to a newer apartment complex in Tempe. Jill's first pay check was a lifesaver. And we had no money problems after that.

Just before the school year began, for both Jill and me, she got a telephone call from Omaha, Nebraska. It was from the sister of Jill's best friend in high school. Abigail Zeigler was her name, and when she found out we lived in Arizona, she decided to call. Abby's husband, Benjamin, had recently gotten back from Vietnam, and wanted to return to college in order to get a teaching degree in Physical Education. He, like I, sought to be someplace where there was no snow and no rain.

The Zeiglers moved into the same apartment complex where we lived, next-door neighbors, as a matter of fact, arriving just a day or two before the fall semester began at ASU.

The Zeiglers became our very good friends. Ben and I had a lot in common, especially our love for sports. He taught me to play golf. We played basketball wherever we found a court. We went to the nearby park to play in pick-up football games. We played water volleyball with many of the apartment inhabitants. What we DIDN'T do was talk about our war experiences. That was still not an appropriate thing to do in 1972. The Zeiglers and we went snow skiing with several other couples to the White Mountains one weekend, too. And, when my best friend from Iowa City, Ike Rutkowski, came to Tempe, (spent a few months living with Jill and me) I'd have to say that was probably the best year of my young life. It certainly was the best year Jill and I had together.

The Zeiglers moved the next year, but I have kept in touch with them ever since, and they are STILL some of my best friends.

Jill and I lived in Tempe for two years, but it was early in that first year at Arizona State, when things REALLY changed for me. I took a class in education. I LOVED the class. And, when Jill asked me if I wanted to be an aide in HER class, from time to time, I accepted. I LOVED being with the kids there. Within three weeks of starting at ASU, I switched all my Liberal Arts classes to education classes. I wanted to become a teacher!

To make matters better, Jill and I ACTUALLY got along during our two years in Tempe. We had fun, too.

After Abby Zeigler's sister, Marion Hazeltine decided to move to Arizona, during the spring of 1974, Jill and SHE re-kindled the tight relationship they had as kids. With those two becoming 'best buds' again, Jill and MY relationship began to lose the closeness we had gained with the move from Iowa.

Marion and Jill had at least two things in common....both had liberal views on just about everything, and both were free spirits. I hadn't really known Marion very well, before she moved to Phoenix....having only talked to her briefly one or two times prior to Jill and my marriage. Just how liberal and free-spirited were they, you ask?

Jill and I had scheduled a vacation for the summer of 1974, which happened to be shortly after Marion had moved to Phoenix. The STEIN original plans were for Jill and me to drive to Canada for a four-day adventure, then stop in San Francisco for three nights. The vacation would be two weeks of travel and fun, just my wife and me.

Marion's move to Arizona got Jill to thinking, "Wouldn't it be a wonderful idea if Marion could join us in San Francisco, then we'd all ride back to Phoenix?" Jill mentioned to me, literally three days before the vacation was to begin. "She would fly to San Fran and stay with us in our motel rooms throughout the rest of our journey. That way Marion and I could have LOTS of time to visit. She was my best friend a long time, and I have to start school shortly after we return. It'll be fun. I'll call her right now."

Like I said, I didn't know Marion very well, but things with Jill had been going pretty well at that point. For me to question her suggestion could have made for a rough go for ME during our two-week journey. The plans were set, and Jill and I had a good time in Canada.

Once in San Francisco, Jill and I checked into our motel, then picked Marion up at the S.F. airport. The first night was comfortable. Due to Marion and my being unfamiliar with one another, extreme modesty was demonstrated in the motel room, by all THREE of us....no snoring, either.

I had made a pretty good friend, during my last year at ASU, and he lived in the San Francisco area. I gave him a call and he invited Jill, Marion and me to visit him. Told me to make sure we had swimming suits with us, since we would likely go to the Russian River for a swim.

My buddy was a free-thinking guy, who lived in a commune with two other fellows and two girls. Just as the three of us arrived at his place of residence, he said, "Let's go." We were headed to the river right way, but as we were leaving, one of the girls asked if she could 'tag along.' SO, we five people AND a huge dog, piled into his tiny car, and we were off to the river.

It took us twenty minutes, but we FINALLY could unfurl from the auto. Breaking through the brush, there were several people already at the river. "We're not swimming Here," the somewhat attractive girl said. "There is another beach where we like to swim. It's down the beach a ways, and then around the bend another quarter of a mile."

As we were walking, the girl ALSO mentioned that the beach, where we were headed, was a bathing suit OPTIONAL beach. I looked at Jill and Marion, while clutching my bathing suit and towel a little tighter.

As we rounded that bend, I saw many people in the distance. It LOOKED like more people were on the second beach than the one near our car. In addition, as we got closer and closer to the crowd, it became apparent that not only were SOME people not wearing bathing suits, NOBODY had clothes on.

I just kept my head down, looking at the sand, but within minutes we all found ourselves right in the middle of dozens and dozens of nudists. My friend and his female roommate whipped off their clothes instantly, and headed toward the water. I looked at Jill, then sheepishly at Marion. THEY were already stripping down, so I said, "What the hell." I quickly got out of my clothes, threw my towel on the sand, and lay down hurriedly....ON MY STOMACH!

We were at the beach for over two hours. Jill and Marion were like rotisseries, but me, I stayed on my stomach the entire time. I COULD have flipped over, as there wasn't anyone looking at us, nor did we stare at anybody else. I have to admit, it kind of felt normal being with ALL naked people....no arousal of any kind, from ANYBODY! The sunburn I got was painful, however.

Jill, Marion and I spent two more nights in San Francisco, and two more nights on the road back to Phoenix, and NONE of us wore clothing to bed....in ANY of the motels. That was a fun trip, and nudity seemed normal for the three of us those four nights, BUT, once we returned to Phoenix, we never talked about the nudity again.

2

THE GOOD, THE BAD, AND GETTING A JOB

E VEN THOUGH I had a little experience with kids in Jill's class, my last education class at Arizona State was a practicum, requiring me to be a student teacher at a school somewhere in the Phoenix area. The premise was that I would learn from a veteran teacher about the day-in and day-out procedures of what it took to be an educator. I would be required to 'learn' the profession, through hands-on experience, for several consecutive months. With this kind of concentrated application, I expected to find out if teaching really WAS what I wanted to do for the rest of my working life.

Having worked with Jill's tough kids in the Inner City of Phoenix, I was hoping that the placement department at Arizona State, would get me into ANY school in one of the toughest parts of town. I was, after all, a recent returnee from the war in Vietnam, and felt that handling tough kids would just be an extension of handling tough, young soldiers. I KNEW I could get the best out of troubled street urchins. After all, the kids in Jill's class seemed to respond positively toward me, and I dealt with THEM like I would with a young soldier....tough, but caring. Yep, I EXPECTED I was going to 'save' a lot of kids, and help them learn that education was THE way off the mean streets of Phoenix.

When my assignment came in, I have to admit I was disappointed. I was assigned to a district that was CLOSE to the Inner City in physical proximity, but one with a reputation for having academic excellence. It was NOT known to be a school with troubled, tough, academically-challenged kids. The students attending Brighton District were concerned with getting the best education possible, where going to college was very much the goal of most of the school's children.(and their parents) What I had learned working with Jill's kids, was that most of THEM were just concerned with surviving each day at school, and MAYBE be fortunate enough to get all the way through high school.

When I arrived at Wilhelm Elementary School, on my first day of student teaching, I was struck instantly by the different appearance of the people at my new school from the Inner City school. While Jill and I were two of the few White people on campus in HER school, Wilhelm seemed to be, maybe, 90% White. I remember only ONE Black student, though there were several Hispanic and Native American students on campus. And ALL the teachers were White. The Brighton District kids appeared more civilized, too. There wasn't a lot of chasing one another, yelling at the top of their lungs, or the use of foul language to express their feelings about things going on around them. The Wilhelm kids seemed more like young people, just being students in a school setting and wanting to learn. They were NOT the kids I was used to being around, using school as a safe haven, trying to avoid the troubling situations in their lives,

which, apparently, were omnipresent before school....after school....
even during school on many occasions.

Behaviors aside, Wilhelm dress code was different, too. At Jill's
school, casual dress for ALL teachers was expected, but NOT at
Wilhelm. Men were wearing white shirts and ties. NO female on
Wilhelm's campus, teacher or student, was allowed to wear pants of
any kind. NOBODY could wear denim, either. Most everybody I saw
had neatly cut hair, too. I, on the other hand, didn't HAVE much in
the way of acceptable school clothing. That first day, I wore the nicest
GOLF shirt I owned, but only had a pair of 'hippie' slacks to wear. I
didn't own ANY dress slacks. I wore my 'marshmallow' shoes, too.
Also, I STILL had hair that had grown to an inch or two below my
shoulders. Still had the Prince Valiant bangs, too. It was no wonder
that everyone stared at me as I walked around campus. I definitely felt
like a novelty character from a fiction book, my first day at Wilhelm,
AND most all the other days I student taught there, as well.

My assignment was in the 8th grade. My supervising teacher was
Abner Caldwell, a teacher who had fifteen years experience working
with junior high kids. He was organized and efficient, but had a play-
ful side to him, as well. When teachers would gather in the teachers' lounge before school, Abner would keep people entertained. He
pulled pranks, told jokes, and started interesting conversations. He
enjoyed playing Devil's Advocate to anyone who had an opinion on
politics, sports or any headline in the daily news. His approach to most
topics was one of common sense, and contained many country sayings,
most of which he had learned while growing up in rural Kansas.

For MY first two days in his class, Mr. Caldwell just asked me
to observe him AND the students in all six of his classes. He was
very professional and thorough in his teaching delivery. I chose

to watch his every move rather than take heavy notes. His down-home, personable teaching technique was quite effective, and I knew I would have to change from what I used as a Vietnam leader, which was ordering soldiers to do things, and adopt the more gentle approach of 'teaching.' I saw that I would have to be part sage, and part entertainer, and develop MUCH more patience, if I ever expected to keep the attention of a room full of thirteen-year-old kids.

After my third day of observation, Abner let me know what he was going to cover in his Civics classes for the fourth day, then told me I was to present HIS planned lesson, to the last Civics class of that day. He said he was interested in seeing how I would deliver the required work in my own words and style.... but all I could think about was, 'Me, teaching on the fourth day....REALLY?'

When Abner's next-to-last Civics class left the room, I walked up to the podium. I may have been older than the average student teacher of that era, but I was STILL very nervous. I avoided eye contact while MY class of Civics students entered. I chose to study my notes as long as I could. Then the tardy bell rang.

I looked up and smiled, but felt my stomach doing flip-flops. I scanned the room, looking at the faces, ALL the faces in that room. I had mostly just seen the backs of their heads for three days. But there they were, staring at me, and patiently waiting to see what I could teach them. I saw Abner, too, sitting in the back of the room with a smile stretching from ear to ear on his face. I thought he looked like the Grinch. Silence was becoming my enemy, but I still wasn't too sure how I was going to start the class.

Suddenly, I saw a girl raise her hand, so I called on her. "Are you married?" she asked, and several of the other students began to giggle....mostly the girls.

I was about to answer THAT question, when a young man, who had also raised his hand, but chose just to blurt out his question, asked, "Why aren't you wearing a tie?"

"I heard you were in Vietnam," "Did you ever play football in college?" How long are you going to be our teacher?" Questions began raining down on me. I looked toward the back where Abner sat quietly. Not only DIDN'T he interrupt, he still had that huge smile on his face.

I raised both arms and said, "All right. I don't mind answering, and I will....in time. Mr. Caldwell has asked me to deliver some important facts about today's lesson, and work with you to make sure you learn them today. If you are quick learners, then there should be plenty of time for many of your questions at the end of class. If you have trouble learning today's assignment, then I will have to answer questions another day. Besides, if I can't get you to learn today's lesson, I could get into trouble with Mr. Caldwell, and I don't want to get into trouble with him. You all seem like smart kids, and I've liked this class during my first three days. So, give me a break, learn what it is that you have to learn today, and that will give me some time to let you know all about me."

The class, except for one pain-in-the-ass, whom I will tell you about later, worked eagerly and successfully throughout the lesson. And there were EVEN four or five minutes at the end of class, which gave me time to answer several questions.

I was very proud of myself, and Abner Caldwell said to me at the end of the day, "You might just make a fine teacher one day, if you can get the work done like you did today."

I got to do a math class in my second week, and on the Thursday, of that second week at Wilhelm, Mr. Caldwell asked me when I thought I might be ready to claim a class of my own for the rest of my student teaching assignment.

I began meeting with him after school, briefly, each Friday, and discussed with him what he was going to be covering during the NEXT week. I would go home and work on MY lesson plans, as if I was going to teach. I was anxious to test myself and I felt confident.

In fact, when he, AGAIN, asked if I was ready to handle a class, I became very brave, "Mr. Caldwell," I said boldly, "I DO think I am ready to teach on my own. BUT, if you will allow me, I would like to teach every one of your varied classes....your first math class, your Current Events class, and your last-hour Civics class. THAT will force me to work on three different kinds of lesson plans. I feel that I need to challenge myself with a heavier, and more diverse workload, to see if I can handle it. AND, Mr. Caldwell, I'd like to have the classroom all to myself....I would like it if you weren't in the room. I know you have to evaluate me. But, if you could just do it from time to time, that would be great. I have to find out if I can handle three classes, WITHOUT having you, their REGULAR teacher, around to distract them or me. I need to see what I can do....just ME and the kids."

My mentor rubbed his chin, nodded his head, then said seriously, "Abe, I've never seen a more mature student teacher. The kids seem to like you, so I WANT you to feel confident that you can handle what you're asking." He hesitated for a brief moment, then continued. "I am willing to give you the chance to work three of my classes, and I will come in to observe for a WHILE, but not sit in the room for any extended length of time."

"However, if you start to feel like you are getting overwhelmed, or you need help in ANY way, I will be next door in the Teacher's Lounge. Just come get me. I want to meet with you every Friday after school, like we do now, and go over the material you plan on covering for the next week. If it meets the class work criteria, then I will let you go with it. This is ambitious, Mr. Stein, but if you want to see what teachers face, day in and day out, teaching three classes is a good start. So, I am willing to let you try it, and good luck."

He shook my hand, and I left happy, knowing that I would have three classes, but worried if I did the right thing. I prayed that I didn't chew off more than I could handle.

In addition to the students, I wasn't sure how well the rest of the faculty would accept me. I didn't look like a professional teacher, and felt a little bit shy about getting to know most of the teachers. I was very busy with MY three classes and watching Mr. Caldwell teaching his classes, so I really didn't have a LOT of time to get to know many other adults.

Fortunately, I didn't get much negative feedback from anyone, either. I may have started out wanting to student teach in an Inner City school, but, as time went by, I certainly became more and more comfortable with the Wilhelm neighborhood.

I feel compelled to tell you about the Wilhelm Teacher's Lounge, as it was back in the '70's. The faculty was eclectic for sure. Some teachers would just go into the lounge to use copying machines, the restroom, or to grab their lunches from the refrigerator. Those were the teachers who just wanted to get their business finished, and get out of there. They were NOT lounge people. The 'business' folks were all polite enough, saying 'Hello,' as they entered, but the lounge had some, shall I say, 'interesting characters' in attendance most all the time. Anyone who stayed, and chose to SIT, could become targets. Let me explain.

My third day at Wilhelm was, actually, the first day I wandered into the lounge. I had gotten to school earlier than usual that day, and knowing that Abner Caldwell enjoyed being in the lounge before school started, I went to that room to see if I could find him. He was there, along with 8-10 other teachers. Most of the chairs and couches had people sitting on them already, but I spotted a chair that was empty, and took a seat.

I hadn't said 'hello' to anyone as there was quite a bit of laughing and loud talking when I entered. However, as I sat on the chair, the room began getting unbelievably quiet. In fact, within seconds of my sitting, the room became COMPLETELY silent. It ALSO became apparent that many of the people in the room had begun staring at an elderly woman, who was sitting on a sofa located directly across the room from my chair.

Her name was Verna Street, and I found out later that she was a long-time sixth grade teacher at Wilhelm, who was planning on retiring from education at the end of the following school year.

But, on THAT day in the lounge....my FIRST day in the lounge, I was surprised at the sudden silence. I scanned the area, wondering what was up. It took a brief moment, but it finally dawned on me that not only were several teachers looking in Ms Street's direction, EVERY teacher was looking at her. Soooo, I casually glanced in her direction, too. SHE seemed to be staring at ME. No, let me re-phrase, she was DEFINITELY staring at me....and rather intently, too, I might add. Her steely-blue eyes were fixated on me, and I felt like she was a lioness focused on her next meal, which, in turn, made me feel a little uncomfortable.

Suddenly, she rose to her feet, and dramatically walked across the room, heading specifically in my direction. She stood right in front of me for a few seconds. THEN, she sat on my lap, put her arm around my neck, looked deeply into my eyes, and said in a sultry voice, "Welcome to the lounge."

Everybody else in the room broke out into hysterical laughter. Verna got off my lap, and dramatically vamped her way BACK to where she had been sitting. Abner Caldwell introduced me, and right away, I KNEW I was going to enjoy being in that room with the rest of the lounge lizards.

I made friends, pretty quickly, with the P.E. teacher, Steve Lipinski. We had a lot in common. He, too, was of Polish decent, raised NOT having a father after the age of thirteen, had been married less than four years, and loved playing most ALL sports. He reminded me of me in many ways. As the years would pass, Steve and I became best of friends. He was the first person who made me feel comfortable being a Vietnam veteran. He, himself, had REALLY wanted to join the air force, become a jet pilot, if I am remembering correctly. BUT, he had had some health issues, asthma I believe he told me, that kept him from that dream. Steve wanted to hear stories of MY time in the service, and ESPECIALLY Vietnam, and telling them became cathartic for me. And it was Steve Lipinski who first suggested that I write a book about my experiences. There will be MUCH more about my 'first' Wilhelm friend later in this book, but I can tell you that he and I became the best of friends….to the point that people starting thinking of us as Butch and Sundance, Frick and Frack, Tweedle-dee and Tweedle-dumb, depending on who was referring to us.

I enjoyed most all of the students I taught during my student teaching, too. Some of the girls could be a handful, however. Because of my long hair, and NON-teacher attire, they wanted to hang around me more than usual. Some of them attempted flirting with me, too, which indicated to me they may have had a student/teacher crush. I felt uncomfortable with that, and would send them on their way. They would act a bit pouty before leaving, BUT, there they were the next day, hanging around again.

I also got along well with the athletes I taught. I'd watch the basketball players during lunch, and give them tips on certain aspects of the game that I saw needed improvement. They seemed to appreciate that, too, which made me feel like I was helping improve their game. When the track and field season began, I would watch practice after school, for a while, and give hints to the boys an girls who were throwing the shot put, too, as I threw the implement when I was in high school. I just encouraged the kids of any athletic event whenever I could. That included lunch time, as well as after school. Fortunately, the head coach for both boys' basketball and boys' track, Steve Lipinski, approved.

Wilhelm students were definitely advanced academically, compared to the Inner City kids I had previously been around.

At least three-quarters of the Wilhelm 8th graders could perform at 8th grade level (or above) on most standardized testing. Not many of the Inner City students, (if any) that I knew, seemed to be able to do so. Several Wilhelm students were working in Algebra and Geometry, and had advanced writing and speaking skills. Most Inner City students were still learning how to do the basic skills of multiplying and dividing, learning how to write a complete sentence using subjects, verbs, and correct punctuation.

And trying to teach Jill's Inner City kids to speak sentences correctly....using proper verb tenses and acceptable words from the English language, instead of street slang, had been a REAL challenge to me. I remember one Inner City child telling me, "As long as Ernie know what I'm sayin', I'm good wit dat." Wilhelm students seemed to WANT to learn correct English.

While I enjoyed watching the Inner City kids making strides toward BETTER academic standing, I equally enjoyed seeing MY classes at Wilhelm take on more complex work, AND enjoy the challenges of doing so....well, most of them did.

Even though many Wilhelm students were academically sound, there seemed to be LOTS of them that were no where NEAR as mature-acting as the kids in the Inner City. Living in the 'Project Developments,' and run-down neighborhoods closer to the center of town, forced Jill's kids to grow up faster. It was easy to see that the 'softer' life-style enjoyed by Wilhelm kids, made THEM expect a more 'entitled,' atmosphere, where they could engage in childish actions without being reprimanded in any way. I found myself telling one or two of them, almost every day, to 'grow up,' and act like adults.

One of the students in my Civics class was a particular problem, as far as I was concerned. While he acted childish, and thought he was cute doing so, he also had a mean streak in him, and was ornery toward teacher and fellow student alike. Again, HE thought he could do as he pleased, and shouldn't be reprimanded for ANY of his actions.

Henry Bryson was nearly six-feet tall, and was a star athlete at Wilhelm. His status in school was respected by most of the other students, but his grades were just average. He expected to have good grades GIVEN to him by the 8th grade teachers, as he had apparently received good grades from teachers in all his previous years in Brighton District. But the Wilhelm 8th grade educators didn't respond to his good looks or his popularity. In fact, all members of his all-male teaching staff were particularly turned off by his braggadocios comments and haughty attitude. Naturally, Henry wanted to show me, his student teacher for Civics, that he was top dog in the 8th grade.

My first day as sole teacher, in Henry's Civics class, started off well enough. Students were expected to be in their seats when the tardy bell rang, and they were. As I approached the podium at the front of the room, and it was apparent that Abner Caldwell wasn't around, Henry Bryson's hand shot up into the air. "Where's Mr. Caldwell?" Henry yelled out before he could be called upon.

"Class, I have asked Mr. Caldwell to allow me to teach this Civics class for the duration of my student teacher assignment. I also asked him to not be present, most of the time, while I do so. He will look in at times, and I know how to get hold him if needed. I chose THIS class because I considered you to be amongst the hardest-working, and most respectful students in the 8th grade. I appreciate him giving me your class, and I know that you all are going to show me that I picked the RIGHT class to fly solo," I thought I showed a lot of confidence in them AND myself with that answer.

"Yeah, right," Henry blurted out.

"Mr. Bryson, if I am not mistaken, students are expected to raise their hands, AND be called upon, before speaking out during class. Is that correct?" I said calmly, but with conviction.

"Yeah, I guess," Henry retorted, while having a smirk on his face. The entire rest of the class ignored his rudeness and was well-behaved for THAT day.

Actually, my Civics class, as well as my other two classes, performed fantastically for me, as a general rule. IF, however, any unruliness took place, I would simply speak to them using common sense reasoning. At times, however, I was forced to lay some Jewish guilt on an offender. And, if need be, I would use a simple reward system I devised. Regardless of my tactics, I was fortunate in that my strategies seemed to work most every time, and I'd have the class back on track in short order.

The 'rewards' were, in fact, the first time I started telling stories about my military experiences. I didn't feel the animosity toward my having been a soldier, from those young people.... certainly not like I had, from adults, following my return from Vietnam.

The 'reward stories' began one Monday when I mentioned to all three of my classes that if they had a good week, and got all of the work I needed to get done, DONE, then I would tell them a short military story during the last fifteen minutes on Friday. I would also offer organized discussions on social issues as a reward, from time to time, but it was the boys, in particular, who wanted to hear about the army, ESPECIALLY about what happened to me in Vietnam....some of the girls, too. So, after particularly good weeks in my classes, I took the last few minutes of several Fridays to entertain with stories.

My story-telling became popular, and there were occasions when students began policing themselves and others, into behaving and getting the work finished, in order that a story WOULD be on the agenda at week's end.

They were short, entertaining stories, to be sure, and I NEVER added too much gore, as I just didn't believe gory descriptions were necessary for 8th grade ears to hear. I ended up PUBLISHING a book on my military experiences, too, but many years after I retired from teaching.

The 'story-telling' bribe worked very well for both my Current Events class and Math class, but the Civics class had ONE sticking point that I knew I would eventually have to deal with....Henry Bryson.

He considered himself a lady's man, and I happened to have three of the most popular girls of the 8th grade in the Bryson Civics class. After I began making announcements about there, possibly, being discussions and stories available as rewards on Fridays, I asked those three young ladies if they would help, both me AND the class, control Henry Bryson's efforts throughout the week. It was a simple request. If Bryson decided to present ANY unnecessary distraction during class, one or more of the girls would politely ask the 'brat' to stop. He admired them all so much, it worked every time....thankfully. The trick was that all three girls liked me as their teacher, and they liked rewards on Friday afternoons.

There was, however, ONE time when I kind of lost my cool with Henry Bryson, and his obnoxious behavior.

On that day I had made the announcement for the class to take their seats, just as the tardy bell began to ring. One of the smallest and nicest boys at Wilhelm moved quickly to his seat. Henry was standing near the boy's desk, at the time, and when the small student was about to sit down, Bryson pulled the chair from underneath the little guy, who THEN commenced to crash to the ground and roll backwards....hitting his head on the desk directly behind him.

Henry Bryson let out a loud laugh, and I raced to the two boys. After I asked the smaller boy if he was all right, and he nodded in the affirmative, I grabbed the laughing prankster by the arm, and hustled him outside of the room. "You are lucky that student DIDN'T get hurt," I started to say, with evident anger in my voice. "If he complains at ANY time that he IS hurt, I will hang you out to dry. You are also lucky that you picked on someone you can bully. ONE day you will pull the chair out from someone who will get up and hit you right in the head with that chair. That's what SHOULD happen to bullies, and Mr. Bryson YOU are a bully! The next time you act out inappropriately, I will call your parents and ask if one of them could skip work for one hour, and come into THIS class to sit with you. MAYBE I can get them to sit with you for a WEEK!"

I opened the classroom door and called in for the victim to join me outside. I stared very hard into Henry Bryson's eyes and said,

"You know what I want you to do now, don't you?" He nodded, but still had a smirk on his face.

"I'm sorry I pulled your chair away from you," Bryson said, as the smaller student stood in front of him. But Henry DIDN'T seem to have much remorse in the TONE of his voice, which matched the still-present smirk.

I hesitated for a second, wishing I had the power to do something TO that ingrate. But, instead, I looked at the still intimidated-looking kid, "If you accept his apology, then put your hand out. And Henry, if you are sincere about your apology then you will SHAKE his hand, and this matter is closed."

Bryson gave a quick handshake, then opened the door and went into the classroom. The victim looked up at me and said, "I'm okay now, Mr. Stein." Then with a gleam in his eye he said, "But Henry DID apologize to me….and I like that."

The Bryson bully incident occurred when I had just twenty days left in my student teaching practicum. From THAT moment, until I left Wilhelm, Henry Bryson acted civilly in my class. Apparently, I had spoken LOUDLY enough, while scolding Henry that the whole class heard what I had to say. If Henry even THOUGHT about saying, or doing something NOT acceptable in my class, one of the popular girls would look at him, shake her head, and Henry would choose to behave. I felt VERY fortunate to have so many respectful and responsible students to work with at Wilhelm. When my stint as student teacher ended, I decided that I DIDN'T want to work at a school with disadvantaged kids, but rather at a school like Wilhelm….EXACTLY like Wilhelm.

There is a sidelight story about Henry Bryson that I want to share with you. Steve Lipinski, and a friend of his from a different school district, had decided to invite kids, from their respective schools, to join them for a one-day field trip to San Diego. The trip would take place during the late fall of 1972, and the objective was to go see a professional football game, returning to Phoenix after the game.

The plan was to invite ONLY the students who had displayed good grades, good behavior and good citizenship, after the first quarter of the school year was finished. The hope was to have the trip by THOSE kids inspire the kids who DIDN'T get to go to work even harder in school. Lipinski and his friend wanted to plan a second trip, during the spring, and hoped to entice their students into having better grades AND behavior through-out the remaining part of the year. Steve wanted to invite his best students on a TWO-DAY trip, which would include Disneyland, and two other kid-friendly venues, in either the Los Angeles area, or in San Diego. The trip WOULD require an overnight stay in California, but only the most deserving students would be invited.

For the football trek, Wilhelm had MANY students who matched the criteria well enough to earn an invitation, so the booking was to be based on a first come, first go system. Even though the kids had to pay their OWN way, and it was kind of expensive, there was a long line waiting for Steve Lipinski on the first day he was ac-cepting qualified students with notarized invitations. Sadly, the bus couldn't accommodate all the children, leaving behind several disappointed kids.

Henry Bryson had gotten the AUTUMN invite AND went on the trip. Just as the bus was pulling into the San Diego football

stadium parking lot, a rumor had gotten to Mr. Lipinski that someone had hidden cans of beer in a travel bag, and was going to sneak
a can or two into the game, then drink the rest on the return trip
to Phoenix.

Before Steve had the students depart the bus, he got onto the
bus intercom. "It has come to my attention that one or two of you
MAY have some beer or other alcohol on board this bus. It is against
bus policy to allow people to have alcohol, (Steve didn't know if that
was true or not, but wanted to make sure he scared the kids) and
anyone caught with alcohol of ANY kind will be arrested. AND
because you are all underage, those of you with the contraband will
be doubly prosecuted for having alcohol as MINORS. Your parents
will then be called to come pick you up at the police station. Since
we are NOT looking for trouble on this trip, and I don't believe any
alcohol has YET been consumed, this is what I am proposing. I will
stand in front of the bus where I can not see you. The culprits, having contraband, WILL find a way to get the beer and alcohol placed
on MY seat at the front of the bus....and I mean ALL of the alcohol.
I will then check each of the bags you brought."

"If there is NO more alcohol in any of the bags, we will go to
the game. If there is, however, any alcohol found we will ALL
miss the game. Then I will call the police and ask them to come
and investigate. Word to the wise, kids, put your stash on my
seat, if you have it, and make sure there is no alcohol anywhere
else. If that happens, this matter will end here.

Most of the kids on the bus looked around in horror.

Steve went out of sight, like he said he would, and once the
kids were all lined up in single file, AWAY from the bus, he went

inside. There he found four cans of beer on his seat. He didn't ask whose beer it was, and he briefly scanned ALL bags. Every student looked scared and innocent, according to Steve. However, SOMEONE had to be a very good actor since he/she DID have the beer when they left Phoenix.

The football game was enjoyed by all, and nothing was said about who the 'beer' culprit was.....UNTIL the invitations for the spring, two-day trip BACK to California were being prepared for mailing.

Not one, but TWO different students told Mr. Lipinski, in complete confidence, that it was Henry Bryson who had taken beer to San Diego, and he had planned on sneaking it INTO the football game, too.

Henry WASN'T sent an invite for the two-night California trip, yet, on the first day invitations were to be brought back to Wilhelm for sign-up, Bryson was the first person in line. "I have forgotten my notorized invitation, but here is my money," he said, just as calmly as you please.

Steve handed Henry BACK his money and said, just as calmly, "You didn't GET an invitation for this trip. And I think you are smart enough to know why. Here's a hint....the San Diego trip."

Henry Bryson's face turned beet red, as the students in line behind him just stared at him. He never said a word, just grabbed the money, whirled around, and stormed out the door. He practically knocked his twin sister down as she was entering the room with her SIGNED permission slip. She looked at Henry exiting the room, and queried, "What was THAT all about?"

She hadn't gone on the trip to San Diego, so had NO idea about his taking beer. "Ask Henry. I'd be interested in HIS answer as to why he wasn't invite," Steve answered.

Henry Bryson wasn't a TOTAL bad apple, but he rubbed me, (and apparently many other people, too) the wrong way. He wasn't a TOUGH kid, just a spoiled, rich kid....but, he is one kid I won't ever forget.

Charles Fletcher was the only principal Wilhelm had known since the school's inception, and he believed he ran a 'tight ship.' Personally, I had only two encounters with him during my student teacher days. One was a positive experience, the other one, not so much.

Let's start with the negative event, shall we?

Four weeks into my student teaching, I had my Current Events class take three I.Q. tests, which I had taken during one of my education classes at ASU. I had explained that I.Q. tests were sometimes given to students coming from foreign countries, as a tool to determine placement in several schools in America. The same testing was often given to children of families trying to get out of ghettos and move into more affluent districts.

I explained that different cultures had different standards by which kids were judged for intelligence. Moving from one culture to another can lead to 'new kids' being placed in special education classes simply because of the lack of experiences and knowledge differences between the two groups' ways of life.

I know that I took a Black I.Q. test, an Hispanic I.Q. test, and a Native American I.Q. test in a class I took at Arizona State University. AND, based on MY scores, I would have been placed in special education classes in all THREE cultures.

First, I had my students work on the Black and Hispanic tests in class. Then I asked the kids to take them home, to let their parents test THEMSELVES on various cultural I.Q. tests. I was interested in how 'well-to-do' families performed on questions that might be given to them if THEY lived in tougher neighborhoods....questions which might easily determine possible class placement.... maybe even into Special Education classes.

I realized that the Black, Hispanic, and Native American I.Q. tests were specifically designed to test people's knowledge in those three cultures much as the basic I.Q. testing used in the '70's seemed based on the White culture's educational values and ideals. I was taught, in my college class, that ALL students, regardless of cultural background, were generally given I.Q. tests designed to measure the White Middle Class.

As far as I knew, none of the OTHER three cultural tests had actually been implemented in any American schools.

The Black test had my students failing miserably. The Hispanic test wasn't much better.

The Native American test was difficult, too, and like the first two exams, I had the kids take the questions home to test their parents. HOWEVER, after my NEXT class, my math class, one of the Current Events students came racing into my classroom. She said, "The Home Economics teacher got hold of the Native American test, and took it to the principal, and she wasn't happy."

I didn't have time to think about the comment because my last class, Civics class, was entering the room. Just before I was to start class, however, Mr. Fletcher opened the room door and asked me to step outside. "Explain this to me, will you?" he said.

He pointed to a question that read, 'The initials B.I.A. stand for,' followed by four multiple-choice answers. ONE of the possible answers read, "Bureau of Incipient Assholes." I HADN'T proof-read any of my three I.Q. tests. They were simply copies of the tests I took in my class at ASU. And I had FORGOTTEN about the language on that particular question.

"Sir," I began, trying to scramble for an acceptable answer, "I am quite certain that THAT choice was given to explain how Native Americans actually FEEL about the B.I.A. And I had just forgotten about the wording, which is the same wording I had when I took the test in my college class. Sorry."

Mr. Fletcher looked me up and down….at my longish hair, and my hippie dress, and then he looked back at the paper. "Well," he responded, "Mr. Caldwell has spoken highly of your work with his classes. And I guess one mistake can be over-looked. But, young man, (he didn't know my name) you ARE collecting them all, aren't you?"

"I have to say," I responded, "I DID tell the kids to take the tests home and work on them with their parents if they wanted to. But, Sir, IF you get any calls from ANY parents, I will be glad to talk to them."

Mr Fletcher didn't say another word.....just turned and walked away. But he DID complain to SEVERAL teachers about 'Mr. Caldwell's student teacher,' (told you he didn't know my name) and the 'Stuff being taught in his class.' I never heard from any parent, or Mr. Fletcher, on the matter, again.....thankfully.

I knew I was in the principal's doghouse, and figured my chances of EVER getting a job at Wilhelm was just a pipe dream. However, an opportunity to reverse my standing with Mr. Fletcher came to me near the end of my stint as a student teacher. The principal had devised a field trip for 5th graders....a science field trip. He had done so for many years prior to MY being at Wilhelm, and the spring of '72 would be no different.

It was called an 'out-of-the-box' learning experience. Mr. Fletcher arranged to have ALL the Wilhelm 5th graders leave school one Friday afternoon, and bussed to the Prescott, Arizona area. There was a camp near Prescott which was designed to provide full outdoor experiences for kids....kind of like a Boy Scout Camp, or just a general summer camp, where kids go for a week, and enjoy everything outdoors.

Wilhelm students would get to camp on Friday afternoon, having all day Saturday as a day of learning. Classes in MANY aspects of the forest and outdoor living were introduced....how to identify different animals that might live there, how to build a camp fire to keep warm during cold nights, (or to cook food) teaching about the topography of a forest, and OTHER wilderness-type classes. Basically, however, it was devised to give city kids a chance to discover AND enjoy the outdoors.

It was a big place, with cabins for campers, and one large building where everybody went to eat, or have programs presented. It was a very cool set-up. So when Mr. Fletcher was looking for volunteers to join the regular 5th grade teachers, (couldn't have enough adult supervision) I volunteered to go.

Mr. Fletcher was delighted when I asked to join him for two reasons. First, of the twenty, or so, adults that usually went to the camp from Wilhelm, only the principal and one bus driver were the EXPECTED males at camp. Secondly, since I had a background in the military, Mr. Fletcher thought I could help with discipline, as there were generally 150 students going. I was told that when moments of free time came around, students tended to get a little wild…. the principal thought I could help get them back under control.

He also felt I might be able to run the camp more efficiently when cleaning up the grounds was needed. Apparently, in the past, the women were in charge, and he wasn't always happy with their "tender' approach to leaving the camp looking as good as it appeared when they arrived. Fletcher wanted a more structured style of clean-up, a more military style. I thought I would wear my military soft hat to camp, and a whistle around my neck, for effect.

His idea of me being in military mode worked. I was in charge of ALL formations, whether it be to organize for classes, or going to eat. I taught the kids how to line up correctly, with proper spacing between students. The different cabins formed into their own 'platoons,' and when we moved from one place to another, we marched IN STEP.

The kids seemed to LOVE pretending to be in the army....even the girls. We even cleaned our grounds military-style. (I called it 'policing the area') I would tell all the kids to 'get into a straight line.' I would THEN say things like, 'Let's move out people,' and 'Keep your eyes on the ground, and if you see things that don't belong there, things that HUMANS have put there, pick it up for disposal.' We DID have clean camp grounds before we headed back ro Phoenix.

I even had a class teaching students various ways of identifying animals inhabiting that neck of the woods....scat, nesting areas, clues of recent animal movement, etc. That learning experience was fun for ME, and the kids seemed to enjoy it, too.

Mr. Fletcher made it a point to find me, after we arrived back at Wilhelm on Sunday morning. "You did a good job, young man," he said. "Thanks for joining us." He wasn't too much on giving out a lot of praise, but I accepted those few words as a compliment. I just didn't want him to only remember me as the hippie who gave kids strange I.Q. tests.

I had a few 5th grade classes write me thank-you notes, too, and even a couple of kids came by the room to personally thank me. They were all girls, however, and I think they were just fascinated that I was a teacher with long hair who wore 'different' clothing than other male teachers on campus.

I really had enjoyed my student teaching experience at Wilhelm, but felt my blunder with the Native American test, and my failure to conform to the Wilhelm dress code, would end up leaving me with just a memory of the school....and NO chance of ever working there as a regular teacher.

HOWEVER, during my LAST week of student teaching, Mr. Sam Armstrong came to speak to me. He was a senior teacher, who taught the 8th grade science class, and he thought of himself as the right-hand man to Mr. Fletcher in many ways. So, when he approached me to have a conversation, I paid close attention to him. "Have you considered getting a job here at Wilhelm next year?" He said with the customary dead-pan look he always had on his face, and there was very little excitement in his voice.

"I think I burned my bridges to teach here with an incident in my Current Events class," I answered with some trepidation in MY voice.

"I'm not asking you to tell me the history of your actions while being a student teacher." Sam said, cutting me off before I could continue to down-grade myself. "I'm just wondering if you have any interest in teaching here at Wilhelm next year."

"That would be an honor, Mr. Armstrong," I quickly answered, as I pumped my chest out with pride.

"Then go to the District Office and fill out an application ASAP," Sam said seriously. Then he began walking away before I could say another word.

I hadn't even thought about getting teacher applications for jobs ANYWHERE, up to that moment. However, right after school THAT day I headed out to get a teaching application for the Brighton District.

I had no problem finding the secretary in charge of applications, either. I smiled at her and asked politely, "May I have a teaching application for this district?"

She looked at my hair and attire for a few seconds, then seemed to fumble around while getting out an application. "We have 150 applications already turned in for next year. And I can tell you there are not many slots expected to open up. Are you sure you want to take the time to fill one out?"

That seemed like an unusual comment to make, though I think my appearance MAY have had some influence of whom SHE wanted to get a job in Brighton. But I just smiled and answered quietly, "Yes, I do." I took the application that she was holding out in front of me, and left the building.

When I saw Mr. Armstrong the next day, I relayed what had occurred, and mentioned that I had some doubt about getting a job ANYWHERE in Brighton, let alone Wilhelm.

"Don't you worry about that," he responded. "Just get the application finished and turned in as quickly as possible." I turned it in to the District office the very next day.

Two days before the end of my student teaching, I got a message to report to Mr. Fletcher's office. When I arrived, he motioned me to come into his office and have a seat. It was quite apparent to me that he STILL didn't know my name. "I just want to know if you already have teaching plans for next year?" he stated bluntly.

I told him that when I finished my student teaching at Wilhelm, I would be going to a few junior high schools in the Phoenix area and fill out applications. I DID mention, however, that I had already filled one out for Brighton District.

"I'm glad you got an application for this district turned in because I would like you to work here next year," Mr. Fletcher said with VERY little expression on his face.

"I would LOVE to teach here, Mr. Fletcher!" I blurted out, apparently stopping him in mid-sentence.

"I WANT you to teach here next year, BUT there is a small problem that needs to be dealt with first," the principal continued.

I immediately looked at my clothes and reached for my longish hair. "There is no job at Wilhelm currently available," he continued. "I EXPECT a teacher to quit for health reasons, but he hasn't said anything to me, yet, regarding coming or NOT coming back next year. The fellow I have in mind for you to replace teaches 7th grade Language Arts. What subjects do you think you can teach with some expertise?"

"I was in pre-dentistry, so took a lot of science classes.....science, for sure. BUT, I feel certain I can teach ANYTHING to 7th graders!" I stated confidently.

"You're SURE you could teach Language Arts competently?"

"Absolutely, Sir!" I announced with much bravado in my voice.

"The problem IS," Mr. Fletcher continued, "I CAN'T hire you right now. The teacher I have in mind hasn't declared his intentions, which leaves me in a quandary. I feel good about hiring you, especially after seeing you work at 5th Grade Camp. But I am being forced to wait to hire ANYBODY until he tells me his plans. You understand what I am saying?"

I really WASN'T too sure what to say to that, but, after a short hesitation, I just said, "I can appreciate that, Mr. Fletcher. However, I am applying for jobs in at least three other school districts, and the truth is, I can't wait TOO long before I have to accept one. I NEED to get a job for next year, and I just can't wait too long. I hope you understand."

"Yes, I can understand that, Young Man," he said. "But there are two weeks of school remaining in this year. Can you give me until graduation, so I can find out who is and who is not returning?"

"That I can do, Mr. Fletcher. I really like this school. I will apply for other teaching positions, in other districts, but will tell ALL of them that I can't accept a job until…." I can't remember what the exact date was, but I DO know I gave Mr. Fletcher two more weeks AFTER the Wilhelm graduation, for a total of one month, to find out if he had a job to offer me.

"I should know the situation here by then, so one month from today. That'll be fine." He reached across his desk and shook my hand.

"Mr.Fletcher," I hesitantly said, "when I went to get my application for Brighton, I was told that there were 150 OTHER applications already turned in, and very few jobs to be had, so I was wondering...."

The principal stopped me short of finishing my statement. "I can hire whoever I want," he said earnestly. "So let me worry about who will work HERE."

"Thank-you, Sir," I said. Then shook the principal's hand, again, and walked out. I was feeling giddy when I left his office. Then, I thought to myself, 'I was practically offered a job to teach at Wilhelm today, but ONLY if another teacher quits. What if he decides NOT to quit? What if I can't find another job I like?'....and on and on I rambled. Giddiness turned to worry instantly.

My ASU graduation happened before the Wilhelm graduation, and I got a summer job as a security guard. I drove around collecting check receipts and other paper work from banks....no money, though. However, I had chances to go to Wilhelm to ask what the status was for the 1972-`73 year. Each time I went in to see Mr. Fletcher, he told me he didn't have a job YET, but was sure one would open up.

On the day that my month-long wait was up, I went in to see the Wilhelm principal. "Mr. Fletcher," I began when he invited me into his office, "today is exactly one month for my promise of NOT accepting a job anywhere else. I really want to teach at Wilhelm Elementary. But, if there are STILL no openings here, when I go home from work today, and if I have received any phone calls from any other school districts, I will call back to the FIRST caller and accept a job. I really HAVE to get a job for next year."

The principal looked sternly into my eyes, and said, "I'm afraid no one has told me about NOT coming back next year. BUT, I know someone, eventually, will." He hesitated for a few pregnant seconds, then continued, "Mr. Stein, (yes, he finally found out my name) I am officially offering you a full-time teaching position at Wilhelm for next year. IF a regular classroom teaching job is NOT available, you will be our full-time substitute teacher until one DOES open up. You will get the full starting salary, and I will give you an EXTRA $400 to compensate for the time you were in the service."

"THANK-YOU, Mr. Fletcher," I responded with OBVIOUS joy in my voice. "I am grateful for the offer, and GLADLY accept the job. I know I am REALLY going to enjoy working here. Thank-you, SIR." We shook hands, I signed a contract, (I think I must have signed the contract before I left, but I was just too happy to know exactly WHAT I signed) and then I left campus....EXTREMELY happy!

I HAD MY FIRST TEACHING JOB!

I actually DID get a full-time teaching position at Wilhelm before the 1973-'74 school year, so no subbing for me. What I taught will be told later in this book.

The irony of me becoming a teacher baffled me. I hadn't really enjoyed school when I was a student. Didn't like my teachers very much, either. I wanted to be rich, like ALL young Jewish boys dreamed of becoming....a doctor, a lawyer, a business tycoon, SOMETHING to make me rich. But, at the age of 27, this Vietnam veteran would be working for a salary just over the poverty line, in a profession that was the LAST on my lists of desirable jobs, and I couldn't wait to get started.

Jill and I ended up renting an apartment just three blocks from Wilhelm. The commute to HER teaching job turned out to be only one-third as far as it had been from our place in Tempe. She was happy about that. Really, the only SAD news we got, throughout the rest of the summer, was that our cat died. We let it out during the nights, and someone poisoned it. I seemed actually sadder than Jill about the cat's demise, and THAT surprised me.

3

THE FUN BEGINS?

MY WIFE WAS starting her third year of teaching when I began my first year. However, I started to see changes in Jill during that year, as well. She was looking to move on to high school in the Inner City of Phoenix, which I thought a bad idea. She was small, just five-foot-two and 100 pounds. For crying out loud, her junior high students were bigger than she was, so the high school kids would be able to push her around easily. In addition, the schools she was looking into already had police officers assigned to them full-time....and that was in 1973! We argued about her moving 'up' a lot, but eventually, she became a high school teacher. She QUIT teaching all together, after just a couple of years in high school, but that is another story.

During MY first year of teaching, Jill and I were BOTH very busy with our own schools. We were headed in different directions, as well. I needed to prepare for my classes a lot more than Jill did. After all, she was already an established teacher, and I was teaching curriculum in which I had little experience.

Jill had ALSO started to go see her good friend Marion Hazeltine a lot more, too. To try and strengthen our relationship, my wife and I decided that we needed to have our own 'date night' every Saturday. But, even when she and I were ON our 'dates,' Jill seemed to be developing a wandering eye, and some of her flirting, with men around her, was shameless. I wasn't TOO worried, though, because I knew who she was going home with….on Saturdays.

I was very busy trying to be a successful teacher most other days….always working on my lesson plans or correcting papers. So, on the many times when Jill and Marion were together, I never questioned what they did. Jill and my date nights may have been Saturdays, but on Friday nights SHE began to either go out with her school faculty for some drinks, OR she went to Marion's place, and THEY went out for drinks.

I wanted to question her about her 'going out' on Fridays but that usually caused a quarrel, so I stopped the inquiries. Instead, I, TOO, began going out with MY faculty on many Friday nights. It was NOT a healthy relationship, and both Jill and I felt it. I sought a divorce during the summer of 1975, immediately after she had had a one-night stand with an administrator in MY district. That story comes later. Just suffice to know that Jill and I were NOT happy with each other once we both had teaching jobs.

On a lighter note, I was informed, early in the summer of 1973 that a 7th grade teaching position opened up at Wilhelm. The teacher, who had health issues, decided to call it quits, and I was HIS replacement. I wouldn't meet any other 7th grade teachers at Wilhelm until after the annual District meeting in the fall of '73.

THAT meeting took place one week before students were to report to school, and was used by District administrators as a forum to give all returning personnel AND new teachers, as well, 'pep talks' and general information about changes in Brighton. Following the District meeting, teachers reported to their respective schools where principals held a second informational meeting.

When Mr. Fletcher introduced the NEW teachers in Wilhelm, there were only two names, mine and ANOTHER 7th grade teacher....Sylvester McMeans.

Sly, as he wished to be called, had an interesting story about HIS being hired by Mr. Fletcher. Apparently, his wife had come to the school to interview for a possible job, or at the very least, she wanted to sign up to be a substitute teacher for Wilhelm if she couldn't get a job teaching anywhere else.

She was talking with Mr. Fletcher, when he got a call. It was ANOTHER veteran 7th grade teacher who was calling to say SHE wasn't returning to Wilhelm. Mr. Fletcher was upset that the teacher was calling it quits exactly ONE WEEK before every teacher was to report to work, but he agreed to letting her go without creating a scene over the phone.

Sly's wife, who was pretending NOT to listen in on the conversation, had a more serious demeanor about her, once Mr. Fletcher hung up. The principal, indeed, started talking to her more earnestly....and specifically about her abilities to work with junior high kids. Sadly, according to Sly's telling of the story, the principal told his wife she seemed to be more suited to teach younger kids, and the interview was over. As she was about to leave the office, Sly's wife turned to Mr. Fletcher and informed him that her husband was also a teacher looking to teach junior high kids, and he was sitting in the car.

The circumstances were that the couple had just moved to Phoenix from Wisconsin, and had decided that the wife should get a teaching job before HE started looking, and Wilhelm was their first interview stop.

Mr. Fletcher asked her to have the husband come inside, and after a short interview, Sly was hired on the spot.

Apparently, the Wilhelm principal had begun to see, that as the years were progressing, junior high students were becoming more difficult to handle, discipline-wise. He had HOPED to get more men onto his 7th grade staff, and with the hiring of Sylvester McMeans and me, he ended up hiring TWO new male teachers to work with 7th graders during the 1973-'74 school year.

The three returning 7th grade teachers were all female, but two of them had proven to be weak in the discipline department. One was well into her sixties, and just wanted to survive the classroom until it was HER turn to retire. A second teacher, who was entering her third year, had deep religious convictions. She would rather pray with the unruly students, than discipline them. Most kids respected that, and were well-behaved around her. But the students who weren't interested in prayer, gave her a hard time during her first two years. She would have to survive one more year at Wilhelm before finding work in a parochial school.

The third female teacher was a pretty woman by the name of Ginger Geiger, and she was NOT afraid to dole out discipline to students who acted-out. Ginger had five years teaching experience, was my age, and was a type-A personality. Everything she did was meticulously thought-out beforehand, and run just as she had planned. She could become quite hyper if things were not run accordingly, but her students knew she meant business in the classroom, and did what they were told. Her discipline was always quick, and decisive, and with her no-nonsense approach to teaching, she was definitely known as the leader of the 7th grade. Fortunately, she became a good friend of mine.

Sylvester McMeans had a very laid-back approach to teaching. He taught the reading classes and was very big on students turning in detailed book reports. If students didn't want to read some days, that was OK with him as long as they stayed quietly in their seats and didn't bother any of the OTHER students. Most of the non-reading kids used the time, when they WEREN'T reading, laying their heads down on their desks to get some sleep. However, Sly enjoyed calling parents, and if students were falling behind in their reading work, he would call immediately. Parents at Wilhelm, in 1973, seemed to be VERY interested in their kids' education, and a phone call home would usually get kids back to work in McMeans' classes.

Sly and I dressed quite differently from other male teachers at Wilhelm....no ties or white shirts, mainly. Within months of the start of school, however, I started noticing OTHER male teachers shedding their more 'preferred' clothing, and adopting more casual attire, too. As the years began to pass, pant suits for women, NO ties for men, and the wearing of denim by teachers and students, alike, became standard fare. However, in the `80's and ESPECIALLY with the turn of the century, casual wear went from classy to tacky. That can be attributed to clothing trend and fads of school children throughout the nation. Boys wearing gang-influenced clothing, and girls wearing bawdy and alluring clothing, seemed to become more and more acceptable in public schools throughout America.

With the allowance of tougher-looking, and sexier clothing being worn in the schools, was it any wonder that behavior began changing accordingly, too? Maybe Mr. Fletcher knew what he was doing by enforcing his strict `70's. However, when I began my teaching career, I knew I had to control the students well enough to allow learning take place in MY classroom, no matter WHAT kind of clothing and behavior was being adopted by kids in America.

I soon discovered that using a combination of both Ginger's and Sly's style of disciplining was best for me. I felt I COULD come down harder on students when needed, but using calmer tactics for control seemed preferable to me. I rationalized that junior high kids knew right from wrong. First, I tried NOT to get upset with class disruptions when they occurred. IF a time came when one or two students were interrupting the learning process, I would stop what I was doing. THEN I would calmly give the offenders the consequences of two possible scenarios. First, if the students chose to continue with the disruptions, I could call their parents and have THEM come and sit in class with us for a couple of days. Or, I could just have the disrupters spend several lunch breaks with me. Since offenders disliked BOTH choices, control was gained again.

I also had a POSITIVE choice, which I offered all my classes at the beginning of each week. If we could successfully finish the work I had to get through, I would take the last fifteen minutes of Friday's classes to tell them a personal story about myself. Don't scoff, I have had an interesting life.

I remember, early my first year of teaching, telling a story to ONE of my classes. It was the interesting, and unusual story about how I got drafted into the army. When I finished, the students told me they thought it was a GREAT story. Other classes wanted to hear the story, too, and I accommodated them. When I told a SECOND story about my military life, two weeks later, as a reward for a good week's work, I got the same positive feedback. From then on, I began to use stories as an incentive to get work done.

I believe my teaching and discipline styles worked fine, for me, throughout my career....thanks, in part, to storytelling.

I was very busy during my first year. Not only was I creating my teaching style to match the curriculum, I was coaching every after school sport I could get. I didn't even go to the infamous Teachers Lounge much during my initial year, either. Instead of socializing at lunch, I developed a club....a drama club. We worked on skits, which we performed, and we read one-act and two-act plays, reading them while trying to be in character. We didn't perform in front of audiences, as we didn't have sets, or means of getting costumes. I had 25 seventh graders interested in drama, and our 'club' met in my classroom, for 20-25 minutes, every day after we finished eating our lunches.

Drama went smoothly, for the most part, but there was ONE glaring event that didn't go so well. This, sadly, happened just before Wilhelm was to break for Christmas vacation.

We had just finished reading, and enjoying, a two-act play. With only one week to go before Wilhelm their annual two-week holiday break from school, my students decided to come to my room after eating and sing Christmas carols. On the second day of 'caroling' one of my 'Drama' students suggested we go to 5th

and 6th grade classes and sing to them. The younger kids had class when the junior high had lunch, and vice versa. She suggested we sing and inject a little Christmas joy into THEIR lives before vacation.

I hadn't really thought about entertaining 5th and 6th graders, but my students began telling me how boring their classes had been just before Christmas Break when THEY were in 6th grade. "Teachers don't start new lessons because they know we will forget during our two weeks away from school. They just like to review 'stuff' we already know and that's boring. Come on, Mr. Stein, let's go SING to them," one 7th grade girl dramatically implored.

Being a new teacher, I actually believed my drama kids, but I took it a step further. "Instead of just singing to them," I said, suddenly energized by the suggestion, "why don't we perform a short skit. We won't have time to go to ALL 5th and 6th grade classes, but going to a couple of them can't hurt, right? We'll decide which classes get lucky later."

OK, I agreed that it would be fun to entertain teachers and students, and get them into the holiday spirit, but I had one definite stipulation. Whatever we did MUST involve everyone in our 7th grade drama group. If we practiced on Wednesday (the skit suggestion was made on Tuesday) we could 'perform' on Thursday. The students all agreed. We were going to have a LOT of fun, I just knew it.

The program had to be short enough so we could select four classes, two in the 5th grade, and two in the 6th grade, to 'cheer up.' We all settled on doing pantomime AND caroling as our means of performing.

Here's the way it worked. We weren't going to work on costumes, BUT each 7th grader needed to bring a pair of white gloves (the necessary prop for pantomiming) with them to school on Wednesday so we could practice our skit. We needed to practice EVERYTHING on Wednesday, and get it right the first time, as our lunch break was not long. My students and I were highly motivated.

The following day, nobody ate lunch, and all students reported to my classroom. EVERYONE had white gloves, which was a good start. First, I had them line up in a single-file outside my room. I had them practice marching like soldiers in a military ceremony, VERY precisely and in step, into the room. As they entered they proceeded to form a big circle close to the the walls inside. No noise was allowed during ANY of our marching time.

After a couple of 'runs' and the kids had the marching and circling part down, we practiced showing 'jazz hands,' which was done by exposing the palms toward the audience and spreading the fingers, and thumb, as widely apart as possible. When THAT was done well enough, we practiced our short song, "We wish you a Merry Christmas, we wish you a Merry Christmas, we wish you a Merry Christmas, and a Happy New Year!"

When the song was finished, the troupe practiced making a sharp 'right face,' which is a military expression meaning turn to the right, BUT again, done with military precision. The students would THEN continue circling the room until the leader of the line reached the door. While I was holding the door open, they practiced EXITING quickly. They continued marching, military style, until the whole group got around the nearest corner of the building.

Except for the singing, there was never a sound made by ANYONE, which represented true mime performance. The Drama Club kids were bright and eager. Fortunately, we got the pattern down perfectly just as the bell rang ending the lunch period.

At the start of lunch the next day, (Thursday) my kids lined up quickly, and we proceeded toward our first 5th grade presentation. PERFECTION! The Drama students did the whole routine without a glitch. The second class of 5th graders, and the first 6th grade class went equally as well. All of us enjoyed the fact that there was LOTS of laughter and applause as we left all THREE classes.

The same can't be said about the second 6th grade class we went to. It was our last performance, and my kids did another perfect job on the skit. However, as were leaving that class, there WASN'T any applause OR laughing. We went immediately to our class after that, and just had enough time to take off the white gloves, congratulate one another on how wonderfully the skits were performed, when the bell rang, ending lunch. The kids headed out to their classes.

I had mentioned to them that we were going to discuss the successes of our first three classes and the anomaly of no applause or laughter coming from our last performance, the next day, (Friday) which would also be the school's last day before our Christmas vacation commenced. I, however, learned the reason for us getting 'the cold shoulder' later on that Thursday.

It SEEMS that the second sixth grade class had a teacher who was all business. She would retire, along with Verna Street, after the 1973-'74 school year. However, it wasn't her age OR strict character that was the reason for my performers not receiving applause and laughter. She, apparently, was in the midst of finishing a 'timed' reading test, when my entertainers came in with five minutes remaining on that test. Oooops!

I heard from Mr. Fletcher on the matter right after school. Apparently, the 6th grade teacher went IMMEDIATELY to the principal's office when my class's presentation was over. Mr. Fletcher told me to 'NOT to pull a stunt like that again.' He also subtly let me know that I should be aware that I was on probation for 'THREE YEARS' in the Brighton District, and could be dismissed for 'things like that.'

All students in the 7th Grade Drama Club, and I, wrote letters of apology during lunch on Friday. We apologized to the teacher and her students for interrupting her 'important' reading test. We wrote them quickly and got them immediately to that class. We didn't have time to discuss our successes, and that was a shame. I, thankfully, heard nothing else on the matter.

I DID find out, however, that THAT particular teacher had many, MANY timed reading tests, throughout the year, so missing ONE wasn't going to be an earth-shattering experience for her OR her students. Still, it was a lesson learned by me.

Wilhelm Elementary had a legitimate Drama class. It took the place of one 8th grade reading class, and it took auditions by students to be invited to join.

Alexander Fenstemaker taught all the 8th grade reading classes, which included the ONE Drama class. He held a Master's Degree in theater technology, and his program at Wilhelm had become so successful, the District built him a small extension to his classroom, which allowed Alex to perform one-act plays when he pleased. He was a gentle man except when he got upset. He could really display a wild temper....VERY dramatic!

Mr. Fenstemaker was impressed by the 7th grade students I sent him after my first year with the Drama Club, and when my second year students performed for him one lunch period, he asked if I would want to join him in a combined class starting my third year of teaching. We would have 7th graders and 8th graders joined for one BIG class. I not only did that, I ended up teaching Drama in Brighton District for 16 years. There will be more about those classes later.

While I did NOT spend much time in the teacher's lounge during lunch breaks, (due to coaching, mostly) I usually had my daily lesson plans complete enough to sit in there before school. What a rush! I have told you about the 'business only' crowd, and while they were nice enough, they were just classified as visitors. I knew I could count on the lounge's established 'lounge lizards' to get my day started off on a happy note.

I had mentioned Verna Street welcoming me to the lounge when I was a student teacher, but she didn't frequent the lounge TOO often during my first year on staff, either. (Verna would retire following that year) However, when she did come in, she was VERY entertaining.

One morning, when Ms Street was in the lounge, an unsuspecting substitute teacher entered to use the restroom. But when he heard a lot of laughing, he decided to sit and enjoy the fun. What the sub did not realize, however, was that HE would be the morning entertainment.

The gentleman was in his mid-forties, new to Phoenix, and had to be a substitute teacher until a regular job could open up for him in ANY district. He made the mistake of sitting on the couch which was also occupied by Verna Street. Nobody else was on that sofa, just this fella and Verna. Per usual, the room got silent, as everybody, but this guy, (we'll call him Bud) knew what was happening. Verna had a patsy, and we all just watched her in action.

He sat near one arm of the sofa, Verna near the other arm. Street started staring holes through Bud, with those penetrating blue eyes of hers. Suddenly, she slid toward him, but only until she had gotten to the middle of the couch. Bud looked at her, and she was STILL staring intently into his eyes. She then crossed her legs and started moving the top leg up and down, rather rapidly, like she was nervous. Bud WAS nervous, by the look on his face.

Within thirty seconds, Verna slid again, practically sitting in Bud's lap. The guy was looking at her so nervously, that a bead of sweat came down his cheek and dripped onto his shirt. Verna crossed her legs again AND hiked her skirt up several inches.

It became very obvious to us witnesses that he was staring directly at her much barer, still nice-looking, twitching leg. He started to squirm, almost uncontrollably. Within seconds, AND without making a single sound, that guy shot off the sofa and out the door like a bullet. Though there wasn't a sound made, by anyone, THROUGHOUT Verna's performance, when poor Bud fled the room, we all erupted in laughter.

Jokes, puns, quips, there was ALWAYS some kind of humor being dispersed by the lounge lizards. During the early part of my 1st year, a teacher, and thankfully I don't remember WHICH teacher, said to me, "Did I ever tell you I went to college in the Hawaiian Islands?"

"No," I responded trying to sound gullible, but KNOWING he was going to try to be funny.

"Yeah," he continued, "I was in a fraternity….the….I Felta Thigh fraternity." There was some sparse, yet quiet laughter from a few other teachers.

I sat there dumfounded that he was TRYING to be funny, but not wanting to hurt his feelings, I just gave a small smile, and nodded. "I actually taught one year of school in the Islands, too," he continued, "at the….Comeonya Wanna Lay Junior High School." And with that HE burst into laughter.

"Good one," I said, kind of loudly, and with a small giggle. A couple of female teachers laughed, but the rest of the males in the room just guffawed, while rolling their eyes.

At times some unintentional entertainment visited the lounge. Steve and I played on a recreational basketball league team, during my initial year at Wilhelm. A substitute teacher walked into the lounge, one day, who happened to referee our basketball game the previous night. It was the same ref who had called Steve for a technical foul, which really upset Lipinski. The sub was a heavyset, slovenly-dressed fellow, who didn't recognize Steve or me when he entered the room.

Once in the lounge, the big guy went immediately to a couch, sat down, slouched back, and closed his eyes. There were about eight of us 'regulars' in the room at the time, but he didn't acknowledge anyone, nor we, him. He just sat right down, sprawled a bit, and tried to get some sleep.

The conversation in the room continued, but at a lower level of noise. It was SO low, that after about three minutes, that substitute teacher, who had apparently fallen asleep, let out a LOUD fart.... and it started stinking up the place immediately. We cleared that room in a split second, and once outside we ALL laughed pretty loudly....except Steve. He still remembered he got a technical foul from Stinky, so he just grumbled and went out to the field to wait for his first P.E. class. That ref/sub never returned to Wilhelm, either.

Wilhelm teachers liked to pull sophomoric jokes on one another, too. And sometimes, depending on the victim, several other teachers piled on him/her like sharks at a feeding frenzy.

Alan Portnoy, another 8th grade teacher, was a master trickster. He had a dry sense of humor. There were times when his humor was so dry that the intended target had no idea he/she WAS the target. However, victims just happened to be in the wrong place at the wrong time....which usually meant being in the room with Portnoy.

One morning, Alan, Steve, and Abner Caldwell got into an intersting discussion about women wearing bikinis at public swimming pools. The talk was NEVER downright crude, just suggestive, and all three of THOSE guys were good at sexually suggestive conversation. "It is interesting how women shave their woman parts when they want to wear a bikini," Alan mentioned in passing. "Some shave closer, than others.

Properly titillated, Steve Lipinski chimed in, "There DOES seem to be different levels of taking care of the hair in the nether area, these days. The bikini bottom is getting skimpier and skimpier, and I would think women would be embarrassed to have all that stubble showing.

"Yeah," Alan continued. "Why is it that some women shave so fine they have the look of a hairless, newborn rodent. While other women shave so poorly, they look like a BEAVER with stubble. That has GOT to be embarrassing to women because I know it embarrasses ME to see it. Alan, Steve and Abner began to smile at how cleverly the discussion had been going.

The women in the lounge suddenly started to take offense. "Come on, you guys," feisty Ginger Geiger said. "That is not embarrassing for any of you. I KNOW when all of you would be embarrassed. For instance, if a beautiful woman, in a REALLY skimpy bikini, walked close to where you were standing, say, by the edge of the pool and you were standing in the water. THEN, if she asked you, in a sexy voice, if you minded coming OUT to help her dry off. Things would happen to you, physically, that would make it embarrassing for you to exit the pool. Now THAT would embarrass you guys. Besides, all the women I know DO shave very cleanly. You won't find many beavers around in today's world."

Betsy Shimmel, a very pretty 6th grade teacher, who was known to be quite naïve about MANY things, just happened to enter the lounge just as Ginger was finishing her admonishment of Alan, Abner and Steve. "I was HAPPY to be a Beaver in high school…. and I STILL am!" she said proudly, referring to the nickname of her high school. "Once a Beaver, ALWAYS a Beaver!"

Luckily, it was time for us to go to our classrooms and get ready for the day. BUT, when Betsy made her cheerful and profound announcement, EVERYONE started to laugh while heading to the door....even Ginger Geiger. "What?" asked Betsy, as the room emptied, and Ginger stayed behind to explain.

There was another memorable time when Betsy's gullibility was on display. She came into the lounge, one morning, and declared for all to hear, "I would like to take my class on a trip somewhere. It needs educational value, maybe a place where I can have the kids develop a thematic unit, covering three areas of learning. Anyone have a suggestion?"

Without a second of hesitation, Alan Portney, with his usual expressionless face, piped up, "How about the zoo? Certainly, you could work a science unit there, and have your students include some reading and writing about the animals they see."

"That's FANTASTIC, Alan," Miss Shimmel responded with, what seemed to me, to be a smiling voice. "I think that is EXACTLY what I will do."

"Why don't you call the zoo now to check on admission cost.... find out when they have guided tours for schools....even when any special events might be there?" Alan continued, sounding VERY helpful and serious. But it was Alan Portnoy making the suggestion, and THAT put the rest of us on alert. He was one of the biggest pranksters at Wilhelm, and even though this sounded like a sincere willingness to help, the rest of us suspected SOMETHING was up.

Then the other shoe finally dropped. "In fact," he said, STILL sounding like he wanted to help, "I know someone at the zoo who could likely help you answer all your questions. Get on the phone right now, and ask for Mrs. Lyons. I'm pretty sure she is at the zoo this early in the morning."

Everyone in the room understood the prank Alan was pulling....everyone except Betsy Shimmel. She found the phone number in the phone book and dialed. While she waited for an answer, she faced all the REST of us with a huge smile on her face. And we, well, we had smiles on OUR faces, too.

"Hello," she said cheerily, when it was apparent that someone had answered her at the zoo. "I am calling to inquire about possibly getting a future field trip to the zoo. I was told that a Mrs. Lyons could help me. Is Mrs. Lyons at the zoo right now?"

There was a slight pause, then Betsy continued, "That's right, I was SPECIFICALLY told to ask for Mrs. Lyons to help me. Is she available at this time? What? WHAT are you saying? Oh, good Lord, I am SO sorry." She hung up and looked right at Alan, but STILL with a smile on her face.

"I take it," Portnoy said with his usual deadpan expression, "that Mrs. Lyons will have to call you back."

Betsy looked directly at Alan, "You rat," she said seemingly more embarrassed than angry. "The person at the zoo said there was NO Mrs. Lyons working there...someone was pulling my leg.... that the only lions at the zoo were in their habitat. Alan, you rat!" Just another fun morning in the lounge.

There is one more lounge 'prank' which I think is worth mentioning. It occurred when I was either in my second or third year at Wilhelm, and the joke was pulled on one the least likely victims at Wilhelm….Sam Armstrong.

He had been at Wilhelm as long as Mr. Fletcher. Sam was a man who liked to give an air of supreme confidence, and truly was unflappable in most situations. He was a mainstay in the teacher's lounge, and watched the comings and goings with very little conversation on his part, and displayed very little emotion when there were jokes or pranks. He almost ALWAYS had a stoic look on his face. While he DID laugh….a little, at times….he was a sharp cookie, and stayed OUT of the frays and chicanery displayed by other teachers. Even though he may have enjoyed the various antics, it always appeared as if he was looking down his nose at the teachers who were 'trying' to be funny.

Unbeknownst to everyone else, one fine spring morning, Abner Caldwell had decided to 'get' Sam in front of a packed teacher's lounge crowd. It all began when Abner decided to sit next to Sam on one of the couches.

Caldwell began sniffing the sleeve covering his right bicep, and repeated that action, from time to time, "This is the most unusual smell," Abner said, seeming confused.

Finally, someone in the room asked, "What do you mean, unusual smell?"

"I was filling my car with gas this morning," Abner explained, "when this strange-acting man, who looked homeless to me, came over and threw a small amount of some powder on my shirt. I asked him why he did that. He only said it was pixie dust. Then he scurried away. He was weird, and I brushed the powder off.

But the smell that the powder left behind, DOES have an unusual scent....and I can NOT, for the life of me, tell what this smells like." Abner took another sniff, then continued "But it is strange....kind of intoxicating."

Abner was telling his story with SUCH conviction and so seriously, AND he didn't have the omnipresent smile that he was known for having. While I, and many of the other people sitting in the lounge, became curious as to what that guy had thrown on Caldwell's shirt sleeve, Sam Armstrong, who was sitting just to the left of Abner, neither commented nor reacted in any way to Abner's comments. He just kept reading the magazine he had with him.

One minute passed and Abner sniffed his right bicep again then said, "I can't tell if this is a sweet smell, or a sour smell. I just CAN'T describe its aroma, and it's bugging me."

Steve Lipinski, who was actually sitting next to Abner's right shoulder leaned over to smell the sleeve. He looked at Abner with a look of wonderment, and Caldwell just winked at Steve. A game was on, and Steve realized it. "Yeah," Steve commented, "that is an unusual smell, all right."

With THAT comment, Abner sniffed one more time, then turned toward Sam Armstrong, so as to get his right bicep a little closer to Sam, "Tell me, Sam, what do YOU think this smell could be?"

Mr. Armstrong, still deigning very little interest in the topic, BUT feeling a bit privileged that Abner would seek out HIS opinion, slowly leaned across Caldwell's body to get a sniff of the powdered sleeve.

Instantly, Abner leaned in and planted a HUGE kiss on Sam's cheek. The lounge erupted with laughter, as Sam Armstrong turned beet red. He had FINALLY become the butt of a teacher's lounge prank.

But, with his usual calmness, and lack of emotion, Sam said, "It smells a little SWEET to me." We DID have fun at Wilhelm!

I really enjoyed my first few years at Wilhelm. Both the faculty and students were great, and even the staid principal, Mr. Fletcher added to my enjoyment of the school.

One of the reasons I enjoyed Charles Fletcher was the way he DIDN'T micro-manage my teaching. He recognized that I was part of the 'new breed' of teachers entering the teaching market, and didn't want to squelch my 'different' style of instruction. When he came in to watch me teach, he didn't stay long, and our conferences were short, too. He just wanted ALL his teachers to 'get the job done,' as he put it to me, and he was satisfied I was doing just that. When the results of our standardized tests in language arts (my subject matter) came in, Fletcher saw my students were almost ALL at, or above, grade level average, so he felt justified letting me have more freedom than principals at other schools were doing with their non-tenured teachers. He watched me around the school, too, and I got glowing reports after all three years that he was my principal.

He could be old-fashioned and stubborn to change, though. At our annual Thanksgiving assemblies, Mr. Fletcher INSISTED that all teachers hand out xeroxed copies of his favorite song, and wanted EVERYONE to sing the song during the assembly. I think the name of the ditty was The Gay, Old Turkey, at least it was that phrase that caused a stir. It seemed like ALL the students realized that the term 'gay' had a different meaning in the '70's than it did in the '20's, whereas the principal didn't. Fletcher didn't like that the students would giggle, even laugh, when they had to say the word 'gay,' but he DIDN'T take the song out of the assembly's program while he was at Wilhelm. Taking the song out of the Thanksgiving program wasn't going to happen with Fletcher as principal....it was tradition, and Charles Fletcher LOVED tradition.

However, he began to realize that 'new' programs, ideas, EVERYTHING in the educational field, were developing at such a fast speed, that he was quickly becoming a relic of the times. He retired in the spring of 1976.

The incident that I remember BEST about Charles Fletcher, and the one that showed me how wily he could be, occurred during my second year of teaching.

One day, as I was teaching in my classroom, the door opened, and Mr. Fletcher asked me to step outside for a minute. My room opened up to the school's beautiful amphitheater. THAT was where we held many of the school-wide programs, including graduation. It had four grassy tiers, a semi-circular cement stage with a nice roof over it, for protection against the beating sun, and any rain that Phoenix got. There was also a two-foot wide sidewalk splitting the two grassy areas into two equal halves. On nice days the amphitheater was a place where several reading teachers liked to take their classes to enjoy the weather. It worked for most any class, really, when chalk boards were not necessary.

It was a strange request by the principal, asking me to join him outside, since I didn't think I had done anything to warrant a visit from him that day. I told my class to sit quietly and that I would return in a minute or two.

Bordering the amphitheater was a black, iron railing, and when I went outside I saw one of our special education teachers, Mrs. Boynton, standing against the rail and staring out at the amphitheater.

Fletcher asked me to join her, then told us he needed witnesses for what he was about to do. We agreed to observing, then we both looked out at the grassy tiers, as the principal headed to the third tier. For THERE was a man, apparently a substitute teacher at Wilhelm that day, in his early twenties, lying spread-eagle on his back. Nobody else was near him. He was just laying there, on his back, with his shirt unbuttoned and opened widely, sleeves rolled up as far as they would go. His pant legs were rolled up to make it appear as if he was wearing shorts. There was a gallon jug, of what seemed to be tea, next to his head, and it was, apparently brewing in the warm sun. He was very much asleep when the principal approached.

Mr. Fletcher positioned himself so that when he would begin engaging the substitute teacher in conversation, the young man would find himself staring right into the sun. Our guest would have NO way of getting a good look at who was talking to him. "Good morning, Sir," Mr. Fletcher said in a voice loud enough to wake the prone fellow.

The sub rose so he could lean on his elbows, and while squinting desperately to see who was addressing him, the young teacher replied, "Good morning."

"You a teacher here?" The principal inquired

"Yeah, subbing here today."

"What class are you subbing for?"

"Reading," the guy said, "and I just have them sitting around outside, so we can enjoy the sun's warmth."

"You're teaching now?" Mr. Fletcher asked with a puzzled look on his face, and tone in his voice," Where are your students?"

"They're right HERE," was the answer. But as the sub started pointing to the tiers around him, he saw nobody. He scrambled to his feet, and hurriedly lowered his pant legs, unrolled his sleeves, and buttoned his shirt.

The Wilhelm principal had been walking around campus when he noticed students in the amphitheater. He also noticed the sleeping substitute teacher. As Fletcher approached the kids, he put his fingers to his lips, indicating he didn`t want the readers to make any noise. Quickly and quietly, the students went around the corner of the nearest building to wait for the bell indicating class was over.

Mr. Fletcher introduced himself, then said rather calmly, "Why don't you grab that container of whatever that is, and let's take a walk to the office," THAT was the last day the young substitute teacher worked in the Brighton District.

Teaching 7th grade for my first two years was fine, and I enjoyed the students. However, I saw a noticeable growth in maturity in MY students when they went through the 8th grade, following their 7th grade year. I liked what I saw, and because of that, I absolutely wanted to move up a grade level....sooner, rather than later.

In my school, which taught 5th through 8th grade students, it was apparent to me that the 8th graders ran the school....WITH the supervision of their teachers, of course. Wilhelm's standing in the neighborhood, even the state of Arizona, was based on THAT grade level's academic, athletic and social demeanor, each and every year. I wanted to be part of the leadership working with the 8th grade.

Unfortunately, when I got MY job, all of the Wilhelm teachers in the 8th grade had been fixtures for several years prior. Even though I was unsure when I would get a chance to move up, on occasion, I would mention my desire to be an 8th grade teacher to Mr. Fletcher. On each of those occasions, he would mention that he was pretty confident that NO position was likely to open up for quite some time.

However, as my second year was drawing to an end, I found myself about to experience some major changes in my life.

4

MOVING ON UP

DURING THE YEAR 1975, two events happened which changed my life drastically.

My wife Jill and I had been having some difficulty enjoying our marriage after I got my job, especially after her childhood best friend Marion moved to Phoenix. It seemed to me that my wife was with Marion more than she was with me. I have to admit that I coached every night after school, and didn't usually get home until nearly six at night. So I was busy. Jill's school let out earlier than my school, but she didn't enjoy coming back to our apartment and being alone for a couple of hours while I coached. So, Jill would often go to Marion's place after work, and she always arrived at OUR home a little after I did.

I worried about Friday nights the most, though. When Jill and Marion were together on Fridays, they liked to go out and party. I was constantly wondering what those two were up to, ESPECIALLY since Jill wouldn't get home until late at night. It's true that my wife went out with her FACULTY after school some Fridays, but mostly she chose to go out with Marion'.

Actually, I went out on several Fridays with MY faculty, too. We ALWAYS had a wonderful time. Still, I would get home well before Jill on Fridays, and wonder about any new people she and Marion had met. I had a right to worry because Jill was a natural flirt, and loved it when men flirted back, AND, if I haven't mentioned this before, Jill HAD been unfaithful to me when I was in Vietnam. Yes, I worried about her on Fridays a LOT!

Whenever I would ask Jill about her evening, she would tell me she had a 'good time,' and I would tell her I had a 'good time.' That was it, no details. I was afraid to pry any further, for Jill would most certainly have told me about EVERYTHING. I guess I really didn't want to face the possibility that she might have had 'extra curricular' fun with other men.

Even though Jill and I 'dated' on Saturdays, I generally avoided taking her to do anything with my school's faculty. She 'got off' by arguing with people, and faculty members from my school' were her favorite targets.

Horace Growanger was Brighton's newest District adminis-trator. In fact, in the spring of 1975, he was offered a job at the District office, which would leave his 8th grade teaching position at Wilhelm open. I saw that as my opportunity to move up to my preferred grade level. Therefore, when I was invited to attend the farewell party at his house I gladly took Jill with me.

Since Horace had invited BOTH Wilhelm and District people, hi's home got crowded....LOTS of people attended. Sadly, Jill chose to argue with many of them. When my wife started to become particularly obnoxious, I told her it was time to go home. (which was quite early in the evening, by the way) She and I got into an argument when I made that demand. Finally, Jill told me to go home myself, and that she would find her OWN ride home from the party. I was REALLY upset with her suggestion, so I damn well left her at the Growanger shindig.

Yep, she stayed out until five in the morning, and I was waiting up for her when she finally got to our apartment. I simply asked her if she slept with anyone (knowing the answer) and when she said she slept with Horace, I told her to get her things together and go to Marion's.

On Monday, I went to get a no-fault divorce packet, got a court date as soon as possible, and in no time at all, I was out of a nearly seven-year marriage.

Since I really liked Jill's parents, and she was the apple of her dad's eye, I told her to just tell her folks that I was ready to start a family. She could then say she had told me she wouldn't be ready for kids for quite some time. Jill would just pretend that she was doing ME a favor….not wanting to hold me back from having a family, which would make the divorce more palatable for her folks to understand. IF her father had heard his daughter was a whore, he might have had a heart attack!

I confronted Horace, too. He was practically begging me to forgive him, and was afraid I was going to do something awful, like beat the hell out of him or worse, shame him by telling parents in Brighton District of his indiscretions; thus, giving him the nasty reputation of being a womanizer. Yes, I believe that the parents in the District would have, most likely, NOT wanted him to be around them or their kids anymore. Would you if you were a parent?

I don't know what really happened, but he told me his excessive drinking HAD to be the reason for his screwing my wife'. He told me he couldn't remember ANY of what happened, but that was his excuse. What parent in Brighton wouldn't want a drunk like THAT being an educational leader?

I feel certain, however, that Jill had decided to take HIM to bed that night. When his wife finally went to the master bedroom to sleep, Jill took my, soon-to-be EX-friend, to the spare bedroom. Horace's wife divorced him within the year of 'the party,' too. AND, since I didn't tell anyone (except Steve) about the one-night stand, the incident blew over by summer's end. Growanger worked in the District for a few more years. Suddenly, he was gone from Brighton. All I could say, when I got the news of his departure, was 'good riddance.'

The only GOOD thing that Horace Growanger did for me was decide that he WANTED to move to the District office. However, getting his 8th grade Language Arts position at Wilhelm WASN'T automatic.

Mr. Fletcher KNEW I wanted to move into Growanger's spot on the faculty, but he had a problem. Sly McMeans had decided to work only one year at Wilhelm, which left me as the only male remaining on the 7th grade core team. And Fletcher wanted to have at LEAST one male teaching his 7th graders.

Shortly before the '74-'75 school year was even over, Mr. Fletcher started to have interviews for the one job he had open.

He was bound and determined to get a competent teacher, one who could work with 7th OR 8th grade kids. Mr. Fletcher preferred to have ALL men teach his 8th graders. However, he was ALSO bound and determined to keep ONE male teacher working in the 7th grade, too.

One morning, with only a handful of days remaining in the school year, Mr. Fletcher had an interview with a female teaching candidate. She and her husband were new to Phoenix, and she was trying to line up a job for the following year. Mr. Fletcher felt that he would find a strong female to fill the 8th grade vacancy if no men were applying for the position. Sam Armstrong was in the interview, too, as HE wanted to make sure that anyone hired would be compatible with the rest of the all-male, 8th grade team.

Turns out, the woman was NOT junior high material. Mr. Fletcher suggested the woman go to our feeder school, Richland Elementary. He thought she was more suited to work with grade levels kindergarten through 4th grade. As far as the principal was concerned, that interview over.

As the woman rose and was headed toward the door, Sam Armstrong suddenly remembered the story of how Sylvester McMeans had been hired. He, casually, asked, "Your husband wouldn't be a teacher looking for a job, TOO, would he?"

The young woman looked at Mr. Armstrong. "Yes, he is," she answered, with a furrowed brow, seemingly astonished that she would be asked about her husband.

"Would he happen to be sitting in your car right now?" Sam asked, keeping his usual stoic-look on his face.

The woman shook her head affirmatively, "How did you know that?" she asked with some bewilderment in her tone.

"Just a guess. Could you ask him to come in and interview for us right now?" Sam continued while looking at Charles Fletcher, who expressed no objection to the request. As Yogi would have said in this situation, 'Deja Vu all over again,' and, indeed, lightening DID strike twice.

Byron Freemont came in, had a great interview, and was offered the 7th grade position....MY old position. As his career in the Brighton District progressed, I enjoyed watching Byron Freemont become as good an educator as the District had ever employed. But, I will always remember HIM best as the man who allowed me to become an 8th grade teacher.

One year after I began teaching in the 8th grade, Mr. Fletcher retired. A new principal came in to run our school, and Alan Portnoy, left his social studies position at Wilhelm and joined the Brighton District big wigs at the main office. Steve Lipinski became the new social studies teacher. I had a fun time working with Steve, Abner, Sam, and Alex Fenstemaker. Times in the District were changing, but Wilhelm adapted and seemed to be thriving in spite of the rather massive economic downturn.

Also, I need to mention that the 8th grade staff got along famously for the next dozen school years. One commonality that we all shared was our competitive spirit, which could be entertaining at times.

Thanksgiving was a time that Wilhelm liked to collect cans and donate them to a local charity. The 8th grade ALWAYS collected more cans than the other three grade levels put together. One year, however, the competitive bug REALLY bit the five of us. It became all about who could collect the most canned goods in the EIGHTH GRADE!

Mr. Armstrong and my class each collected over two thousand cans each, with my team losing the school champion's crown by just five cans! My students were quite upset! The other three 8th grade home rooms collected over a thousand cans each, too, and the 8th grade, alone, collected nearly eight thousand cans for the charity. One or two classes from the rest of the school TRIED to compete, but could only collect a couple hundred cans. The majority of the homerooms, however, did the usual, averaging less than a hundred cans each. (some got as few as fifteen to twenty cans) Our school total was nearly TEN THOUSAND CANS! We filled the large truck, which the charity sent for collection. All in all, there was happiness at Wilhelm with our ability to help the needy.

HOWEVER, other schools were gathering cans for charity as well. And when the city newspaper had an article written, expressing how 'giving' schools were in their canned food drives, it decided to write about a local parochial high school, which had collected around 1300 cans....TOTAL.

Some of Wilhelm's students were furious, and wanted the 8th grade teachers to complain to the newspaper. We teachers simply used the 'shun' as a teaching lesson, and tried to convince them that we should be satisfied knowing how well our school did, and accept that our happiness should come from knowing we helped feed lots of people.

The teachers realized that the newspaper often felt compelled to honor HIGH SCHOOL kids doing something important, so we simply explained 'When older kids get involvement in charity events that almost ALWAYS trumps grade school kids getting involved.' At least that was the message we TRIED to convey. Our students STILL grumbled about the whole situation, and I wasn't happy, either. The competitive spirit in me wanted Wilhelm to get recognized....I just didn't let that be known.

Brighton District remained elite for the first five or six years I taught there, but change came fast. The economy was in trouble, and our district started losing some of the local businesses in the area, which caused our tax base to dwindle quickly. Many of the well-established families, that had kids attending Brighton schools for decades, began to move OUT of the Brighton neighborhoods. Those folks began selling their homes at less-than-market-value prices. Families, looking to move OUT of the Inner City's tougher neighborhoods, began purchasing the bargain houses in droves. Wilhelm became a transient district, with families, teachers and administrators moving in and out at a high rate, and it would only get worse as time went on.

I was oblivious to the change for many years. I had a routine that I enjoyed. I had the structured classroom environment in my English classes. I had a nice dose of creativity with the Drama class. AND I got to relieve any stress I received throughout the day when I coached after school. Coaching gave me a chance to YELL, and yelling relieved my stress...most of the time.

Change came in my coaching, as well. In my second, fourth, and sixth years at Wilhelm, I got to coach the 8th grade football team. Steve Lipinski, the school's MAIN coach, and I, decided we would each coach the 7th grade football team one year, then follow by coaching the same boys during their 8th grade.

It worked well. BUT, it was working SO well, we dominated the other two schools in our district.

My team practiced during every lunch period, (yes, the kids ate first) AND every day after school. We got to be a very good team. SO good, that, during my fifth year of coaching football, my 8th grade boys won our conference championship game 56-0, and I didn't even allow three of my best players to start the game....for disciplinary reasons. We also played two teams from other districts, as each of them claimed to be THEIR respective conference champion. We won both handily. Wilhelm's 8th grade team was not only undefeated, they were not scored upon....not one point allowed, in any game.

At the end of the year, (I believe it was the 1978-'79 school year) all the district football coaches were told 'football is NOT going to continue in Brighton, soccer will be replacing it.' The Wilhelm football players, Steve Lipinski, and I were disappointed. We asked for explanations, but the district administrator, in charge of athletics, would only say, 'For insurance reasons.' That was my FIRST disappointment in the Brighton District. I didn't like, or even understand, soccer so I didn't coach the sport.

His name was Curtis White. While Wilhelm had had some tough kids during my first five years at the school, when Curtis arrived, at the start of the sixth year, I finally understood what a really tough kid was. He was the first authentic gang member that I met while teaching. His mother and her boyfriend, two younger sisters, and the 13-year-old Curtis, had moved to Phoenix from Los Angeles in order to take young Mr. White away from the destructive environment of gang warfare. Curtis had been in several 'scrapes' in L.A. and had the scars to prove it. The White family moved into a one-bedroom apartment, which was located about six blocks from Wilhelm.

He was a big kid, maybe 6'2" and 165 pounds. He wore the hairstyle of the day, having an Afro that stood five inches tall, and puffed out on all sides. While his grade SKILL levels were only in the 4th grade range, I knew Curtis was no dummy. He was in my homeroom, so I took particular interest in his academic progress. "I never liked going to school," Curtis told me one day. "But Wilhelm is aw right." He grew two to three grade levels in reading, English, AND math, during his 8th grade year.....according to standardized testing, which were tests determining such matters, and were issued toward the end of each school year.

The kid had a constant frown on his face, more like a scowl, which was intended to let people around him that he didn't like to 'be messed with.' He wasn't a student who had a lot of fun times, either. Everything was serious to him.

He was pretty talented athletically, too. He played very well on the school's LAST football team, and finished 2nd in the season-ending county wrestling tournament, where I entered him as a heavyweight. (giving up nearly sixty pounds to some opponents) He was a tough guy, and EVERYBODY knew it. Curtis played prominently in three stories from that year.

I taught an English class immediately after the junior high lunch break. My classroom door opened up to a tarmac play area, and the girls' P.E. dressing room was located about 30 feet from my classroom door. The school's huge, fenced-in playground area was just on the other side of that dressing room.

While I had a class to teach, after OUR lunch break finished, the 5th and 6th graders would eat and head out to the field for THEIR playtime….many going right past my classroom door to get there. Sometimes the younger kids got a little noisy, but it never really affected my class, except for ONE day.

I was just getting my class into that day's work, when we heard a lot of yelling coming from outside my door. I told the class to sit tight for a minute, and opened my door to see what the racket was all about.

I saw a large circle of 5th grade kids, boys and girls, and inside that big circle were two boys rolling around. While they must have been fighting, I didn't witness a single blow. "HEY!" I yelled, trying to be heard over the din. Everyone seemed surprised at how loudly I could yell, and ceased making noise immediately. "You two boys get over hear RIGHT NOW!" They got off the ground and angrily came toward me.

"First, did you know that there is no fighting allowed at Wilhelm?" I inquired, sounding as serious as I could be. "And secondly, I'm teaching a class in here now."

Both boys were STILL staring meanly at each other, but both nodded that they knew that. "So, what happened?" I said trying to get this over with and get back to class.

The two kids started chattering about name-calling and this and that, but I couldn't make heads nor tails of it. "ALL RIGHT!" I yelled again, and that got them to both look at me. "Here's what I want you to do. Don't talk to each other, and go to two separate spots on the playground and stay away from each other for the rest of lunch. Understood?" They both nodded 'yes,' so I said, "Now go out and play," and I went back inside.

I no sooner closed my door and the loud yelling started AGAIN! "HEY!" I shouted when I saw those two imps were on the ground, trying to hit each other. "GET OVER HERE, NOW!" Once they were standing in front of me I said rather calmly, "SO, you want to fight, do you?

Once again, they stared angrily at one another, clenched their fists, and said, almost in unison, "YEAH!"

Curtis and my biggest 8th grade football player, a strong-looking chap, by the incredible name of Sampson Dillon, happened to be in that particular class. "Curtis...Sampson, can I see you here for a minute?"

Curtis WAS six-foot-two, and with his hair he looked all of six-seven. And Sampson was a solid 6-foot, and weighed nearly 220 pounds....and he WASN'T fat. Both of them came outside to where the smallish combatants and I were standing. "These two 'tough' 5th grade guys just told me they want to fight," I said while looking at my 8th grade giants. "Who do you each want to fight?" I said in all seriousness.

I must preface the rest of this incident by telling you that Steve Lipinski usually allowed disputes to be settled by having fighting students go inside the boys' dressing room, put on these HUGE boxing gloves, and hit each other until they were tired. And while Steve was teaching social studies during that year, the practice was still in use by the new P.E. teacher. Hell, I wasn't even sure those two little guys would even have been able to lift their arms chest high, let alone be able to hit one another....but I knew Curtis and Sampson could.

"I'll take him," Curtis said, while pointing at the kid standing closest to him.

"Then I got him," Sampson said, pointing to the other 5th grader.

"I don't want to fight HIM," said the kid Curtis pointed out. And that little fellow got tears in his eyes almost immediately. And the other kid looked in shock, just hearing that he might have to fight with Sampson Dillon.

"I TOLD you there was no fighting at this school, but as soon as I close my classroom door, you guys are fighting again." Now BOTH 5th graders looked like they were about to cry. "If EITHER of you feels the need to fight again, or DO fight again, I will take you to the boys' dressing room, and have you fight THESE guys, while using those great big boxing gloves. NO MORE FIGHTING! Do you understand?"

They nodded again, and I told one of them to 'go that way,' and the other one to go the opposite way.

Here's the real kicker to this story. ONE of those 5th graders made it into our 8th grade. And on the first day of class came up to me and said, "Mr. Stein, do you remember me?" When I told him I didn't, he proceeded, "I almost had to fight Curtis White when I was in the 5th grade."

"So YOU'RE the one?" I said with a wry smile on my face.

"Yep, and to this day I haven't been in another fight with ANYONE!" the kid said proudly.

Curtis never looked for trouble, but sometimes he just couldn't seem to avoid it.

I was teaching one of my English classes one day, when an 8th grade student came running into my room. "There's a fight in Mr. Armstrong's room, and he sent me to get help!"

Sam's classroom was right next to mine. Stopping in my English-oriented mid-sentence, and telling my class to 'stay here,' I hustled to see what the trouble was all about. If Mr. Armstrong needed help, I thought it must be SOME melee.

When I dashed into Sam's room, I saw him struggling to get two boys separated, but was NOT having any luck. He was on top of one student, trying to stop the kid from flailing away at the second kid, who was on the ground. I saw Curtis White, sitting on Jamaal Cople, and he had Jamaal's head on the ground, while continuously slapping his victim on the sides of the head….not punching, thankfully, just slapping. Mr. Armstrong could simply NOT get Curtis off Jamaal.

I walked around so that Curtis could see me and said, rather loudly, "It's OVER, Curtis, get OFF Jamaal." I was Curtis' football coach, at the time, he was one of my homeroom students, AND I knew his mother pretty well, I was hoping he understood those things. I wanted to persuade him to stop hitting before he got into MORE trouble by actually hurting Jamaal Cople. Curtis stopped at my request, thankfully, and rose to his feet. Jamaal just lay there, rubbing his head.

I helped Sam get to his feet, and HE sat in a chair, exhausted. "Do you mind if I handle this, Mr. Armstrong?" I asked. "I'm going to try to explain to these guys why they should NOT be a disturbance in your classroom, or any other place, at Wilhelm."

Sam Armstrong was a by-the-book disciplinarian, and if he had taken them to the office, both boys would have been in a LOT of trouble, and I wanted to try to figure out what I could do FIRST, in order to keep both students from facing, perhaps, some severe consequences.

"That would be OK with me, Mr. Stein." Sam responded while continuing to gasp and catch his breath. "I'm too tired to do anything with them now, anyway."

Jamaal Cople had come to Wilhelm three weeks after the school year began. He was immature and couldn't stay out of trouble because he chose to shoot his big mouth off at the wrong times. He actually wanted to be Curtis' friend, but Curtis recognized him as a trouble-maker, so chose NOT to be Jamaal's friend.

"He's been talking 'smack' to me, Coach. Been doin' it a LOT lately, so when he started up wid' it again in this class, I had enough." Curtis said in a matter-of-fact tone.

"C'mon, MAN," Jamaal interrupted rather loudly, "you know I was jus' jivin' ya. Ain't no big THANG. You had no call to go all cave man on my ass, Man!"

I raised MY voice so I could have a say on the matter, "JAMAAL, has Curtis ever told you he DIDN'T like you bothering him with your jabber? Has he ever told you to STOP annoying him?"

"He say 'at ALL the time, but he don't mean it."

"I'M a witness now. Curtis, do you enjoy Jamaal trying to get your attention all the time with his constant jabbering?"

"No. I HATE it!" Curtis said while giving Jamaal one of his most glaring frowns. "I'm just trying to keep myself clean at this school. This guy is ALWAYS talking at me, and today he wouldn't shut up. So I dealt wid it."

"Jamaal, I could take you guys to the boys' dressing room, put those big boxing gloves on you, and let Curtis punch you around the room, if you'd like," I said, trying to avoid taking them to the office.

"Oh, Man, Curtis wouldn't do dat, would you, Curtis?" Jamaal joked while displaying an ear-to-ear smile.

Curtis' frown got even MORE menacing. "If Coach gives me the chance, I'll beat you 'til the sun go down. I'm tired of all yer crap. I just want you to leave me the hell alone."

"The way I see it, Jamaal, Curtis DOESN'T appreciate it when you bother him by talking nonsense to him all the time. I'M just trying to keep the peace at this school. And Curtis, you don't REALLY want to have trouble at Wilhelm because of Jamaal, do you?"

Speaking with a tone that told me he was attempting to keep his pride, Curtis replied, "He stays away from me, no trouble. He starts talking 'crap' to me, I'm goin' to take care of business. It won't be here, though, but I'll get 'im. That's just the way it is."

I had Curtis apologize to Sam Armstrong later in the day, but Jamaal didn't think he needed to apologize for being beaten on. The principal's office wasn't notified by me or Mr. Armstrong. The science teacher had NO more problems with those two students.

Jamaal lasted just a little over two more months at Wilhelm as he and his mom moved out of the Brighton District. I have mentioned that the District was becoming VERY transient, and I offer Jamaal Cople as proof of that.

Curtis was involved in one more story that put him into Wilhelm Elementary folklore.

Teachers really enjoyed going to the teacher's lounge during their lunch breaks, to relax and gear up for the afternoon stress, which wound-up students usually brought back with them from an active lunch period.

In the mid, to late-'70's, the children were pretty well respectful at Wilhelm, and weren't looking to get into any trouble. Therefore, lunch playground supervision was only needed to be done by one teacher, who would roam the play areas, being the visible symbol of authority.

One day, in the spring of my sixth year of teaching, Alexander Fenstemaker was doing his lunch duty rounds as usual. He had JUST come onto the large, grassy playground when he noticed a car slowly moving past the big grassy field, but it was located WAY down at the furthest end of the schoolyard. There was a small group of 7th grade boys in that area, as well. Suddenly, Alex SAW a Wilhelm student hurl an object at the car. (turned out to be a small rock, according to the thrower)

The slowly-moving vehicle stopped immediately, and four high school boys jumped out of the car, and scaled the small fence that surrounded the entire playground area.

The Wilhelm students took off like being shot from cannons, and headed toward the basketball courts where a LOT of other kids were playing. The high school boys were in hot pursuit.

Alex, seeing all this happening, began to shout at the intruders, and even though he was small in stature, he was like a wet hen when riled, and he was PLENTY riled seeing high school kids chasing Wilhelm kids on our campus. Fenstemaker began moving as swiftly as he could to intercept the high school boys.

Suddenly, those older guys saw Alex, and, for some reason, the would-be bullies turned course and started to run toward the teacher. Alex immediately turned around and headed in the direction of the main building. Fenstemaker feared HE would become the target of their anger.

Suddenly, from around the corner of the girls' dressing room, Curtis White came ambling out to recess. Alex saw White and yelled, "Curtis, go get me some help!"

The tall Wilhelm student saw what was happening, quickly reached into his pocket, pulled out a nine-inch long, metal chain link object, and while wrapping it around the knuckles of his right hand, he ran toward the teacher. He DIDN'T head back to get help.

Once the trespassers saw the size of Curtis, AND that he was preparing to do battle, they couldn't get back over the fence fast enough. They quickly jumped into their car, and speed out of the area, while shouting obscenities in Curtis' direction.

When Curtis White got to Mr. Fenstemaker, he had an angry scowl on his face, and watched menacingly at the car as it sped away, never saying a word. He ALSO put his chain back into his pocket, trying NOT to let Alex see it.

"Thank-you, Curtis," Alex said with MUCH relief in his voice.

Young Mr. White just looked at his teacher, and nodded approvingly to the appreciation. And, with the omnipresent sour look still on his face, the hero started heading toward the basketball courts. He didn't utter a single word, just kept walking.

Mr. Fenstemaker came to my room, as lunch ended, and told me his story, using all the dramatic hyperbole a theater major could muster. Speaking very rapidly, Alex me about how heroic Curtis was....and about the chain which he DID see.

Since I had White in my class after lunch, I asked to see him outside for a minute, right as the tardy bell rang. "Mr. Fenstemaker just told me how YOU stopped trouble during the lunch period, and I want to thank-you for doing that."

"The man needed help, so I went to help," Curtis said in his usual non-emotional, hard-core manner of speaking. "Didn't have no time to get nobody else."

"And, while I appreciate, very much, what you did, Curtis, Mr. Fenstemaker DID mention that you had a chain on you. You are a hero in my eyes, Curtis, but you KNOW you can't have any weapons on the school grounds."

Without a word, Curtis took the chain out of his pocket, handed it to me, and we went back into class. Very few teachers knew about the incident, and the principal never heard. But, the students knew, and Curtis White was practically a cult hero, all the way through graduation.

The Whites moved during the ensuing summer, and nobody heard another word about what happened to Curtis. Unfortunately, NOT hearing about kids after they left Brighton, was common. But, Curtis White, I will ALWAYS remember you, and the positive effect you had in the District.

The school year, 1978-'79, was one of my favorite years at Wilhelm for several sporting reasons. There were our tremendous football teams, for sure, but that was ALSO the year the school had an outstanding basketball team, with my friend Steve Lipinski coaching, and I had my first successful wrestling team. Sports aside, that was the year I got to have Daniel Zwang as a student in my English class.

The Zwang family consisted of five people. The mom had been an educator in a village in rural China, working in a Christian school. Dad was an uneducated peasant, who worked a farm, but was barely making any money with his crops. Then there was Daniel and two brothers, who ALL had been fortunate enough to be students in China.

In the summer of 1977, the Zwang family was sponsored by an American Christian group, (based in Phoenix) and given permission by Chinese authorities, to have the family of five leave China and move to the United States. The group could only manage to put the family into a very small house, BUT the mortgage had been paid in full. Sadly, that Christian group could only afford to give the Zwangs a meager amount of clothing and food. The family, however, considered themselves VERY lucky to have a chance to improve their future by living in a democracy, so they never complained about anything

Mr. Zwang had gotten a small job delivering a small newspaper, which specialized in listing job opportunities and special deals for certain businesses. I'm not sure what Mrs. Zwang did to bring money into the family. BOTH parents, however, knew they would have to rely on the boys if they were ever going to leave the poverty they had always known. Education was the answer, and it was in the Brighton District where the Zwang brothers began their outstanding educational prowess.

Daniel was fourteen years of age when he was enrolled in Wilhelm, and was placed into a sixth grade, where it was thought he could get more one-on-one learning of the English language. He had a wonderful teacher, by the name of Sarah Wright. Sarah was a nurturer, and she was like a mother hen to Daniel. She pushed him educationally, and that was good, as Daniel WANTED to absorb as much American education as he possibly could.

His two brothers were younger than Daniel. They were twins, equally hard-working, and were in the 4th grade at Wilhelm's feeder school. Mrs. Zwang, who could speak some English, was very pleased with the progress her boys were making in the Brighton District.

In fact, Daniel, who could speak very little English when he arrived in the States, carried a Chinese/English dictionary with him where ever he went. When he saw a new English word of interest, written somewhere around Phoenix, or heard an English word he didn't know, (which he asked to have written down FOR him) he would quickly look it up. Then he would practice using it in English sentences. To say Daniel Zwang was bright AND motivated, is an understatement. With Ms Wright pushing him at school, and his mother pushing him at home, Daniel learned English quite well in just a matter of a couple of months. Daniel was passed into the Wilhelm 7th grade halfway through the school year.

Not everything went smoothly for Daniel in the 7th grade, however. For the first few weeks, some of the junior high bullies made fun of him. After all, he was small in stature, and had very few different clothes he could wear, so he appeared as poor as he was. It should be noted, though, that he always LOOKED neat and clean, but bullies, being bullies, gave him a hard time.

Daniel would hear 'slang' or 'cuss' words that he didn't understand, and couldn't be found in his dictionary. He would ask people to explain the meaning to him in words that he DID know, which he would look up. Often times, Daniel blushed when he found out what certain words meant. He wanted to fit in socially, and it WAS his innocence with the English language that often saved him from physical contact at the hands of ruffians.

Daniel had a constant smile on his face, and because he never showed a threatening demeanor and would indicate that he DIDN'T understand, he would just nod, smile, and go about his business. He just didn't show an inclination toward violence, so bullies left him alone after while.

To nobody's surprise. Daniel Zwang could hold a very coherent conversation in English by the end of his first year at Wilhelm. The next year he moved on to the 8th grade.

By the time the school was going to let out for Christmas Break, Daniel was quite accomplished in his English skills. Yes, he STILL carried his dictionary, but he didn't need it much at all. His church sponsors had given his family more clothes, too, so he looked like every other student in our 8th grade. He had assimilated very well in just one and a half school years in an American school.

I had developed a rather time-consuming, and challenging English assignment, which I sprung on my classes two weeks BEFORE the 'break' started. It was a 1000-word-plus research paper, COMBINED with a five-minute speech. The individual projects were to be presented AFTER we returned from the Christmas holiday, and I felt that could give students a lot of time to polish their writing and speeches while on vacation.

Schools had a penchant for slacking off a bit before the two-week hiatus....school assemblies, room parties, and the like. MY feeling was that the children were already getting two weeks off school, and I didn't believe it should be three or more weeks; thus, we worked on the tough assignment every day in class for two straight weeks, so that the kids could get MOST of the hard work finished BEFORE being away from school for such a long time.

First, I would sign the students up for specific days they would be doing their speeches in class. Then, I would talk to each person about the topic of the combo-assignment, and I wanted to have them narrow their topics greatly, so they could give specific information, not just an overall view of any subject. For instance, if a child came to me and told me he wanted to do the project on 'cats,' I would begin to ask him what he had specifically in mind. Did he want to talk about big cats like: jaguars, or lions, or the pre-historic Saber-toothed Tiger. Perhaps they would be more comfortable talking about regular house cats like: the Siamese cat, various long-haired breeds, or perhaps they wanted to just inform the class on how to care for, and feed a domestic pet. I WANTED all my students to have to do some research, however, so we would discuss how to that, too.

This always sounded daunting to the kids, so to ease the burden, I invited them to join me at the city library, which happened to be located right near our school district. I would be there for them the first three nights of the assignment only, but I wanted to be able to help them locate resource books, etc....to help get them started on the research.

On the day of their presentations, I also allowed them to bring visual aids to class, including live animals. Since I was aware that many young people had trouble facing an audience when speaking, I gave them instructions on how to use note cards. The cards, and/or visual aids were meant to help the speakers feel more comfortable in front of a crowd. I DID tell them, though, that they needed to speak TO their audience, not the cards or aids. They needed to try to scan the room, moving their eyes from left to right, and front to back. Staring at one particular spot was a no-no. For most of my students, this assignment was going to be a precursor of what will face them when they move to higher education....doing research papers and giving speeches. I knew this would be the first experience, in either writing research papers or giving speeches, for many of my students. And even for those who had done similar work in the past, I felt it important that they get more practice on these skills before they moved out of Brighton District.

Sadly, as the years went by, fewer and fewer students could achieve the standards I set. Papers less than 1000 words, speeches less than five minutes, were becoming all too common, and the students' grades reflected that. As time went by, and I recognized that the students didn't seem to care about receiving poor grades for poor efforts, ('too much work' many of them told me) I stopped the project before my nineteenth year of teaching.

Daniel Zwang DID care about grades, and he absorbed every bit of writing technique and speaking skills as he could. He was like a sponge, and HIS research paper/speech combo may have been the best I ever had.

It started with the topic, 'China,' which he announced when I asked him what he wanted to do for his project.

"That topic is WAY too big," I suggested. "Can you narrow it a bit?"

"I want students to know about my country, ALL about my country. I will do this. You will see." And with that I allowed Daniel to tackle the topic of 'China.'

He never joined us, during my invitation to help students the first three nights at the library, but I was told that he went to the library every day he could go, over the two-week vacation. AND he spent several hours working each time he went. His end-product turned out to be astonishingly good.

Making FIVE minutes was NOT hard for Daniel. In fact, he had SO MUCH information to give, that he talked for the entire period.....for two straight days. He was such a strong speaker that word got around about his presentation going a second day. A couple of teachers, who had that particular time period free from their own classes, and had heard how well Daniel was doing, came the second day to hear the second half of the speech. They were so engrossed; they stayed until Zwang was finished. They seemed impressed.

Daniel knew HOW to get his audience's attention, too. I had instructed the class to make each new topic of the subject matter interesting. That meant giving a dynamic first-sentence introduction each time the topic changed. This was done to keep the audience's attention when something new was being introduced. Daniel became a master of the technique. For instance, when he decided to let his classmates know about the education system in China he began, "In United States, students are lazy. They expect EVERYTHING, but don't want to do work necessary to EARN everything."

That got most every student to sit up and listen intently, and some of them looked a bit perturbed that this foreign student would talk about them that way. Daniel then continued, "In China, it is different than America. Not all children in China get to go to school. Many just become peasants, and start to work in fields when they are four-year-old. Education is for the few. When a child is four, parents are required to take child to get tested. If child is thought to be smart enough he is put on waiting list. There not that many schools in China, like here in United States, so children wait turn to go to school. If they are not smart enough on test, they just return with parents and begin work in the fields. China family very poor, children need to help make money."

"In China, teachers are revered higher than parents, and must always be respected. When I was younger I had math class, and teacher show us how to get the answer to one problem. I saw different way, and told him I could show him. He got very mad, and I was sent to spend the day in a small room to think about how I embarrassed him in front of students."

"Next day, I required to have parents come to school, and I face that teacher, and three school elders. I need to apologize and that teacher have to accept. If he don't accept, I placed in same small room for a second day, and have to think about BETTER way to apologize. Next day I go to school and parents do, too. This mean Father lose TWO day pay working in fields, and he get VERY angry with me. If my teacher accept second day apology, I return to class. If not accept, I leave school forever and go to fields to work with Father. NEXT student on waiting list allowed to take my place. For me, my teacher accept first day apology, so I NOT get Father angry with me for second day. I don't make mistake again, but I see many students removed from school."

Daniel was one of only a few students who bothered to use note cards. He would look at his short notations, then embellish on his topic. It was easy to see that not only did he KNOW his topic, he had practiced it a LOT. His 'scanning of the room' technique equaled that of any student I had that year. In short, Daniel Zwang did VERY well at the podium.

His paper was much longer than 1000 words, even though he did NOT embellish his writing with stories....choosing to give only the facts. But he had LOTS of facts, and his paper was amongst the best I ever had turned in. It was easy to see Daniel Zwang had put in a LOT of time on my English assignment.

To prove just how much more Daniel worked on his school projects than the average student, I had a 'different' assignment for my students. I asked them all to keep a chart, a weekly chart for one whole week. It was to be a 24/7 listing of how they spent their time during one specific week. They could use any type of chart they wished. The math class had covered charting at about the same time, so I was using MY charts as an over-lapping thematic unit with math.

The object was for the students to account for every minute, of every day, for one straight week. They were allowed to 'block out' certain times of the day....like the seven or eight hours of sleep they got each night, and all the hours they were in school. BUT, I wanted them to account for every hour of the time they were NOT in school. I told them they would get their grades based on how detailed their work was, NOT on what they did with their spare time. This would give the below average student a chance to get a high grade WITHOUT learning anything....just reporting on everything.

The kids loved the idea of that assignment, and were actually kind of hung-ho about telling me ALL about their week. SOME of the work was turned in on one huge piece of construction paper. (bar graphs, were popular to list the seven different days) Some students chose to use seven, smaller pieces of blank papers, one page representing each of the seven days. Pie charts were used, and some kids decided to write out, paragraph style, all their hours. I didn't really care HOW they got the information in to me, as long as they told me EVERYTHING they did for the week.

What I wanted to keep tabs on was the amount of time students spent watching television, speaking with friends on the phone, goofing around with their friends, and most of all, how much time they spent doing homework for one full week.

When I totaled the hours of ALL my classes, on my four major topics of interest, I discovered that the average amount of time spent per student, on doing homework, was ONLY three to four hours of homework for the week....FOR THE WEEK! And THAT average was helped, greatly, by Daniel Zwang's announced homework time, which was 26 hours of homework that week. To nobody's surprise, Daniel Zwang was my top English student for that school year.

He attended a prestigious high school in the Phoenix area, during his next four years. His family was forced to move close to Daniel's school, as the family did not own a car, and they all had to walk everywhere they went. I never got to work with his twin brothers, and that was sad for me. I had hoped to hear about Daniel's progress throughout his school career. Someone got word to us, however, that Daniel finished at the top of his graduation class, and had scholarship offers from several prestigious schools throughout the United States. I was not surprised, and I knew that Daniel Zwang would be doing SOMETHING important, where ever he ended up after his schooling. I take pride in knowing that I had a hand in his progress.

I was very fortunate, at Wilhelm, to be able to work with students listed as gifted for a few years. However, there became a HUGE controversy, in the late '70s-early '80s, when District administrators decided to bus ALL the junior high-aged 'gifted' children to Pfister Elementary School, where they would be taught by one of THAT school's teachers. Both Alfred C. Cahill and Wilhelm were being depleted of their brightest students, and the junior high teachers, from both schools, protested bitterly when the academic leadership was taken from their respective 7th and 8th grades. I was particularly sad because it was the four years PRIOR to the 'bussing,' that I got to teach all of Wilhelm's brightest 8th grade English students in ONE class, which was called the Advanced English class. I loved it.

The Wilhelm Advanced English class came about because Alex Fenstemaker and I taught the combined 7th/8th grade Drama class, which consisted of MOST of the junior high's brightest students. The Drama class was labeled Advanced Reading, so it was decided that those students should, ALSO, be tracked in an Advanced English class. Byron Freemont taught the Advanced English class in the 7th grade, and I was VERY happy to teach the 8th graders.

My other Wilhelm 8th grade English classes had some good students, too, BUT, the Advanced English class was special. It couldn't be called a 'gifted' class because, in truth, Wilhelm may have had only five or six students that had tested high enough to be called gifted. However, since the Drama class had ALL the gifted kids, and many of the OTHER top academic students, it was not difficult to put the best of the rest English-skilled students, in the 8th grade, to help fill the Advanced English class.

But my four 'special' years working with the best of the best in one classroom, allowed me to see what highly motivated AND competitive students could do if given the opportunity. Since most of the 'brightest' students had very solid backgrounds in the structured side of English....namely grammar, punctuation and spelling, they could learn those skills much faster than my other classes. The Drama class took care of a lot of their speaking shyness, too. In fact, presentations of ANY verbal nature (debating, delivering timed speeches, extemporaneous speaking) were picked up and mastered rather quickly. I, therefore, decided to work on writing skills much more with my 'advanced' students than any of my other classes. And THAT meant entering writing contests! And all FOUR years of Advanced English classes had success in the writing contests we entered. Not a year went by that I didn't have at least ONE student win or place in MOST of the city-wide, county-wide, even state-wide writing contests being offered by various groups throughout Arizona. I was a VERY proud teacher!

One contest sticks out as an absolute favorite of mine. A group from Tucson decided to hold a state-wide, PLAY-WRITING contest for junior high students. They were offering four place winners, and ten honorable mentions, with the OVERALL winner having his/her play produced by the Tucson Children's Theater. Entrants were given two weeks to send in their entries.

This tournament was right up our alley. Not only were the majority of my Advanced English students DRAMA kids, we had recently worked on play-writing fundamentals like: how to write directions for stage movement, learning all the punctuation required for writing plays, and how to write character's dialogue to indicate proper emotion needed in various scenes. We had also worked on the writing of stories, as well, and we wrote LOTS of stories. I was confident that my students were well-versed on foreshadowing, developing plot, creating the climax, maybe having an anti-climax, EVERYTHING that it took to write a successful story, and put it into a play. In short, my students were prepared to write their own scripted plays, as they had had an abundance of background experience to do a good job.

And do a good job, they did. MOST of the plays turned in to me showed exceptional ability in setting the various scenes and creating effective dialogue. I was impressed with 16 of the entrants I received, and those were the plays I forwarded to Tucson.

A couple of weeks after the contest was over, I got the results of the winners. One of my students, Natasha Beddington, WON the tournament, and it was announced that she and her family were to be the guests of the Tucson Children's Theater. She would have to give written permission for her show to be produced, but if she did, the play would be put on for one special night, and Natasha and her family would be the guests of honor. They would stay in a fine hotel, too, so that they would not have to drive back to Phoenix after the play finished. Natasha, of course, was ecstatic when I gave her the news.

My Advanced English class was happy for her, too, BUT, were even MORE excited when they heard that our one, single class had students finish third, and fourth, AND occupied nine of the ten honorable mention spots in the contest. I was SO proud of those kids. I wasn't sure how many OTHER classes had had the experience WE had in the field of drama, but I do know this....it was the last year the state-wide, play-writing contest was put on by any Tucson groups, or any group ANYWHERE, as far as I had heard.

At least I never got word of another tournament. I guess I really couldn't blame anyone for shying away from offering drama-writing contests. After all, my ONE class of students garnered 12 of the 14 places offered in THIS contest. We DOMINATED!

Natasha reported back to the class, naturally. She said it was a wonderful ceremony, and she enjoyed getting her 1st prize trophy. By the way, there were no trophies or medals given to the 2nd through 4th place winners, or honorable mentions, either. Ribbons were, however, mailed to those students. Natty mentioned that the kids producing her play did a 'marvelous' job, too. She was only disappointed that the theater was so small, holding less than 100 people, she guessed.

I had kind of wondered why I wasn't invited to see the play. After all, I WAS the teacher of, not ONLY the winner, but most of the other outstanding plays, too. It MUST have been the size of the theater, and I would have taken some parent's place, or something. I don't know.

All right, THAT comment might be a bit facetious, as I DID think I warranted an invite. However, my BIGGEST disappointment came with the District office....even our own school principal. I DIDN'T get ONE congratulatory word from the District, and I certainly do NOT remember our principal ever giving praise to the class's fine effort. Come on, administrators, we DID represent Wilhelm and the Brighton District in a prestigious, state-wide writing contest, AND we did well.....DIDN'T WE?

While I enjoyed teaching the Advanced English kids, during those four years, it was getting clearer that the District was losing many of its more academically-talented students. By the fourth year, some of the children being placed in the top

English class were struggling to keep up with their brighter classmates.

One incident occurred that year, which pointed that out to me.

Heath Ambrose WAS a smart boy, but had been having trouble receiving the grades he used to get when he wasn't being challenged by the more advanced, and more quickly moving tasks that my top class was required to do. In previous years, he had been lazy, and was STILL capable of pulling off the marks that kept him right at the top of all his classes. However, being placed in the Advanced English class, was a challenge that wouldn't allow him to be both a top kid in class AND lazy, at the same time. Didn't mean he didn't try. Here's an example of what I mean.

Poetry was fun for most of my top students. They enjoyed writing Haiku and other forms of 'patterned' poetry styles, and Heath was as good as any of the other students in those forms. Young Ambrose's problems came when we were working on Free Style poetry. He was more of the Roses Are Red, Violets Are Blue type, NOT the creative, soul-searching poetry that the other students could do masterfully.

When the FINAL piece of Free Verse was turned in, and had a major grade attached to it, I received an unusual piece of writing from Heath. It just didn't SOUND like Heath, whose voice was more jovial, less thought-provoking, and WAY less complicated than the work he turned in. I KNEW he couldn't have produced the intricate writing, with its unusual wording and punctuation.

After collecting all the poetry, I took Heath Ambrose's 'original' work into the teacher's lounge at lunch, to see if other teachers agreed with my assessment that a thirteen-year-old, 8th grade student, would NOT be able to produce that writing. I KNEW it had to be plagiarized, but couldn't prove it.

Byron Freemont, who was a HUGE fan of poetry, took one look at it and said, "OH, this is 'Desiderata,' a poem that Max Erhmann wrote in the 1920's. And you're saying one of your students is claiming it as his? I have a book, with this poem in it, if you'd like to see it."

When Byron got me the poem, I asked to speak with Heath Ambrose immediately after school, for a minute. Heath, who always seemed to be in a good mood, came in, and I asked him to sit. "Heath," I began "I've been reading the class's poems, and yours was outstanding. It is not, however, like ANY work you have turned in this year. Where did you get the idea for this poem? It doesn't sound like wording that people write today....sounds like language that people USED to use." I was trying to, effectively, let Ambrose know, that I knew his poem was a fraud.

"I know," answered Heath, in his usual up-beat tone. "I WANTED it to sound different than the other kids, so I worked VERY HARD at getting the words this way."

"You wrote this poem all by yourself, making up all the words and everything? You didn't get help from anywhere else, or from anyone?"

Heath's constant smile turned into a little frown, but he stuck by his guns. "I asked my mom for some help on a couple of words, but the rest is mine."

I was dumbfounded that such a nice kid could, so blatantly, lie to me. He was a good student, not one, whom I thought, would stoop to cheating in order to get a good grade. I knew several kids who WOULD, but Heath Ambrose wasn't one of them....or so I had thought. "All right, Heath, you may go. Thanks for talking to me," and with that the young man smiled again and left my room.

I called his mother and asked if SHE could come to Wilhelm to talk to me about a piece of work that her son turned in for home-work. I didn't want Heath to get home and be able to talk to her before I could, so I asked if she could come right in, and that our conference wouldn't last very long. She was at my door fifteen minutes later, having taken off from work for a break. Since she was a single mom, and Heath was her only child, if there was ever any school business having to do with Heath, her workplace excused her to deal with it.

"Glad to meet you," I said WITHOUT showing any worry on my face, she had a worried look on HER face, though

"What's wrong, Mr. Stein? Has my baby gotten into some sort of trouble?" she asked quickly as I motioned for her to take a seat.

"Did you know, Ms Ambrose, that Heath and the rest of my top English class have been working on composing an original Free Verse poem?"

"Oh, yeah," she said with a face that still showed concern, "and he worked VERY HARD on it, too!"

"You saw him sitting down and writing the words, and he didn't have any help from any other sources?"

"I saw him write EVERY word onto a piece of paper, and, NO, I didn't see him copying it, if that is what you are asking."

"Heath told me you helped him with a 'couple of words.' Is that true?"

"Sure, when he got stuck with a word or two, I helped him, but he wrote most ALL of it by himself. I saw him"

I handed her Heath's work and had her read the first line. She seemed pleased.

Then, I handed her Byron's poetry book, which was opened to the page with Desiderata on it. "Ms Ambrose, would you read, out loud, the first line of this poem for me?"

She started to read, but stopped short, "Where did THIS come from?" she asked, with a quizzical look on her face.

"It's an established piece of poetry, written in 1927, Ms Ambrose. And not only did Heath copy it, word for word, he has every piece of punctuation written exactly like the original author, Max Erhmann, did in the book." I stopped to let Ms Ambrose say something....she didn't. "Heath will receive a failing grade on THIS work. But, I am willing to give him extra credit if he writes one of his own original Free Verse poems, and turns it in within the next couple of days."

With a look of, well, hate, she looked at me, rose from her chair, and exited the room without uttering a single word. Heath did NOT turn in an extra credit poem, and THAT, for me, made me realize that the quality of student I had in Advanced English was steadily diminishing as the years went by.

That particular year WAS the last year for me teaching English to the brightest students living in the Wilhelm neighborhoods. The following years our VERY brightest were bussed to Pfister to learn, and compete, with the top students from all THREE district schools having junior high-aged students.

5

TIME TO GET DRAMATIC

I WAS UNHAPPY with the brain drain from my English classes, but I DID get to work with our top students every day....through Drama class.

Getting to work with Alexander Fenstemaker was a dream job for me. We got along famously, AND we divided up our responsibilities according to our strengths. He was a genius at set design, lighting, sound systems, literally anything to do with stage preparations. He didn't really have the patience to deal with 8th grade angst in the theater, as he was always going a mile-a-minute in production preparations.

I, on the other hand, was more familiar with the disciplining of a large group of students, especially when only a few of them were in action at a time. Going over blocking in a scene, while keeping control of many more students just sitting on the sidelines, could cause problems for junior high teachers at times. Fortunately, coaching gave me the experience I needed to deal with antsy kids, so discipline of 'extra' players wasn't a particular problem for me.

I, ALSO, seemed to have a knack for getting the most out of character interpretations. Getting students into the proper frame of mind, having them get 'in touch' with their various characters' specific traits, and getting the students to deliver the lines as the author intended them to be delivered, I considered strengths of mine. Alex enjoyed working with the 'things' involved with drama, while I enjoyed working with the humans. After each presentation, we were quite happy with our end results.

During my fourteen years of teaching Drama at Wilhelm, Alex Fenstemaker and I put on some VERY challenging three-act plays. Our successful process started with the students that were selected from the 7th grade. Most of the EIGHTH GRADE Drama students were carried over from their first year, and many of THEM were rewarded with the prime roles for our productions. In fact, the plays we selected were CHOSEN with particular returnees in mind.

One year Alex and I chose to produce Arsenic and Old Lace simply because we had several students who could carry off five of the six major character parts in the play. We were VERY fortunate to find a 7th grader who could deliver, perfectly, the remaining main character, that of the humorous Dr. Einstein. In fact, HE stole the show.

Arsenic and Old Lace was a very popular play for schools to produce that particular year. In addition to Wilhelm, one of our neighborhood high schools put it on, and so did the junior college located within our district borders. Alex and I, along with several of our students, went to observe those two productions, and we unanimously believed OUR Dr. Einstein to be superior, to his older counterparts, with his interpretation of the wacky character. OK, maybe we were a LITTLE prejudice, but we also thought that

NONE of our students gave inferior performances, either. Arsenic and Old Lace was one of my two favorite productions. Oliver Smithson, the student who played Dr. Einstein, was fabulous in his 8th grade year, too. Sadly, he died in a car accident while still in high school. R.I.P., Ollie.

The second production, You Can't Take It with You, had many, MANY unusual characters, and we felt we cast the parts very well. The play, however, had ONE central character. The character, Grandpa, was on stage much of the play, and most of the action revolved around him. Alex and I truly believed we had a very strong boy, coming up from the 7th grade, who could handle Grandpa, and we were SO correct. James Cooledge was a smart, quiet kid in his everyday life, but put him on stage, and he became THE star of any play. He held 'center stage' as well as any student actor we had go through Wilhelm, and made teaching enjoyable for me, as did a LOT of drama students. However, we DID have exceptions to the 'enjoyable' side of teaching student actors.

Seventh graders, who hadn't been involved in theater before, COULD be a handful. Sure, they had been recommended for drama by their 7th grade teachers, and went through try-outs before being selected for the class. And all of them were placed in our class for their 'potential.' But, smart kids who AREN'T the center of attention....let's just say they WANTED to be the center of attention, and some of them found a way to GET it in unusual ways.

Garth Ewing readily comes to mind. When HE was a 7th grader, Alex and I had MANY good 8th grade students in Drama. One of the plays we selected was an entertaining two-act play called, Clown Prince of Wanderlust, a story based on the story of the princess who couldn't smile. There were SO many parts to cast, that we also thought this a wonderful opportunity to get several 7th grade students involved on stage.

Garth played the part of a magician, and in the first act his character was given a chance to make the princess smile....but she didn't. Garth had to stay off stage for the rest of the play. MOST of the characters had to wait in the wings, for their turn to 'emote.' But, for the most part, the Drama kids usually were respectful enough to sit quietly while the actors on stage proceeded with the action.

Neither Alex nor I was ever backstage to help maintain discipline. Our students were to police themselves, and usually did a wonderful job.

Fenstemaker would be in the dressing room helping put on make-up, or working with either the props or lighting crews. My job was to stand at the back of the auditorium, evaluating the performance. I had two rules the students needed to remember. First, the characters needed to speak loudly AND clearly, enunciating their dialogue well enough so that I could hear and understand them from behind the audience. We didn't believe in using microphones during most of our performances. Projection was stressed by us.

Even more importantly, under NO circumstances could the players on stage break character....at ANY time. I told the students that it didn't matter what distractions were going on ANYWHERE, or how many people were watching the play, they only had to worry about pleasing ONE person....and that was ME! I was the one giving the grades. And, with high-achievers, like the students in our Drama class, grades were VERY important. I would tell my kids that if they had to adlib, then so be it….just stay in character. If they don't SHOW the audience they are making mistakes, the audience would not KNOW that there were mistakes. Adlibbing was acceptable, but it had to help the flow of the action. No matter what, the actors knew to STAY IN CHARACTER!

And now, the Garth Ewing incident.

Our Drama class had become well-known for producing quality performances, year in and year out. In fact, the year we had Ewing, Gilbert, Arizona….a small town Southeast of Phoenix, asked if there was ANY way we could take one of our programs to Gilbert, and perform for one of their schools. The request came early enough in the year that we evaluated our resources.

Since we had a lot of talented 8th graders, and a huge class, we knew we would have to find a play that could involve most ALL of our students; thus, we decided to take The Clown Prince of Wanderlust to Gilbert.

Alex built a BEAUTIFUL stage set. He designed it so that it could be folded up and taken on a bus. We scrounged for, and had made for us, outstanding costumes. One of the more important scenes of the play is when a zoo comes to town to try and make the princess smile. The costumes of our animals were beautifully made. We practiced hard, and finally the day arrived to take the play to Gilbert.

It was a long ride to that little town, but we had no trouble with students. Most of them were nervous and anxious to perform in front of kids from another district. In fact, the play, itself, looked GREAT from my vantage point in the back of the Gilbert school's auditorium.

It wasn't until we got on the bus and headed back to Wilhelm, that I discovered the cast had had a problem.....with Garth Ewing. An 8th grader came to sit with me, when we were on the road, and told me that Ewing wanted to create havoc backstage when he wasn't performing. After all, his time on stage was miniscule, and he was a hyper kid anyway. The 8th grader told me that the other players had to try to keep him quiet, and that was hard on them as they were trying to stay in character, and NOT miss their cues to enter the stage. It got SO bad, that during the second act, Garth crawled up into the rafters of the stage, shinnied his way to Center Stage, and started spitting down on the characters, TRYING to break their concentration. The 8th grader told me that the other kids wanted to beat Garth Ewing to a pulp when they returned to school.

I told the informant NOT to jeopardize his, or ANY of the other students' good standing with the school by fighting. I would take care of it. Ewing had been in the back of MY bus, and I immediately went back to where he was, and sat next to him for the remainder of the journey home. He wanted to be funny to make me laugh....I didn't. He wanted to leave his seat and sit somewhere else.....I didn't let him. FINALLY, when we returned to our school, I had him sit on the bus with me, and let him know I knew what he had done at the Gilbert school. He sobered up quickly. I then told him to help with the unloading of the set WITH me, and that I wanted him to report to me first thing in the morning.

No one 'messed' with him that night, and on the following day, when I told him he was being removed from Drama class, and placed into a general 7th grade reading class, he seemed genuinely relieved....and so were the other Drama students.

I was proud of that particular class of students for controlling themselves and adapting to the situation. And I told them I was PARTICULARLY proud of those on stage, who were spit upon, for not breaking character.

While we DID receive congratulatory letters from many of the Gilbert students, and teachers. Sadly, we heard NOTHING from any Wilhelm administrators, though they knew of our good will trip, and our success.

Through the years we had a few disruptions and accidents.... like the year we were supposed to have a cherry PIE come onto the stage. Much of the dialogue, for that scene, centered on that pie... the baking of it, the eating of it. But we had NO pie around the stage area at all. So the actors had to think on their feet.

The character in charge of getting a fresh pie to school, forgot it at his house. He didn't have time to call home, so he went onto our all-purpose stage with a medium-sized, empty cardboard box he just 'happened to find lying around somewhere in the cafeteria kitchen.' From that point onward ALL characters had to INSINUATE that a pie was inside. It was supposed to be removed and passed around during the scene, too, which didn't happen, obviously. With the characters adlibbing masterfully, and with the audience never having to actually SEE a pie, the action flowed perfectly.

One year we were putting on a one-act AND a two-act play for the Wilhelm's fifth grade classes. The one-act play was billed as the shortest play ever written. It was about an elderly woman who was having a birthday. She lived alone, and tried several times to call people to come celebrate her birthday by eating some of her birthday cake with her. Sadly, no one could join her, and she ended up lighting one candle, placing it on the cake that SHE had bought, and singing (sadly, and with tears) Happy Birthday to herself.

Alex and I had presented the play on a previous occasion, and it had students, and teachers alike, wiping their eyes as the curtain closed.

On the SECOND year we were presenting it, the mother of the girl cast to perform the old lady, called and told us her daughter had come down with the flu....ON THE MORNING OF THE PLAY! So, we either had to scrap the one-act, or find a replacement who could learn the lines and blocking in half a day. After all, the play only called for ONE character. I selected another 8th grade girl, who, previous to that day, had been reluctant to act on the stage. She preferred to work with props or be the prompter in our productions, and she had done so on several occasions. She had let Alex and me know how 'terrified' she thought she'd be if she ever had to be on stage.

I gave her no time to give me any excuses when I recruited her to step in to play the character. Just gave her a 'pep talk' about being able to step up for the class when they needed her, then I told her she needed to learn the part in three hours. Talk about pressure!

She not only did a GREAT job, she had ME sobbing with her ending song. Wilhelm had talent oozing out of their students, and I loved working with them in drama.

However, when I moved on to DeWitt School, the program died after two tough years. You'll find out more about the demise of Drama, AND DeWitt later in the book.

Communicating with parents was always an important part of the teaching year. If a student wasn't performing up to par, or if he/she had some problems at school, teachers were NOT reluctant to get into touch with parents.

At Wilhelm, I didn't usually have to call a parent, or arrange for a meeting to discuss urgent problems. The school held parent/teacher conferences twice a year, so there was ample opportunity for both me AND the parent to discuss any student's progress. I used to encourage the parents to come to the conferences and bring their child with them. I never wanted any 'he said, she said' situations. When ALL the parties were in the same room, the REAL story usually came out....and usually the kids didn't like what they heard if they were 'screwing around' at school or getting poorer grades than parents wished.

Wilhelm parents were good about making conferences, ESPECIALLY those whose children were doing well in school. Teachers didn't NEED to talk to parents of great kids, but the parents liked the reinforcement of knowing THEY are doing a great job, too. THOSE conferences were a delight. However, even the best of parents could be tested during conferences.

Evelyn Holliday was one of those parents. She MAY have been my favorite parent of all time. I knew her as a single mother, who was trying to get her boys to be respectful, hard-working citizens, and I think she did a GREAT job. All four of her sons were honor roll students, and all four were respectful to adults and authority figures, AND all four went to college on football scholarships, earning college degrees, too. She was a wonderful mother, who cared deeply about keeping her boys on the straight and narrow.

The first conference I had with her, however, was an eye-opener in a DIFFERENT way. Wilhelm held their conferences in both the individual teacher rooms and the library. I was in the library on the afternoon that Mrs. Holliday came in for HER first conference, and she brought all of her sons with her, too. Steve Lipinski and I decided to hold a co-conference with her, as her eldest son was in the 8th grade, and was just a great kid. We wanted to let her know what a fine job she was doing with Tyrone.

I had already been teaching at Wilhelm several years by then, and had seen a lot of changes in both Brighton District and my school over that length of time. As the years passed, several of the conferences had become almost punitive for the parents, as their children weren't the good academic students, or the respectful children I had been teaching at Wilhelm much earlier in my career. So, having a parent of an all-around 'good' kid was a pleasure, and Steve felt the same way. He and I decided to make Mrs. Holliday feel EXTRA good by having TWO teachers tell her, at the same time, that Tyrone was a delightful child, and that we both enjoyed having him as a student.

Mrs. Holliday was smiling when she and her young men came into the library. Both Tyrone and David (three years younger than Tyrone, and a 5th grader at Wilhelm) sat at the table with hands folded on top. Mrs. Holliday was in a joyful mood because she knew Tyrone was doing well, and was looking forward to hearing about HOW well he was doing.

The two younger sons, Aaron and Nathanial, were in the second and first grades, respectively, at our feeder school. They DIDN'T want to sit with the five of us at the big conference table. Instead, they both appeared a bit 'hyper' and curious, which made them decide to walk around the library, looking at all the books.

As soon as the conference began, and both Steve and I were starting to lay all the 'good stuff' out for Mrs. Holliday to enjoy, she got a rather serious look on her face. Aaron and Nathanial had stopped looking at books, and had decided to run around the library. "Boys," the mother began, "you get over here RIGHT NOW, and sit here with me!" Her voice became quite forceful, and Aaron hustled to a chair at the table and folded HIS hands on top, like his brothers had done.

But the little brother, Nathanial, wasn't quite convinced that his mother was serious, so he looked at her, gave a huge smile, and started running around the room again. "NATHANIAL!" she yelled, loud enough for everyone in the room to hear, "you get over here right NOW. Don't make me have to get up and come get you!"

Nathanial, seeing his mom meant business, ran to get on the seat his mother was patting for him to occupy. He STILL had a huge grin on his face. His mom, seeing that he wasn't QUITE getting the message of respecting the situation, took the tip of her middle finger and THUMPED little Nathanial on the forehead. I'm sure I saw an instant red spot develop, and I DID see Nate's demeanor change instantly, as he, TOO, put his folded hands on the table. Mrs. Holliday enjoyed the rest of the conference, and walked out cheerfully, with all four of her sons following her in a respectful manner.

She had it all, a strong desire for her boys to get a good education, a pleasant personality when speaking to school personnel, and the ability to have her sons 'get in line' when she needed them to do so. I had MANY successful conferences with her over the next several years, and she even had her three youngest boys graduate from DeWitt School. At DeWitt, she became an oasis of happiness for me, as most of the conferences at my NEW school became a lot tougher to get through.

At Dewitt, conferences were held in either the library or cafeteria. It had become such a dangerous neighborhood that female teachers weren't feeling safe being in their individual rooms alone....especially at night.

Many of my conferences, at DeWitt, seemed to follow a terrible, desperate pattern. Parents OFTEN said, "What can I do?" or "He/ She won't listen to me." One parent even told me, "My son runs the house."

"He is thirteen, how can that be?" I questioned.

"He just does what he wants," that particular mom complained. "I can't get him to do ANYTHING. He has a terrible temper," and on and on she went. I talked to her about several solutions....take away his privileges, get help from OTHER family members, (grandparents or uncles who might have influence on him) seek help from her church (mom was very religious) or government agencies with programs for troubled youth. I even asked if she was willing to sit with him and ME, together. Perhaps we could convince him that his mom needs his HELP not his disobedience. She kept wringing her hands and saying over and over again, "Please, Jesus, help me."

Other parents faced many of the circumstances she faced, they just didn't express the despair as strongly. Desperation appeared in many conferences at DeWitt. With each different troubled parent, all we teachers could do was council them, recommend experts in the District who might be more able to help in the situations, or give them a plan for success to try at home.

Poor organizational skills, and failure to follow through with devised plans, were the usual culprits keeping the weaker parents from being successful at home. Teachers NEVER stopped trying to help moms and dads by offering solid ideas that have been tried and true with other parents. But each parent was different. Sometimes the 'plans' worked, sometimes they didn't, and the less-than-successful, yet MOTIVATED, parents might call teachers for more ideas. Sadly, I was seeing more and more parents just giving up when attempting effective discipline on their offspring.

I constantly felt like I was treading water, too. Besides the failures of a lot of 'motivated' parents, there were so many other parents we NEEDED to see concerning their troubled children. Sadly, most of of THEM chose not to come to conferences at all. It was terribly frustrating! Conferences at DeWitt were rough, and not as successful or as fun as they were at Wilhelm. There were some UNUSUAL moments at my new school's conferences, however.

I remember ONE mother, in particular, who came to an afternoon session of DeWitt's parent/teacher conferences. Three blocks from our school was located a, shall we say, 'gentleman's club.' It had small locations, located throughout the place, where women would 'dance' in various stages of undress. This mother worked there, and yes, she was a dancer.

When she walked onto the campus, and headed to the cafeteria where the 8th grade teachers were doing conferences, people stopped in their tracks and stared. She was pretty, facially, and she had a figure that was outstanding. However, she was between shifts at work, and was in a hurry, so she wore her 'work' clothing to school. Specifically, she wore a sheer blouse that was so transparent, it left NOTHING to the imagination, and a VERY short wrap-around beach cover-up over her g-string. She walked into the large room, and without ANY apparent uncomfortable feelings of shame, she headed right to MY table. Steve hustled over to join me, as ALL of her son's teachers wanted to see her, and Steve wanted to make sure she got to see HIM! The mom's son was one of our most difficult students to work with that year, and after meeting the mom, it was not difficult to understand why he was rebelling EVERYWHERE....at home as much as at school.

She basically told us that she had LOTS of boyfriends who would visit her at their home, and the son hated them all. She even told us that she had tried to ship her son to stay with her father, but dear, old dad refused to take the boy. And the kid's birth father was in jail. She liked her job because she could make good money, AND her boyfriends were generous to her, too. Her son had run away from home once, but came back because HE felt he couldn't leave her alone with some of the rough-looking characters his mom entertained. The son COULDN'T win! He didn't like the men in his mother's life and they didn't like him, BUT they would buy his mom things. (we're talking groceries here as well as girly gifts) Just another lost boy with a mixed-up mom, but there was nothing we could figure out that would help her in her current situation.

FINALLY, the mom and son moved out of Arizona, and back home with HER mom. It was a sudden move, and I'm not sure the boy was happy with THAT arrangement, either. At least we had gotten her to come to a parent conference so WE could learn more about why her son was the way he was. After stripper-mom's conference, most of his teachers tried to adapt to the troubled youth's moods, but he never really was much better behaved. The boy and his mom needed help WAY out of our capabilities, and I STILL felt like we failed them. The situation of boyfriends at homes was familiar in a lot of households of the district. But, again, I feel confident saying that the DeWitt teachers NEVER gave up trying to help all our desperate children and their families.

We had ONE night conference that turned out to be rather funny, though. A 7th grade dad came in for his conference, and was sitting at the first table inside the cafeteria. One of his daughter's teachers happened to be occupying that particular table. Sadly, he had ill-fitting denim pants on, and his butt-crack was VERY visible. Every parent AND child who came through the door could NOT miss that man's pants halfway down his rear-end, AND he wasn't wearing any underwear, either.He spent a long time talking to that teacher, who had no idea what was going on behind HIS behind, as she had a LOT to tell the dad. Finally, another 7th grade teacher asked the dad to 'step outside for a moment.' Most of the kids who saw the 'crack' had smiles on their faces, parents had frowns, and teachers....well, we displayed BOTH reactions. Hey, it was getting late and we were getting tired, all right?

It seemed like there was one tough conference after another at DeWitt, but Wilhelm, ALSO, had had a few tough conferences. One incident, that comes to mind, was one of Steve Lipinski's conferences, and MY table was very near Steve's, so I could hear most of what was going on. First, it seemed like the father, Steve was talking to, had been drinking, and I'm not talking a swig or two. He seemed TOO loud and combative even as he walked over to Steve's table. He had his son right behind him, and when he arrived at Lipinski's's table he shouted, "So, what's this JERK done NOW?"

Steve began getting upset while listening to this man 'riding' his son, and finally asked the boy to leave his dad and him alone and to wait outside. "Look," Steve started with SOME anger in his voice, "your boy may not be a top student, and he may play around too much in class, but he IS a good kid. If you keep being abusive to him verbally, and maybe physically, too, my guess is that your son will grow tired of it and turn against you.....maybe end up beating you to a pulp." I agreed with Steve's assessment, but just sat quietly waiting for the dad to come and see me next.

The father, however, got up and stormed out of the building. Steve and I heard, maybe three or four years later, that the son actually DID take a baseball bat to his dad. Never found out what happened after that.

Wilhelm had a lot of great parents, most of the time, but as the drastic economic changes began to take place in Brighton, it seemed that more and more parents of my school were becoming less easy to work with. By the time we junior high teachers moved to DeWitt, the little elite district that I had grown to enjoy immensely, had as many tough-acting kids and disagreeable parents as any Inner City school in Phoenix.

When I first started teaching, in 1973, discipline was accomplished pretty easily. I could use physicality to stop fights, simply by gently pulling or pushing any particular student to get him/her to go where he/she needed to go. I DID once have to pick a big kid up and carry him to the office, as he refused to go on his own, but that was a rare incident. I don't remember parents ever having a problem with teachers getting a little physical to stop inappropriate behavior.

I was given the right to paddle a student, once, after he had given me 'the finger' because I wouldn't let him beat up on another student. The pummeling was occurring on campus, which was a no-no, so I stopped it. I only spanked him once as I didn't want to hurt him. And ONE smack was all I needed to get my point across....no flipping off teachers!

I had four principals, through my career at Wilhelm, and they ALL defended their teachers in any kind of disagreement, or any accusation made by students or parents. However, as the economic 'slide' was infiltrating our district, it seemed that more and more discipline restrictions were being put on teachers. By the time I went to DeWitt School, most of the teachers that I knew were AFRAID to touch a student. Hell, yelling at kids, or even looking harshly at students, could bring reprisals against teachers.

Students at DeWitt KNEW that they could get a teacher into hot water just by telling their parents they felt abused. The parents would then complain to administrators, who, themselves, seemed to be afraid of backlash from the public. No 'boss' wanted to face a lawsuit, so many of us teachers felt like we were just left out to dry, when asking for discipline help and support from administrators.

Where once I could stop fights by grabbing two combatants and holding them apart, by the time I was ready to retire, I was reduced to taking a legal pad and a pen with me wherever I would go. IF I saw a couple of kids fighting, (the usual big crowd of screaming kids in a circle was a dead giveaway) I would approach the group, and start shouting, "I am taking down names of ALL witnesses!" The crowd usually dispersed quickly, leaving me with just the two battlers.

"All right," I would calmly say, "your fans have gone away, and it's just you and me now." I had earned respect by being a long-time coach and teacher, so kids watching the fighters didn't want me to think THEY were trouble-makers, too. Once the innocent bystanders scattered from 'the scene' as quickly and unobtrusively as they could. I had little trouble stopping the combatants. Other teachers didn't have it so easy, as you will find out a little later.

By the year 2000, in Brighton District, most teachers had little to NO control over the behavior of students; thus, respect gotten FROM students toward teachers was nearly non-existent, from what I could ascertain through conversations with peers. Educators throughout Brighton began leaving in droves....senior teachers taking any good early retirement packages that were offered....young teachers fleeing to districts where respect was still given to authority figures. To ME, when a person loses respect, the will to succeed deteriorates. I remember the very first time that support from one of my principals, for me, wasn't what it should be. The incident took place during my 6th year of teaching at Wilhelm.

In the school year 1978-'79, Wilhelm had a principal named John Peabody. He was a former teacher of the Brighton District, and had worked in the District office for a few years, too. However, he had wanted to become a school principal. When Charles Fletcher retired, Peabody jumped at the chance to lead Wilhelm. He wasn't a great principal, and I didn't really have much to do with him. Basically, he pretty much left me alone to 'get the job done,' just as Mr. Fletcher had done before him. That was fine with me, as I DID get some top-notch learning from my students that year.

Unfortunately, there had become such a huge occurrence of transient families, moving in and out of Brighton, that by 1978, newer students were presenting themselves to be more difficult to discipline.

Simon Miller wasn't much different from most of the newer students we had enrolling into Wilhelm. He was an only child, living with his mother, and they were poor financially. Not Daniel Zwang poor, but not much better off. The difference between Daniel and Simon was attitude. Daniel's was always positive, Simon's was always negative.

Simon was in my 3rd hour English class, and one day he came into the room looking angry. The tardy bell rang, and I was anxious to get the day's work going because I had a lot of it to do that day. Simon was fiddling around in his desk's book compartment. Since the compartment was low, on the side of his desk, Simon was on his knees, and just kept shuffling papers around, NOT trying to get anything out....just shuffling.

The class was quiet, and looking at Simon, and I finally said, "Simon, I need to get class started now. Would you sit in your seat, now, please?"

The boy never raised his eyes to let me know he heard me, just kept pushing papers around for no apparent reason. "Simon, did you hear what I said?" No recognition of me whatsoever. "Simon," I continued with a little more urgency in my voice, "I need for you to look at me to know you hear what I am saying."

The kid just kept his head in the compartment and the shuffling got more animated....so I moved to his desk. "Simon, can you hear me?" I said while getting more impatient. "I want you to look at me, in fact, I NEED for you to look at me so I know you understand what I am saying."

Simon wasn't handicapped in any way, just a product of a broken home living on welfare, and he always seemed angry about that. But, by 1978, Wilhelm had begun having more and more families living on welfare. He was just being obstinate toward me, and his behavior wasn't letting me get my class started. I just plain got tired of the game.

I got down on my knees, so we were at the same level, cupped my hands over both his ears, turned his head slightly, so I could see him looking at me, and said sternly, "Can you see me now? I want you to stop this nonsense and let me do my class."

"My mom is going to SUE you," he said with a truly evil look in his eyes.

THAT was it....I was FED UP! "Let's go, Mr. Miller," I said while feeling my blood pressure rising instantly, "You and I are going to see the principal."

I took his arm, lifted him to his feet, and headed out the door. The other students were, thankfully, quiet, and I said to THEM, in a serious tone, "Stay quietly in your seats, and I will be RIGHT back." I didn't really care what the other kids were going to do at that moment, I just knew I had to get Simon to Mr. Peabody IMMEDIATELY!

I had never taken a student to the office before, so was unsure what the procedure would be. I was hoping to tell Mr. Peabody my story quickly, then hustle back to my class. Even though the principal was IN his office, when young Mr. Miller and I arrived, he seemed content to be having a jovial conversation on the phone. My class disruptor and I sat in the secretary's office for nearly ten minutes. I was getting antsy about leaving my class, but I WASN'T going to let the words 'sue you' go by the wayside.

Finally, Mr. Peabody came out of his office to get us. He then asked the two of us, while displaying a big smile on his face, to come inside and have a seat. He saw me perturbed, yet he was smiling....must have been a great phone call.

Simon sat directly across from the principal, while I sat in the seat closer to the door. I wanted desperately to get back to my unattended classroom. AND when the principal said, "What's the problem here?" while maintaining that smile on his face, I told him the whole story.

Peabody FINALLY got a more serious look on his face then addressed Simon, "Is what Mr. Stein has just told me the story the way you remember it?"

The student nodded affirmatively, so Mr. Peabody continued, "Well, Simon, your mom CAN'T sue him for that. You were rude, and NOT letting him teach his class, which is his job. All Mr. Stein was doing was getting your attention. He certainly wasn't hurting you. You owe HIM an apology."

"My mom's going to sue YOU, too!" Simon blurted out.

The principal jumped to his feet instantly, and got a VERY serious look on his, suddenly, purplish-red-hued face. He reached across his desk with the speed of a lightening bolt, and grabbed BOTH of Simon's arms. Mr. Peabody pulled that kid straight out of his chair while shouting angrily, "WHAT DID YOU SAY?"

"MY mom's going to sue him, you, the school, AND the district,! My mom is going to sue you ALL!" Simon shouted, though he was trembling. That kid was not backing down.

With the principal now FULLY engaged in the situation, I said calmly, "I'll be getting back to my class now." And I left. There were NO questions from my students when I returned, which kind of surprised me. I guess they never saw me upset in class before.

However, when THAT class ended, I stepped outside for a second, and saw that Mr. Peabody was heading toward my room. "Why did you have to grab that kid, Stein?" he blurted out WELL before he got to my room's door. I was surprised at the anger he was showing toward ME. I was feeling attacked simply by hearing the tone in his voice AND due to the fact that he was addressing me by the usage of just my last name....something he had never done before.

"You grabbed him, too, Sir," I said defensively. "And a lot rougher than I did."

I saw the exasperation slightly leaving his tense face. "Nothing's going to happen, Mr. Stein," the principal said while trying to act a little more professional. "I talked to Simon's mother and she seemed surprised at what her son had said. She never talked to him about suing anybody, and will talk to him when he gets home today about his class behavior. I will have him in the office for the rest of the day." Then the principal looked at me, and suddenly, with the exasperation fully returning to his face, he said, "BUT, Mr. Stein, QUIT grabbing your students."

Simon Miller was the last kid I ever physically responded to while I was angry.

Indeed, disciplining of students was changing quickly for Brighton teachers. We were being restricted in how to deal with kids. Molly-coddling, especially by administrators, had suddenly become the disciplining fad being introduced into Brighton schools as the `70's decade faded away. Students began NOT to fear retribution for disrupting education. When I was a kid, I HATED to be sent to the office. If I got into trouble at school, I got into MORE trouble when I got home.

My first principal, Mr. Fletcher, was a throwback to days gone by. Kids respected him as a hard-nosed principal, and shaped up instantly for their teachers if they thought they might have to see him for discipline reasons.

Gentler and kinder ways of dealing with poorly-behaved children were suddenly being demanded by government at the State and Federal levels, parent groups and school boards at the local levels, and administrators EVERYWHERE. Strict discipline had quickly become a dinosaur in education.

By the time I retired, there was no paddling allowed by anyone at schools, teachers were told to keep their hands OFF students, (even while trying to stop fights) Yelling was out. Hard looks were taboo. Discipline at Brighton schools had become a joke.

Teachers were told to send disruptive students to the office for discipline. In MANY instances the miscreants were sent BACK to class before that class was even over for the day. When that action was taken, teachers were told that the malcontents agreed to behave themselves, therefore, being allowed to return to class.

Is it no wonder that other students, seeing students quickly return to class, figured out nothing 'bad' would happen if THEY were to become agitators, too. I heard some teachers say that there were times when they (educators) were spending more time sending students to the office then being allowed to teach the lesson of the day.

Students did NOT seem to be held accountable for poor behavior, and teachers began to feel helpless when trying to control class discipline. It was becoming apparent me, as school discipline began waning, student learning began waning, too, and at an alarming rate. I was not surprised to see more and more teachers looking for opportunities to get out of education.

Even by the mid-1980's, my fellow teaching friends and I began realizing that educational achievement was taking perceptive steps backward. We were reading where decline was happening NATIONALLY, as well. Our once proud district was struggling to even score SATISFACTORILY on skills being tested by national tests. My hypothesis was that there had to be a definite and direct link between students' achievement in academics, and discipline plans being implemented on campuses, both in the Phoenix area, and in schools throughout the nation.

Take a look and see how THIS works. Teachers are TOLD to have students get better grades....even 'threatened' to have salaries tied to student achievement. Those teachers, however, have been given more and more restrictions put on them on how to discipline their charges. Students, realizing that discipline in the classroom has become nearly non-existent, decide they can 'act out' as much as they want as reprisals are laughable. This scenario causes teachers to struggle in maintaining a good learning environment WHILE trying to control student behavior. With increased disruptions in the classroom, time has to be taken away from the learning process; thus, less is being taught, AND students are learning less. No WONDER learning has been on a decline!

Many of us working in the Inner City experienced this 'happening' to us first hand, and were insulted when we were blamed for poorer test scores on those national standardized tests. I feel pretty confident, even in my retirement of more than ten years now, that the situation in many of the poorer neighborhood public schools hasn't changed much at all. Those schools are likely still rife with poor discipline plans, which, I believe to be directly

linked to having poor scores on national tests. The whole situation may even be getting worse, based on what I am hearing and
reading.

But, I ALSO believe that the 'powers to be' don't really feel
the NEED to do what is necessary to help improve education in
ghettos. Oh, they say what people want to hear....that they are
working on the 'problems' in education. But it seems that the rich
only take care of their OWN children by enrolling them in private
schools, or OTHER similar institutions that wealthier folk can afford, while the poor are forced to fend for themselves in poverty-
stricken neighborhood schools.

Educational politics in this country is....well....people can SEE
what is happening in the increased disrespect and miscreant behavior being displayed by young people throughout our country.
Respect, discipline, and a solid educational background go hand
in hand, and apathy by people in power can only mean further
back-sliding of what made this country strong.

But, I am straying, here. I have more to tell you of MY experiences.

Setting discipline aside, I can say that my work with Brighton
kids in drama, sports and something called the California Trip, was
very satisfying....especially my sixteen years at Wilhelm. DeWitt
was more of a nightmare. Read on to see what I mean.

6

AH, THE SPORTING LIFE

PLAYING SPORTS, ANY sports, while growing up, taught me responsibility, teamwork, and skills that would help me deal with life. When I began teaching, I ENJOYED working with children in my English classrooms....rote learning, rules and exceptions to the rules, spelling....time-tested learning skills that put structure in students' lives. I thoroughly enjoyed working with the students in Drama classes, too. I enjoyed the creativity of visiting make believe lands, and watching the students emote with ACCEPTABLE means of expression. But it was coaching athletes, in both my schools, that made me a truly happy camper much of my career.

Coaching was MY way of dealing with the daily stress that most teachers faced back then....ESPECIALLY when we were given less effective ways of disciplining students around school, or even in our own classes. Stress just piled up on me by the end of each day, and I needed a release... I needed to YELL! Yelling WAS allowed when coaching teams, and I felt SO much better when I went home at night. Coaching athletic skills, and getting to yell while coaching, allowed me to have nearly perfect days at school.

As soon as I was ready to begin a practice for ANY of my teams, I simply had to yell, "ALL RIGHT, LET'S GET STARTED!" My stress level diminished instantly. I never TRIED to discourage or demean any of my athletes by yelling. The occasional, "You've GOT to start focusing," or "Don't DO that again!" bothered no one, and I don't recall any of my athletes taking my yelling to heart, as a way for me to belittle them due to lack of talent. Sometimes, however, when I was having practice, and some of the members of the team were 'horsing around,' I got unhappy and yelled (never cursing, though) and that would get EVERYBODY'S attention, which gave me control again.

I screamed at ALL of the athletic games and tournaments my teams participated in because I knew my athletes were still kids, and they had LOTS to learn. I was just telling them, in a loud voice, what needed to be done next. I am a very competitive fellow, and I wanted to help my teams NOT lose. Sometimes I screamed encouragement....in fact, a LOT of times I screamed encouragement. Sometimes I screamed about points that were concerning me. The point here is that I USED coaching as a way to release all the pent-up stress that the rest of my day had built up.

While student teaching, I volunteered to assist ANY Wilhelm coach, in any sport his/her kids were playing. I got to help Steve during his track and field season, and loved it. I was even asked one day, by Wilhelm's girls' P.E. teacher, Sarah Collier, to run her softball practice. She had an appointment, and needed someone to step in for her, lest she would have to cancel practice. It must have been an important appointment because Sarah NEVER missed practice. I was excited for the opportunity to help, and couldn't WAIT for school to be out! Since most of the girls on the team were 8th graders, I knew of their academic skills, but I was curious to see them in action OUT of the classroom. I wanted to see if any of them had athletic talent.

I was pleased with a couple of the girls and their skill levels, and thought things were going swimmingly UNTIL there were five minutes to go before I wanted to end practice. I simply told the girls to line up in the outfield, so we could run a couple of 30-yard 'wind sprints.' "Mr. Stein," one of the girls complained, "Ms Collier NEVER has us running AFTER practice. I don't think we need to run."

I told them that practice wasn't over yet, and that conditioning was an important facet of being a good athlete, etc., etc. But the girls had already tuned out. Several of the girls, who had agreed with the complainer that running was NOT a 'thing' that Coach Collier would do, decided their practice was over, and immediately headed off the softball diamond. Two other players saw a slow-moving car, loaded with high school boys, rolling slowly past the practice field, so they took off to say 'Hi.' One girl said she wasn't feeling well, and another two girls just started wandering away in animated conversation. Needless to say, practice was over.

The next day, I told Ms Collier to not ask me to coach her girls' softball team again. She just laughed when I told her my story and said, "That's junior high girls for you." Then the coach looked at me and continued with some advice that stuck with me throughout the rest of my coaching days, "TELLING what to do is not, necessarily, the technique you should use on teenage girls who aren't star athletes, and most of the girls here do sports because their friends are doing them. You should try to COAX the girls into understanding that they NEED to do what you say because it will help them succeed."

Quite honestly, I ended up using that technique my entire coaching career on boys, too. I DIDN'T raise my voice to make DEMANDS. I raised it to free stress that I had building up inside. Once THAT was done, I did what I did best, and that was explaining why certain strategies worked, while showing my athletes how to perform the skills.

Of course, we practiced, practiced, practiced, so urgency of learning was relative. In the classroom, I HAD to teach many different skills, and sadly, I only had just so much time to do it. Practice on any English skill was limited. Coaching, on the other hand, allowed me to take as much time as is necessary to achieve learning a new skill. There was no bell to move them from one class to another. No detailed daily lesson plans to follow. I could take my time and pratice until all or MOST of my athletes showed a high level of understanding of what was being demonstrated. This allowed us to practice, practice, PRACTICE without constraints. I LOVED coaching!

The only GIRL'S athletic team I really coached, in my 16 years at Wilhelm, was the track team, and I 'inherited' them the third year I taught 8th grade.

I had helped both Steve Lipinski and Sarah Collier with the boys' track team, and girls' track team, respectively, during my first two years as a certified teacher. In fact, I coached 'weight' throwing, specifically the shot put, for both boys AND girls, and worked with sprint starts, too. Mostly, however, I just helped to make sure everybody was doing SOMETHING track-oriented, as there were kids EVERYWHERE, and the coaches could only be in one place at a time.

However, at the end of MY second year, Sarah had an 'incident,' which had her turning over the reigns to me, and I ended up coaching girls' track for the next fourteen years.

That second year, Ms Collins had ONE outstanding athlete out for track. Esther McCloud could run like the wind. Unfortunately for the team, there weren't too many other girls who had top-notch talent. Oh, they tried to compete, but the talent pool was more on the mediocre side than gifted. Esther was gifted.

The local Optimist Club held a big track meet every spring, for 4th-8th graders, and many teams were invited. Everyone called it the 'State Meet,' though not all teams in Arizona were invited to compete, not even all schools from the Phoenix area, let alone outside Maricopa County. Short sprints, jumping events and throwing events, were the only events...no long-distance or relay events were on the agenda EXCEPT for ONE short relay. The track, where the meet was held, was only 300 yards in total length, so all running events were limited. Therefore, the LONGEST event was the 240 yd. relay, for both boys and girls.

Esther won the 'open' 60 yard dash (the longest individual girls' race) with ease. Then she won the long jump with ease, as well. She was to anchor the girls 4X60 relay, and if Wilhelm could win the event, Esther would be awarded the outstanding girl athlete of the meet. A nice trophy was given to the outstanding boy and girl, so Sarah Collier was excited that she FINALLY had an athlete who stood a chance to win the prestigious trophy, AND she told the relay team that a WIN would ensure the Wilhelm girl of the award.

The team had three 'fairly fast' runners in front of Esther, but Coach Collier was CONFIDENT that once Esther got the baton, no matter if she was, maybe, five or six yards behind the leaders, McCloud would get to the tape first.

Wilhelm drew a middle lane for the Finals, and there were four teams outside of them. They all had staggered lanes, but to our girls it looked like they were giving up a lot of track to their competitors. Collier explained, during the preliminary heat Wilhelm ran, (and our girls drew the OUTSIDE lane for the preliminaries) that the girls on the inside would be catching up to the outside girls who looked like they had a big lead. She assured her team that every runner ran the same distance, and that the STAGGER was an allusion of being ahead. The coach also explained that, by the time the LAST handoff was made, ALL anchor runners would be running down the straightaway at the same time, the staggers would be made up, allowing the fastest girl to win the race. She just told her team that EVERY girl had to run just as hard as she could. Wilhelm won their preliminary race by SEVEN yards.

Drawing a middle lane for the Finals had the girls doubting themselves again, SO Coach Collier explained, again, what a stagger meant. THREE of the girls got what the coach was explaining right away. One girl, Betsy Unger, really had trouble understanding the concept of staggers. She kept saying it looked like cheating to her.

Betsy was considered a 'sourpuss' by many Wilhelm teachers, in the classroom. She was smart enough in her class work, but tended to be quite moody, and had a temper, too. If Unger decided she wasn't going to do something, she didn't do it. In fact, Betsy Unger had butted heads with Coach Collier a couple of times BEFORE the 'State' meet came around.

During one of the practices for State, Betsy told the coach that she didn't LIKE to hand-off, just liked 'getting' the baton. Betsy even suggested that SHE should be anchor instead of Esther, then pouted when she was told she wasn't getting her way.

EVEN when the relay teams were being called to the starting lines AT State, Betsy pleaded with her coach to change the two positions. Ms Collier told the girl that she wanted the judges to SEE how easily Esther caught her opponents in winning the relay, making sure that the Wilhelm runner would win the outstanding girl athlete award. The coach tried to explain that Esther and Betsy hadn't even PRACTICED switching handoff positions, and that trading places would surely lead to disaster. Betsy was pouting again, but went to her position on the field....where the third runners were to report.

When the race started, the first two Wilhelm runners were holding their own....I'm thinking adrenalin was at work here. There WERE some pretty fast teams, but nobody appeared to be pulling away with the race. The hand-off to Betsy went smoothly, too. But ALL the girls to her outside still had a lead due to the stagger. Betsy took five steps, after she got the baton, then THREW the baton on the ground and walked off the track.

Esther McCloud looked in amazement when she saw Betsy stop running and heading to the infield. She then looked at the finish line, where Coach Collier had been waiting for the victorious

Wilhelm team. The coach IMMEDIATELY headed toward Betsy Unger. Seeing how angry the coach looked, I headed in Betsy's direction, too, to see if I could help in any way.

Betsy, for her part, saw her coach running in her direction, so she stopped, folded her arms, and looked up into the air as the coach started to rant. "WHY DID YOU THROW THE BATON DOWN, UNGER?" the coach said, loud enough so that people within fifty yards of her could hear.

Betsy never wavered a bit. She kept staring up to the sky, and with the usual sour look on her face, and her customary caustic attitude, she answered, "I wasn't catching anyone, so we would have lost ANYWAY!"

Sarah Collier walked angrily away, definitely showing frustration. Esther didn't win the outstanding female athlete medal at the meet, and Betsy Unger wasn't given a track certificate at Wilhelm's spring athletic presentations, either. It was at THAT awards assembly that Sarah told me I could coach the track team if I wanted them, and that is how I came to coach my only girls' team.

During the next track season, and every season that followed, I had the girls practice relay hand-offs at lunch, EVERY lunch. We practiced getting fast exchanges against boy volunteer runners, too. Funny thing, though, the boys ALWAYS thought they would be able to beat the girls on handoff exchanges, but they never did. One special year, I had a team with FOUR fast runners. They even broke the Optimist's relay RECORD that year, and held it for a few years thereafter. I NEVER had a Betsy Unger on ANY of my teams, thankfully, but DID have two Esther-type runners, the year the re-lay record was broken.

With the move to DeWitt, however, I was replaced by the new school's female P.E. teacher, as the girls' track coach, and I wasn't sad.

I DID, however, get a chance to work with Jerry Randolph and the boys' team at DeWitt. I worked ONE year on relay handoffs with a special team he had that year. Jerry knew of my reputation at getting runners to make great relay exchanges, and he had two boy runners who were VERY fast, PLUS two other boys who were pretty fast. Jerry wanted them to run the perfect relay, and he thought my 'handoff' method would help them succeed.

One of the star runners was Aaron Holliday. His older broth-er David was even faster than Aaron, but when HE was at DeWitt, there was no supporting cast for a fast-running relay, so Jerry used his relay methods of training, and was OK with it. In fact, David Holliday went on to be the Arizona State 100 meter champion his senior year in high school, was an all-state football player, was the star back on his university's football team, AND played profession football for three years. He was a great athletic talent, and all three of his brothers were just a step behind him.

During Aaron's 8th grade year, there was another very quick runner, named Dorian Cummins. Those two guys were SO CLOSE in every 100 meter dash, that when they had race-offs, one of them might win one race, with the other guy winning the next race between them. I called them dead-even in speed. When I realized there were two OTHER fast runners on the relay, I knew the school had the fixings for a GREAT relay team....and I wasn't disappointed.

Aaron was the leader of that team. With my positive history with his mom, and ALL the Holliday brothers believing I knew what I was doing as a coach, Aaron made sure that the other three guys were at every practice, and doing exactly what I asked them to do....no goofing around, no coming late to practice, either. Aaron was ALSO a lady's man, of that there was no denying. But while I was in charge of that year's relay, he was all track business, AND he made sure the other three fellows were serious, too.

Like I used to do with my girl relay teams at Wilhelm, we practiced our 'blind' hand-offs constantly. It didn't matter that all the other teams we faced were doing very SIMILAR techniques of hand-offs between runners, my style was definitely different.

I YELLED to get my point across. I yelled whenever ANY of the runners started off too slowly from his mark, yelled when anyone took off too quickly, too. And I ESPECIALLY was loud, if I saw ANY of them looking back for the baton, once the in-coming runner hit the mark indicating it was time for the out-going runner to take off. I wanted each 'receiving' runner to sprint away as hard as he could go, and to TRUST that his teammate would get him the baton. AND, I wanted each receiving runner's start to be identical to every other start he practiced....same speed, same hand position, same trust of in-coming teammate. I wanted the perfect exchanges of the baton. I told every relay member, who was to hand off the baton to the next runner, "When you are approaching your teammate, and you are getting READY to give the baton up, I don't want you to yell 'HAND' until you can actually GET that baton handed off in LESS than one second...no sooner....no later.....

make your exchange in less than one second. If you CAN'T make the exchange in less than one second, you don't yell 'hand.' at all."

I also had specific instructions for the RECEIVING runner, as well. "When your take-off mark is hit, you take off like a bat out of Hell, and it doesn't matter if you run all the way to the finish line without the baton, you do NOT slow down OR look back until you hear your partner say, 'HAND.' Understood?"

"When you DO hear 'hand,' you snap your hand down like THIS," and I would demonstrate the technique once again. "Once you RECEIVE the stick, you get that baton to the next guy just as fast as your legs can get you there. Aaron, once YOU get the baton, you don't slow down until you are FIVE yards past the finish line. Don't slow down AT the finish line, run THROUGH the finish line for five extra yards. Understood? The bottom line IS, relay runners, I mean, CHAMPION relay runners, you run as hard as you can at all times, and you NEVER look back!" Yep, gave the same speech every chance I got. OK, I was an emotional coach, but the boys GOT the message.

We went to practice at one of the local high schools one day, and some of the track guys on THEIR team wanted to race our relay. The high school boys hadn't practiced hand-offs, amongst themselves, even once, and it showed. Our team won by nearly seventy yards, and the high school runners were impressed.

I usually had Aaron anchor, and Dorian run the second leg, where HE would be able to impress everyone else, in the race or watching our relay team in action, with HIS speed....and it worked. When Dorian would receive the perfect hand-off, WHILE running at full speed, he would pass ALL the other second-leg runners, no matter WHERE their lanes were. And the crowd would start to murmur louder and LOUDER as Cummins blew past all his competitors. By the time Aaron Holliday got the baton, he could beat ANY team of 8th grade runners, by NEARLY 60 yards. I just watched the relay with pride, and the boys LOVED winning by such great margins.

We had ONE incident, a missed hand-off. It occurred at a big meet in Prescott, AZ. DeWitt's third runner hit Aaron's hand incorrectly, causing the baton to drop to the ground. Holiday stopped, went back to pick up the stick, then ran to a twenty-yard victory anyway. The best junior high relay team I ever saw!

After watching so many failures by America's Olympic relay teams, I wanted someone to call me and ask if I would help the U.S.A. team with relay hand-offs….just kidding…no I'm not. Let's just move on.

I never heard if three of the boys, from that relay team, ever ran track after OUR fabulous year….not even about Aaron Holliday. I did, however, hear that Dorian Cummins chose to play baseball instead of run track. Nonetheless, for one sweet year, those four guys were the cream of the junior high crop, and I was proud to be a part of it.

The competitive spirit I felt, every time I was involved in any sporting event, had always been a driving force in my life. (still is) NATURALLY, when I began my career at Wilhelm, I told Steve Lipinski I would help coach ANY team that he had available. I wanted to see if I could bring out a similar desire to win in kids that I coached.

Football was Wilhelm's first athletic program every year, and since Steve had the varsity (8th graders) during my first year teaching, I had the junior varsity. (7th graders) Steve had been the coach of both teams, prior to my getting to the school, and was delighted that he could concentrate on the one team. However, his coaching techniques were different than mine, SO, when my second year at Wilhelm came around, we decided Steve would take the NEW junior varsity team, and I would continue coaching MY team through their varsity year. THAT way, the boys wouldn't have to learn a new system each year. As I have previously mentioned, the 'system' would only be in place for six years before soccer took football's place, and that made me quite sad.

I have to mention here that Brighton's OFFICIAL reason, for the change in going to soccer, was their declaration that the District's insurance had increased a great deal BECAUSE we had football. With soccer, our insurance rates would be MUCH lower, we were told. All I knew was that Wilhelm never had a football player get an injury, during my six years coaching, and I never heard Pfister or Cahill complaining of injuries, either. How could soccer generate LESS insurance? After all, wouldn't a kid, trying to stop a kicked soccer ball with his HEAD, seem more likely to create an injury than pulling a flag? And kicking each other's legs all game....that has GOT to be painful.

I had never played soccer, therefore, I couldn't coach it. A number of boys, who loved playing football, chose to 'skip' soccer, too. Participation by Wilhelm boys on the soccer team was pathetic compared to the numbers that football had produced every year. That left a lot of boys, doing nothing after school, which could only mean more time for the guys to get into trouble....or so I believed. Brighton

District had soccer teams for girls, too, so that was a positive point. I just felt sour grapes at the time because I loved coaching football.

In the '70's, basketball was the king sport around Wilhelm. Steve Lipinski was a basketball fanatic, and he had a pretty good system worked out at Wilhelm. He had Abner Caldwell coaching the 7th grade boys, and Abner had played college ball, so he was really knowledgeable with his coaching. Caldwell worked hard on basic basketball skills, which gave more time for Lipinski to work on the intricacies of more complicated offenses and defenses.

When Steve asked me if I would mind coaching the 5th and 6th grade boys, he knew I knew basketball pretty well, also. He had had volunteers in previous years, who didn't have the competitive spirit that Steve and Abner had for the sport. But both knew I DID, so Steve asked if I would mind taking over the 5th and 6th program. Since I would be working hard on the basics of basketball with the younger guys, Caldwell could work HIS team with more intricate skill sets more quickly. The Wilhelm basketball system was in place for many years with our 'farm' scheme....and it worked.

It didn't matter how much the District was changing, Lipinski ALWAYS was able to put a quality team on the court. Steve never had a kid over six-feet tall, but his 8th grade teams never failed to be competitive....even in large tournaments. No matter the larger populations of other schools, who had many, MANY more players from whom to choose the best players and form teams, Wilhelm had the reputation of being a formidable basketball opponent. It was a reputation that the school cherished. However, the basketball fortunes changed when DeWitt was built, but THAT gruesome story will be told later in this book.

As a school with good athletes, Wilhelm was known as a tough competitor during MOST of the sports seasons. There was ONE glaring over-sight, as far as I was concerned, and that was when the wrestling season came around.

Lipinski had studied the basics of wrestling, and presented what he knew in his P.E. classes. Since there also was a lull between basketball and track seasons, Brighton P.E. teachers taught wrestling AND decided to have a wrestling tournament. If Steve and the other two coaches decided to coach the sport after school, too, I was unaware of it. But I DID hear they were holding a tournament when the wrestling unit was finished. I couldn't wait to be there for that.

I was a 7th grade teacher for my first two years at Wilhelm, and 8th graders were usually the primary source of the wrestling team's entrants in the Brighton tournament. For THAT reason there was NO chatter in my classes about the sport. Actually, NOBODY seemed to be 'fired up' about wrestling at all....not the kids, and not Steve Lipinski. I might have been surprised about the total lack of enthusiasm if I didn't remember that Wilhelm was a BASKETBALL school, and Steve was really an expert in THAT sport. But I only heard about the tournament through a fluke conversation I overheard. One kid was telling another kid that he would be late to his house because he had to 'wrestle in a tournament after school.'

EVERYONE seemed to view wrestling as a 'filler' sport at our school. Therefore, I WASN'T surprised when I discovered that several of our school's top athletes didn't view wrestling as 'their thing.' Many of them chose, instead, to take time off after b-ball and rest before track season started. I saw that as the way for athletes to get out of shape, and, possibly, give our star athletes time to get into trouble….idle hands, you know.

I went to the tournament, and was terribly disappointed at what I saw. NONE of my school's students attended the tourney. It was held at Cahill Elementary, but that was fine. Wilhelm fans attended our football and basketball tournaments no matter where they were held. Besides Steve and his team, and a few parents of the wrestlers, and I mean a VERY few parents, I was the only Wilhelm school member at the meet, and that made me sad. I was NOT surprised that no administrators were there….they never seemed to be at ANY of the District's sporting tournaments….EVER!

The school hosting the meet, Alfred C. Cahill Elementary, was located in the toughest neighborhoods in Brighton District. It was pretty much known that the kids from that area were brawlers, and would be using the wrestling tournament as a way to take out their aggression on the wimpier kids who attended Pfister and Wilhelm schools. Jerry Randolph only had to teach most of HIS wrestlers the 'basics' of a takedown and the two other starting positions (top and bottom) to start each round, then he let the kids' aggressive natures take over. However, NOBODY was really adept at doing wrestling moves from any school. Cahill guys would simply walk in to their opponents, take them down any way they could, and turn them over if they could. It was terribly sloppy wrestling, but I guess I shouldn't have expected any more, since the whole wrestling experience was so short, and no coach really had a background in wrestling.

I grew up in Iowa, where wrestling was practically a religion of its own. If a boy in the Hawkeye state didn't start to learn how to wrestle by the time he was FIVE years of age, he would just get beaten up by those kids who WERE learning how to wrestle. I LOVED wrestling, so I asked Mr. Lipinski if I could take the program over in my second year of teaching. He was much obliged to let me do that.

To tell you how lop-sided Cahill's victory was, at the first tournament I witnessed, let me just say that there were 18 weight divisions being contested. Cahill won 16, with Wilhelm and Pfister winning just one each. According to Steve, that was the usual way the tournament went during HIS time at Wilhelm. I was bound and determined to make changes.

When it was time for wrestling to start, the next year, with me as the coach, I started by making the wrestling season longer…. six weeks. Cahill stayed with the customary two to three weeks of instruction in the sport. I sought out non-basketball athletes, in both the 7th and 8th grades, and convinced them to give wrestling a try. I might have STILL been a 7th grade teacher, BUT I had taught the current 8th graders when they were in the 7th grade, so I still believed I had some influence with them. We even started the 'season' three weeks before Steve began wrestling instruction in P.E. My team practiced after school though we just had tumbling mats to practice on….which belonged to the P.E. classes.

Fortunately, the 5th and 6th grade boys' basketball season ended earlier than did the varsity, so I could coach THOSE boys for the extra couple weeks, too. And I got several 7th grade basketball players to try grappling, too, as their season ended earlier than the 8th grade. I didn't want to upset Steve's season, by trying to recruit his players and have them think about joining my team. But as soon as

the 8th grade season was over, I pushed hard to have the older basketball players join Wilhelm's wrestling team, too. I had SO MANY
wrestling candidates, that I couldn't teach everything I needed to
during my six-week season.

When the tournament was held, during my first year coaching, I asked that it be held at Wilhelm. Steve was there, and so
were MANY more Wilhelm fans. Our school was FINALLY getting
spirit for a wrestling team. However, Wilhelm only won SIX weight
divisions, with Cahill winning eleven and Pfister its usual one. But
MY school was on its way to having success on the mats, and I was
happy, happy, HAPPY!

By the time I started my third year of teaching, which was my
first year teaching 8th grade, and second with the wrestling program, I had SEVERAL boys asking about joining the team BEFORE
the season was to start. I even invited the fourth graders from our
feeder school to come and join us. I got to extend the season a bit
longer, too, maybe one more week longer than the previous year. I
actually started my FIRST wrestling practice the Monday after my
basketball team coaching assignment was over.

When the wrestling tournament came around, I had experienced wrestlers back from the previous year, and MORE 8th
grade star athletes joining my team. It didn't matter that the
tournament was, once again, being held at Cahill Elementary,
Wilhelm won 16 weight divisions, Pfister its customary one,
and Cahill could only claim ONE champion. My school had
become dominant, and BOTH of the other school's knew it and
chose to NOT have a District wrestling tournament the following year.

That put me in a quandary. I wanted to coach wrestling, and there were many boys at Wilhelm who looked forward to wrestling for me. I volunteered to coach ANY interested boy in wrestling, in the Brighton District. And I would start that program the following year.

My plan was to have wrestlers from the other two schools simply get on a school bus after school, get off at the bus barn, which was three hundred yards from Wilhelm and come join the team. Steve made arrangements to have ONE bus drive the Wilhelm neighborhood kids home AFTER practice, but the wrestlers from both Cahill and Pfister had to find their OWN ways home. That didn't seem fair to me, and held the participation down from those two schools, but that was the 'Best the District could do,' according to what Steve was told by District administrators.

The bussing situation DID hurt a bit. In fact, only two boys from Pfister showed up for my initial District-wide wrestling practice. Cahill only had three boys choosing to join us, and they came late because the bus they rode took quite a while to get to the bus barn. All the Pfister and Cahill wrestlers complained that they would have to walk home after practice that first night....wanted me to drive them. I didn't. The next practice I noticed that ALL of them found a way to get home. In fact, the boys from the other two schools liked the new wrestling set-up so much, they arranged transportation home after EVERY practice, and that took a lot of pressure off me.

Cahill had the only wrestling MAT in the district, and it was very small. It used to be shipped from school to school when the District tournaments were held away from Cahill. But, once I started my program, Jerry Randolph 'donated' the mat to Wilhelm. We ended up with 45 wrestlers, that first year, and had to use Wilhelm's tumbling mats, which were placed around the edges of the lone wrestling mat. That gave the appearance of a bigger surface on which to wrestle....though we had to keep tucking the tumblers BACK against the Cahill mat, as they slid so easily when the boys were practicing.

With so many boys, coming from four schools, (this included our 4th graders from our nearby feeder school, Richland) I could see I needed help coaching. The very first year, I told the 8th graders from ALL schools that they needed to help me keep order, or the wrestling season would be cut short. It worked so well, that I got help from 8th graders EVERY year, even when I DID have an assistant coach.

I ALSO called around, to many Phoenix-area schools, to inquire if any of them had wrestling programs. Some of the schools who DID have wrestling told me that they had their schedules filled already for that year, but wanted me to call for the NEXT year. I was fortunate enough to find four schools, however, who wanted to put us on THEIR schedule, that first year I coached the District's wrestlers. Two of them were much bigger and more experienced than we, and had had wrestling programs for years prior. I believed that THEY believed the Brighton fledgling wrestling program could be used by them as a kind of 'practice' meet....you know, so their kids could work out with new 'meat.' At THAT time, though, I had wrestlers who had wrestled for me for three years, so I felt my boys would NOT just roll over and be humiliated.

I had to make arrangements with the District for an after-school bus to take us to the bigger schools, and Brighton came through.

I DIDN'T want to rely on parents to drive. I had a lot of kids, and I wasn't sure about what kind of insurance Wilhelm would need to have if I had parents driving students OTHER than their own, and an accident occurred.

Our first wrestling meet was scheduled after just three practices for us. It was the only time that one of the big schools had left on its schedule, and I was anxious for my kids to have some experience against students from outside Brighton District.. Fortunately, that big school had a lot of inexperienced wrestlers, too, so their coach and I just matched wrestlers up according to ability, as best we could. We didn't win the meet, but Wilhelm had several winners, so we felt pretty good about ourselves, and practices became more fun. There was no 'practicing' on us by wrestlers from that school, that's for sure. My kids were happy with their efforts, which gave our next practices more energy, too. I was developing a tight-knit wrestling team, and that made me a happy coach.

Things got better for us, as the next two meets were with newer programs, and neither of them had more than twenty wrestlers. My kids looked good compared to either of the other schools, and we won both meets.

Shortly after our third meet, I got an invitation to compete in the Maricopa County Tournament, which would be held on the weekend after our last scheduled practice, and I loved that. We would see how we fared against wrestlers from SEVERAL other programs, AND it would happen after our initial year was just finishing. I accepted the invite, and paid the entry fee myself.

On the Monday, just before we were to be in the county tournament, we wrestled in our last dual meet. This school was different from any of the other three schools we faced. Sure, it was a 'big' school, but we had already wrestled a big school, so that wasn't different. The coach and the quality of wrestlers at the last school WERE different, however. This second big school coach had a GOOD program up and running, as he had for more than a decade. They had a reputation of putting really good wrestlers on the mat. What's more, we had to travel to THEIR school, which meant we needed to wait for our district's travel bus to finish taking home kids from school before they could come get us. I knew it would be a late night.

I didn't mention the other school's reputation to my wrestlers, but as soon as we entered the gym, we ALL knew we weren't wrestling just any old school. There were pennants on the walls, and trophies in a case, and the crowd.....they were ELECTRIC! They had a big crowd, and all of them were cheering for their wrestlers, and LOUDLY, too. It was pretty intimidating for all of my wrestlers....even for us just entering the building.

And THIS coach wanted to match up the 'varsity' wrestlers by their weights NOT by abilities, as we had done at our other three meets. That was fine by me as we were going to have Wilhelm wrestlers in the Maricopa County meet, a few days after this dual meet, and my kids could ONLY wrestle other kids who were in their own weight divisions. The other coach and I DID, however, match up several 'exhibition' matches, and we chose to ability group for that, as we both wanted to get as many matches in as possible....you know, give a lot of kids wrestling experience against kids from another school. And my kids wanted to wrestle someone other then themselves, for a change, too. We had over forty matches. It WAS a long night!

I had two wrestlers that I thought were really good. Mikey Strong was a Wilhelm wrestler, who wrestled for me in both his 6th grade and 7th grade years. He was a good natural athlete, and HATED to lose. He had learned a lot in his three years with me, and I felt he could hold his own against most wrestlers his weight. He was very excited about getting to wrestle his big school opponent.

The second good wrestler, Ruben Cordova, was from Cahill. He came from a tough family, and had been Cahill's ONLY district champion the last year Brighton had a tournament. He was as close to a natural wrestler, with raw ability, as I had seen through my three years at Wilhelm. I wasn't too worried about how he would perform at the big school, either.

This school, from the Moon Valley section of Phoenix, had MANY good wrestlers, and they were pretty tough on my guys in several matches. But I had a few kids surprise themselves at how much they learned, and beat wrestlers they weren't supposed to beat. And I had several of the 'exhibition' wrestlers from Wilhelm win, too. Most of THEM were underclassmen, so I was excited when thinking about the future teams at Wilhelm.

Young Cordova had NO problem beating his opponent, and he CLEARLY looked like the better wrestler.

Mikey had the match of the evening. I hadn't told Strong, but HIS opponent was the best wrestler at his school, and besides wrestling for his school, he had additional experience wrestling for an All-Star team of junior high wrestlers from throughout the Phoenix area. When I told the opposing coach that Mikey was one of MY two good wrestlers, he licked his chops and said, "Let's save THAT match for last," and I agreed.

Talk about noise. When the two 'best' wrestlers from the two schools headed to the mat, the gymnasium was in pandemonium. Wilhelm had very few parents attend the meet, so 98% of the noise heard in the jam-packed gym came from boisterous fans rooting for our opponent....and, have I mentioned, they were VERY LOUD!

I thought I would have a heart attack, I was yelling instructions so loudly at Mikey. But, whether he could hear me or not, he never looked my way. With the match tied and only ten seconds to go, Mikey drove into his opponent with a double-leg tackle, and the opposing wrestler was knocked backwards. Strong scrambled on top of him to take control, and was given a take-down with five seconds remaining. I'M having heart palpitations just REMEMBERING that moment NOW! Mikey Strong had won our school's first really competitive match against an outstanding wrestler from another school, and he was a Wilhelm wrestling hero for WEEKS afterwards, too.

Mikey went to high school, but never wrestled. He got involved with girls, I was told, and just kind of gave everything up OTHER than to be with his girlfriends. It would not be my FIRST disappointment from Mikey Strong, however. He never showed for the County Wrestling Tournament, either! He just didn't go, and I wanted to know why.

On the Monday, following the Maricopa County tournament, I sent for Strong to come see me, before school even started. When I asked him what happened, why he didn't show, he simply told me that his family had gone camping out of town, and while he COULD have stayed with a friend, and been involved with the wrestling tournament, he loved going camping more. After that declaration, he just shrugged his shoulders then went about his business. I, on the other hand, was pissed! My jaw just dropped, rendering me speechless. I wanted to scream at the kid, but I liked him. So I stood there silently, while I was being eaten up with rage inside. His attitude SHOULD have been a strong (no pun intended) indication to me, of the change in MANY of the students, who were beginning to enroll in Brighton schools.

Mikey had a mind of his own, and while he did have SOME allegiance toward Wilhelm, his desire to make HIMSELF happy was SO strong, (OK, pun intended), that he didn't allow any room in his conscience to think about what his absence might mean to the TEAM. In addition, he never told anyone about his camping plans, so I didn't even have a chance to get a replacement for him in the tournament. Mikey Strong displayed both selfishness AND inconsideration, but he DID teach me a good lesson....to work harder on developing team unity, giving that concept the highest accolades I could. Team FIRST was my motto, even though wrestling was an individualized sport.

I had one OTHER surprise take place at the Maricopa County Tournament, too, but THAT one I found out about AT the tourney.

Weigh-ins took place well before the competition was to start. Even though I, and all the other coaches, had sent in team rosters, there were ALWAYS changes to be made....wrestlers moving from one weight division to another, kids who had been ill, or had informed their coaches that they would not be able to wrestle for a plethora of other REASONS. (I expected Strong to be there so took no extra wrestlers)

When a coach had his team roster finalized, he had the team members weigh in, then maybe have them eat a little something before matches began....a couple of orange slices....some honey on a piece of toast....not a large breakfast, but something to tide them over until the event began. If a wrestler did NOT make weight, initially, he had an hour to shed the necessary weight, and try 'weigh-ins' again. However, there was a time limit, after which, the scales were closed.

I had my team weigh in, leaving a spot for Mikey, as he could come make weight ANY TIME during that weigh-in session.

When Ruben Cordova stepped onto the scales, my eyes bugged out of my head. He showed he was nearly four pounds over his weight division....FOUR POUNDS!

"What happened, Ruben?" I said in disbelief at what I saw on the scale.

"My mom wanted me to be strong today, so she took me to Village Inn for pancakes."

It's NOT like we hadn't talked about what it took to make weight....we had. Ruben's mom was the power in his family, and he never wanted to upset her, so he ate like he was told.

I put him in LAYERS of clothing, placed him inside the Phoenix College's steam room, turned up the heat, and had him exercise for the entire rest of his allowable hour. In retrospect, that was dangerous, and wrong, but I hadn't seen Mikey yet, and I wanted to have ONE good wrestler representing Wilhelm that day. And no mom was going to deny me that opportunity.

So Ruben did jumping jacks, ran in place, and did squats, RIGHT up until it was just a couple of minutes before the weigh-ins were closed.....AND I STILL DIDN'T HAVE MIKEY STRONG, EITHER!

I had Cordova peel ALL his clothes off, had him wipe off his sweat, and watched him drag himself onto the scale. The judge, doing the weigh-in, held the balance bar at the top of the bracket. He told me, "If the bar falls, even a slight bit, he makes weight." He knew how hard Ruben was working to cut the extra weight, too. Ruben stood still, the judge released the bar, and there was just the minimal break from the bracket. "He's in," said the judge, expressing himself as being the most important person in the room.....which, as far as I was concerned, he was.

I went to the gym, happy about Ruben, but still upset by Mikey not being there. Suddenly, wrestlers were being called for their first matches of the day. There were four large wrestling mats on the gym floor, and four different weight divisions had been designated to start on those mats.

Just as Cordova appeared from the dressing room, I heard him being called to one of the mats for his first match. The kid had barely had fifteen minutes to rest after he made weight, he didn't even have the time to get a slice of an orange in him, just a quick drink of water, but he was already being called to the mat to wrestle.

I could see he was exhausted, and the other kid looked pretty tough. But looks can be deceiving. This time they weren't. Ruben and his opponent wrestled into overtime, with Ruben getting pinned in the extra period of wrestling.

I was furious, but couldn't show that to Ruben. All I said was, "This is why you watch your weight to make sure you don't have to work more than necessary to drop it." I also told him he would be placed into the consolation bracket, after his loss, and would have at least one more match that day. He dragged himself to the bleachers and lay down.

Within minutes I heard the announcement, "Will the Wilhelm Coach please report to the scorer's table?"

When I got there, an official told me, "Coach, we made a mistake. Cordova had been moved into the next higher weight (Strong's empty spot) when we THOUGHT we saw he didn't make weight. We just assumed that because he DIDN'T make weight, he would fill your team's empty roster spot. We do that sometimes, so the kids don't get disappointed if they don't make weight....gives 'em a chance to wrestle anyway. That is what we did with Cordova. THEN, when his match was over, we noticed that the weigh-in judge wrote that he DID make his original weight, we just misread it. It's a mistake, and we are sorry."

My blood pressure was sky high, by that time. "You mean Ruben wrestled in the next higher weight instead of his OWN weight?"

"Yes, Coach, and we are apologizing for that. Does he want to wrestle at the higher weight, or go to his original weight?"

"You've got to be kidding me. That kid killed himself to make his own weight, and now he is completely worn out because of a tough DIFFERENT weight-division match. He wants to wrestle kids his OWN size, BUT he will need an hour to recuperate."

"That is perfectly fine with us. His division will be called shortly, but we will make sure he has the last bout of the round."

There were at least thirty teams at the meet, which meant that there must have been twenty or more wrestlers in each weight division. Ruben Cordova went on to finish 3rd in his own weight. Got a nice medal for his effort, too. I never heard if he wrestled in high school however. But for one year, he was MY team's star. No one else placed, though we had a few wrestlers win their matches, and THEY were happy. My first year being Brighton District's head wrestling coach was over, and the track season got started the next Monday. THAT'S how coaching went at Wilhelm....never a dull moment.

As for the County Wrestling Tournament, Curtis White finished 3rd in the heavyweight division two years later, and we never went to County again because it wasn't HELD again. We started to go to the State Tournament after White's year. Wilhelm's wrestling program was starting to develop a good, competitive reputation, even amongst the bigger schools, and that made me happy.

While Ruben Cordova represented Cahill's toughness on the Wilhelm wrestling team, AND there were several more good wrestlers, through the years coming from BOTH Cahill and Pfister, I need to tell you of a failed, yet successful, story about ONE Cahill tough guy. Confusing? Read on.

I don't even remember the kid's name, but the event took place when our district wrestling program was in its fifth year of existence. We had started practice one day, during our second week that year. All the wrestlers from both Pfister and Cahill had already arrived, so we had begun working on skills review. I had a big team that year; more than sixty wrestlers had showed up. It seemed like there was a lot more interest being generated amongst 4th-8th grade boys to become wrestlers as the years went by.

Five minutes into drills, three more boys, suddenly, meandered into the wrestling practice. They just stood against the wall, and seemed totally content watching us work out. It was my policy to have NO other students watching us practice, simply because it was hard enough keeping track of all my wrestlers, let alone OTHER kids. Plus, I didn't know these three new guys. They weren't from Wilhelm, though.

Two or three minutes more of practice progressed when I decided to confront those characters and ask why they were in our wrestling room. A wrestler from Cahill quickly approached me, when he saw me headed toward the three strangers, and said, "Coach Stein, that big guy," and he pointed toward the biggest of the three, who, by the way, had removed an over-shirt, stripping down to a tank top revealing his muscularity, "he is new at my school. He's kind of a bully, bragging all the time about how tough he is. And he is mean to some of the kids at school. The other two kids (quite a bit smaller than the bully) follow him around like puppies."

I thanked my informant, and proceeded to call the three of them over to the edge of the mat to talk. "Can I see you guys for a minute, please?" I asked politely.

The big guy, puffed out his chest, gave a sniff of derision, strode confidently toward me trying to flex to show how 'bad' he was. The other two smaller kids just stayed against the wall. "What's up, Man?" Bully said, when he got close enough to talk to me.

"Well, first off, my name is Coach Stein, and this is the Brighton District wrestling team practicing here. I do not allow spectators to watch our practices, so am I to assume that the three of you want to join the team?" I was still trying to be polite.

Big guy looked back at his followers, smiled, then looked at me. "Yeah, maybe. What we gotta do?"

"First, you take off your belts (they weren't wearing them, but that was always part of my spiel) take off your shoes and jewelry, and get rid of anything in your pockets," I proceeded while looking him right in the eyes. "You are a bit behind, since we started wrestling over a week ago, but you seem plenty smart. We will go through wrestling moves, and practice them enough so we can do well against opposing teams. We will wrestle several other schools this year, and I want to put a good team against all our opponents." Then, with a smile, I began to schmooze him. "You look plenty tough, too. Perhaps you could end up helping this team....your buddies, too. Are you interested?"

"Rasslin? I already know how to rassle, Man," the kid said with his voice loud enough for everyone in the room to hear. "Who I got to whup to prove it to you?"

"Once again," I said, while still speaking calmly, "when you are speaking to ME, you can call me either, Coach Stein, or just 'coach,' and nothing else. Understood?"

The kid looked at me with a dumbfounded look on his face. I don't believe he was used to anyone talking to him like that, BUT he didn't say a word, just gave a curt nod.

"What we are learning here," I continued, "is called folkstyle wrestling. That is the kind of wrestling where you, and you alone, will step out onto the mat with another kid who is your weight. A referee will give you the signal to wrestle, and you both try to take each other down to the mat. The ultimate goal is to pin both of your opponent's shoulders to the mat at the same time. That is an automatic win. If you can't do that, then there is a point system which will determine who wrestles best, and when the match is over, the wrestler with the most points is declared the winner. MY job is to teach you how to do both.....pin your opponent's shoulders to the mat, as well as teach you how to win the match by getting more points than the guy you are wrestling, if, somehow, you CAN'T get a pin."

"Aaah, THIS sounds like a piece of cake, Man," and I gave him a frown and a hard stare. "I mean, Coach....WHATEVER!"

"Coach is fine," I said, now eager to see if this cocky kid could back up his bravado. "This is not professional wrestling, young man. You can't hit your opponent, gouge him in the eyes, kick him, or any OTHER moves intended to inflict injury. None of those spectacular moves you may have seen from acting wrestlers on TV. The blood may be real, but the so-called 'wrestling tactics, are scripted. This is as real as wrestling gets. You understand THAT, too, don't you?"

"Sure, Man....I mean Coach. You told me to just take down my victim and pin his shoulders to the ground. I can do that. It'll be a piece of cake."

"How much do you weigh?" I asked while sizing him up.

"About 170, I think, and most of me is ALL muscle," the kid bragged. He looked at his two buddies, still standing away from the rest of us....then the three of them laughed.

Everyone had stopped practicing, and were just watching and listening to the blow-hard from Cahill Elementary. I saw Doug McGuire, and asked him to join Big Mouth and me in the center of the mat.

Doug was going to be our regular 167 LB. wrestler for the season, though he weighed 159 pounds soaking wet. He was a well-muscled kid, too, but definitely smaller than the braggart. However, Doug was the only kid in the room, whom I felt could wrestle with the wannabe, as our two heavyweights that year were kind of soft and very inexperienced. Doug had wrestled with the Wilhelm team for four years, and was easily the best wrestler the team had that year.

"This guy? You want to wrestle THIS guy?" The big kid from the Cahill neighborhood gave a sneer while puffing out his chest even further. Then he looked around at other wrestlers in the room. "I'd destroy THAT guy, too!" he suddenly stated with extra bravado as he pointed at one of the heavyweights watching the proceedings.

"If you do a good job with Doug, here, then we can see where you fit in with the other big wrestlers we have on the team. I was actually setting the bully up to lose, but I WANTED it to sound like I was testing him against a smaller guy before putting him against the biggest kids I had. I had a feeling that the kid COULD hurt one of the heavyweights in the room. Both of the team's big guys were roly-poly and, as I have mentioned, VERY inexperienced wrestlers. But I was pretty certain Muscles wasn't going to hurt McGuire. In fact, I was pretty sure Doug was going to teach the big mouth a lesson in wrestling.

"This guy's nothin'," the mouthy Cahill kid kept snarling, as he once again looked at Doug McGuire. "All I got to do is put him on the mat and get his two shoulders down flat at the same time, right?" Doug just looked, well, almost sheepishly at his bigger opponent. He was the most unassuming good wrestler I ever would coach, AND he was a genuinely nice person, too. No bragging, just action.

"That's right," I said reassuringly. "But remember, this is NOT a street fight....just get hold of him, take him down, and put him on his back. No rough stuff....which is actually ILLEGAL in high school wrestling."

"Don't worry, I GOT this," said the big fellow as he took off his tank top and joined Doug at the middle of the mat.

I told the boys to shake hands, and with the Cahill wrestler not looking so confident anymore, I said, "Wrestle." Doug immediately reached up to cup his opponent behind the head. The challenger started to reach behind Doug's head, as well, but as soon as his hand touched McGuire's neck, Doug executed a move called a duck-under, where he slipped under his opponent's reaching arm, and while moving forward, Doug dipped down to where he barely touched his knee to the mat. The forward momentum carried the smaller wrestler under his bigger opponent's raised arm, which had the Wilhelm wrestler standing BEHIND his statue-like opponent. At the same time he was getting behind the challenger, Doug had slid his own right hand down to grasp the Cahill kid's left wrist. Then, while quickly securing that same 'grabbed' arm with his second hand, using correct technique, Doug sat down and rolled backwards, causing his opponent to fall backwards, too. McGuire rolled to his left until the big fellow was lying flat on his stomach, with Doug ending up on top of the startled guy.

Instinctively, while still on his stomach, Bully Boy reached around to grab McGuire, and Doug performed a Half-Nelson, which meant he quickly moved his own arm UNDER BULLY'S raised arm, getting it to the point where his hand was securely attached around his opponent's neck. Then Doug, sliding to a hip, started walking his body toward the 'hooked' fellow's head, using the hand-on-the-neck as leverage and his chest as a bulldozer. Big Mouth rolled onto his back instantly. The bully WANTED to do something to counter his position, but was flailing around helplessly. I saw both his shoulders, flat as could be on the mat. I slapped the mat, and said, "Pin!" The match was over in less than fifteen seconds.

Doug got up, then Muscles shot to his feet, and declared, "Hey, I wasn't really ready when you said 'Wrestle.' That was unfair."

"You're probably right. Most wrestlers know to defend themselves after shaking hands, so I assumed you understood it was time to wrestle," I said, trying to sound sympathetic.

"Well, I wasn't, and I KNOW he couldn't do that again if I was ready." Then the Cahill kid looked at his two little followers, standing near the mat, and nodded his confidence.

"You're telling me you want to try again?" I questioned, hoping he would say 'yes.'

"This time, this dude is MINE!" bellowed the spectacularly out-classed visitor to the gym.

I had them shake hands again, asked SPECIFICALLY if the big guy was ready. He nodded, and I said, "Wrestle."

The Cahill kid feigned a move forward, with his hands, toward Doug's face, a movement which kind of had the look of what a bully would do to intimidate weaker kids. He also bellowed a 'HEY' sound, like he was trying to scare, McGuire.

As the kid stepped back from his feint, Doug strode forward, bending down and grabbing a single leg of his opponent. When McGuire raised the leg high into the air, Bully Boy lost his balance, and went immediately down to the mat, turning to land on his stomach, while using his hands to brace the fall.

Doug scrambled to get on top of the kid again, and then Bully made the same fatal error of reaching back to grab the kid who was on top of him. Once again, Doug executed a Half-Nelson, moved quickly around his opponent to put him on his back, then lay, chest-to-chest while forcing all his weight straight down.

The Cahill kid lay flat on his back, once more. And while he TRIED to struggle, AGAIN, the efforts were futile. He could NOT get his shoulders off the mat.

I smacked the mat a second time, while saying, "That's a pin!" We'll call that an 18-second pin this time.

The Cahill loud-mouth got angrily to his feet, looked at his underlings, and shouted, "Let's get outta here. This is crap!" He grabbed his two shirts, and the three of them were out of the gym in less than thirty seconds. That was too bad. He likely COULD have easily defeated either of my heavyweights; thus, helping the team in meets. But his ego was crushed. I feel confident that I would have reached him if he didn't have his little admirers with him. I never got the chance as he never returned to Wilhelm.

The experience had an unusual GOOD result, though. No, not having the other wrestlers see the humiliation of a bully, though that DID seem appropriate at the time. I got a report from one of the other 'true' wrestlers from Cahill, later in the season. Word got around about what happened to the new kid when he tried wrestling, so whenever he started to brag on how tough he was, OR showed bullying tendencies, one of the popular girls of the school, (whom he desperately wanted to impress with his bravado) would say to him, "If you were really as tough as you say, then you would go back to the wrestling team and prove it." That was usually enough to quiet him. By the end of the next three months, HE moved out of the Cahill neighborhood, never to be heard from again.

Doug McGuire, on the other hand, became the District's FIRST State wrestling champion. He was, however, unique to most champions. Doug never bragged on himself, and ALWAYS seemed humble, even caring, if he thought he had hurt anyone. THAT was proven perfectly when McGuire wrestled in the championship match at the Arizona State Wrestling Championships at the end of our season.

He was matched up against a kid from Tucson, who was a good six pounds heavier than Doug, AND was undefeated, too, when the match began. McGuire frustrated his opponent while wracking up points, winning 7-1. The Tucson wrestler was so upset, that when the match ended he just lay on the mat and was sobbing uncontrollably. Normally, kids winning State championships are SO elated that they jump and down with joy, or maybe run to jump into their coach's arms. Not Doug McGuire.

The Wilhelm wrestler looked at his opponent, who had dropped to the mat and had begun weeping. Before ANYTHING else, Doug McGuire bent down and put his hand on the down-trodden wrestler's shoulder. Then the champion said in a TRULY sincere and caring voice, "Are you OK?"

It wasn't until McGuire's arm was raised in victory, and he came back to me and heard ME say excitedly, "Doug, YOU'RE the State champion," that's when I saw him smile, for the first time, about his outstanding achievement.

Doug wrestled four years in high school, but only finished 3rd in his weight division as a junior in high school. He was injured most of the early part of that junior year, to boot, AND he was injured during the last two months of his SENIOR season, which kept him from wrestling at State. Still, he was MY first champion, and I would end up coaching four grade school champions in 22 years. I DID have wrestlers with better results at State, though, as two of them (neither had been grade school champions, however) going on to win an Arizona State HIGH SCHOOL wrestling title.

Still, Doug McGuire, put the Brighton wrestling program on the State's wrestling map when he became the District's first champion.

Sportsmanship is not easy to teach kids these days. They see their heroes grandstanding, self-promoting their achievements with up-stretched arms, asking for more recognition of their latest good play. By far, the worst display of sportsmanship is the trash talking that goes on. Just play the game, respect the other player's effort, and go out with your friends to celebrate the TEAM'S efforts, NOT your own. After all, how many times have you seen a player ask for recognition when he/she has made a BAD play. Let the crowd determine how well a player does, on any play, and take THAT as your compliment or detriment. It's a poor attitude that is shown through poor sportsmanship, and teaching young athletes the right way to participate isn't easy when 'star' athletes don't display good behavior themselves.

The FIRST lesson taught to MY athletes is how to display good sportsmanship before, during and after the games. Wrestling is pretty easy to understand. It is an individual sport, so when the referee raises the hand of the victor, only one of two hands will be raised.

Nobody likes to lose, and IF a young (and sometimes NOT so young) athlete loses a contest, of ANY sort, they like to blame others for the loss. Comments like, "If I would have gotten the ball toward the end of the game, we never would have lost," "The referee should have called a foul on the other team, and if he did, then we wouldn't have lost."

It is NEVER the player's fault if a contest is lost...it is ALWAYS somebody else's fault, and those are excuses heard in team sports on occasion.

Wrestling isn't exactly like other sports. One athlete competes against one other athlete of approximate size. The wrestler displaying the better skills is USUALLY the winner. There CAN be some exceptions, and I will grouse about them later in the book, but, generally speaking, a wrestling match is won by the better wrestler.

MY first lessons, concerned good sportsmanship and they went like this: One....shake hands with your opponent BEFORE you wrestle...it shows respect. The ref MAKES opponents shake hands, so that is automatically taken care of. Two....wrestle the best you can, and when the match is over, whether you've won or lost, shake the opponent's hand. AGAIN, the referee will make that mandatory, but I needed my wrestlers to hear me tell them THOSE rules of sportsmanship again and again. Finally....MY most important rule of good sportsmanship was this.... it doesn't matter if you win or lose, you do NOT show any emotion while on the mat....no temper tantrums if you lose....no gloating or preening if you win. JUST hold any emotions you have in check. Shake your opponent's hand, the opposing coach's hand, THEN come back to see me. IF you have a complaint, about ANYTHING, tell me about it. But NEVER show the audience, your opponent, or the referee WHAT you are feeling.

The ONLY exception would be if my wrestler won a huge tournament. Then, and ONLY then will it be acceptable to show how happy the wrestler feels in becoming a champion. Anything OTHER than my three rules, made me unhappy. I just didn't appreciate, after a match, my wrestlers showing spectators that they have NO class through selfish behavior like griping OR self-grandizing.

I've had wrestlers come back to me and say, "Coach, I wasn't pinned!"

I would counter, "Were you on your back, or stomach?"

"On my back, but I wasn't pinned."

"The referee is specifically down on the mat to SEE if both your shoulder blades are touching at the same time. And IF he sees them both touching, even for a split second, he can call a pin. Now, if you DON'T go to your back, he can NEVER have a chance to say you were pinned." That would usually end the discussion.

I would THEN recommend a vanquished Wilhelm wrestler to do three things: learn what his opponent did to beat him, figure out a way to STOP that the next time it is tried, and thirdly, learn how to do it, too, so HE can use the move on future opponents.

The economic changes Brighton District experienced in the late '70's/early '80's, was a force that couldn't be stopped. The affluent families were leaving in droves. In their place came financially struggling families. There seemed to be an increase in dysfunction behavior, as well. Kids were growing up faster and looking for support from their peer groups, as much, if not more, than from their family members. Gang behavior, though light at first, was definitely creeping into Brighton schools more and more as the years passed. With the rougher personalities, came an increase in drug use, violence, crime, even sexual experimentation.

It became more difficult for me to convince my wrestlers of the proper behavior I expected from them when wrestling. Too often, I would notice that if a kid was NOT getting his way at home, there was no 'good sport' behavior displayed anywhere. Many parents were becoming more and more frustrated with the 'me, me, me' attitudes displayed by their children, too, and after while just gave up, from what I was seeing.

Life had become all about getting what the boy/girl wanted, and he/she got it by any means possible. Threats, posturing, tantrums, bragging, these were traits that were all too commonplace with our new students' personalities. They didn't take losing OR winning well, The new breed of kid EXPECTED to get what they wanted, and working for it wasn't in their repertoire. They made demands of the parents, and discipline at home was sketchy in SO MANY households. Kids were losing respect for parents, and authority figures, alike. The face of poverty was NOT pretty in Brighton District, from the mid- '80's onward.

Teaching good sportsmanship was an every day event for me. Sadly, as the years passed, I kept seeing more and more attitudes that reminded me of the big bully from Cahill.

I have to give credit to Brighton District at this time. As I started my third year of coaching, (my first year coaching all District wrestlers) I convinced the Board and chief administrators that buying a brand new wrestling mat was a necessity. The old Cahill mat was too small and in bad shape. I told them that since wrestlers from other schools would be coming to Wilhelm, it would be nice to show them how well the wrestling program was being treated. In all sincerity, I would like to say NOW, "Brighton, THANK-YOU for helping my wrestling program get started."

That, however, would be one of the LAST times I felt support from administrators, at ANY level, in Brighton.

It didn't matter what changes were occurring in Brighton's neighborhoods, more and more kids wanted to give wrestling a try. For the 1983-'84 season I had 119 students try out for the team. Even though some kids discovered that the sport WASN'T for them, Wilhelm ALWAYS had at least sixty wrestlers on the team at any given time.

I knew I needed help controlling so many bodies in the room. Yes, the 8th graders, of each new season, helped me when I asked, but that STILL wasn't enough help. For the '83-'84 season I enlisted my new bride, Katherine, to help me coach. She was athletic and eager to help. She worked particularly well with the 4th graders....and we had a BUNCH of 4th graders that year.

With our new mat AND the tumbling mats, we still didn't have enough room to get all the kids onto the mats, at the same time, for instruction. I worked in shifts....lightweights got the mats first, and this is where Katherine was most effective. I would hear her say, "No, your OTHER right leg, Honey," to 4th graders who were watching me instead of listening to me....and we could get all of the 4th graders on the mat at the same time, but ONLY the 4th graders. The other athletes were instructed to watch and learn; thus making THEIR time on the mats less time than the little kids needed.

Next, I would work 5th-6th graders on the mats, while Katherine helped me AND kept watch on the 4th graders. When the 7th-8th graders were on the mat, she watched the 4th through 6th graders, which was important because the younger kids could get squirrely without supervision. The older wrestlers got the same amount of time on the mat, but, because they had been 'paying attention' when the little guys were on the mats, I could run more repetitions with the older kids. They liked that.

Katherine came when she could, and her help was GREATLY appreciated, but she was busy with her own school activities, too.

(she was a teacher in a different district) I knew I had to find a permanent assistant coach to help me. I ESPECIALLY knew I needed more help after one incident that happened during a wrestling match, that '83-'84 season.

We had a home match, and Katherine couldn't be with us. Even though I had harped on sportsmanship MANY times, there were SO many kids on the team, it was difficult to know if all of my wrestlers understood what I meant by 'good sportsmanship,' whether they won a match or lost it. My answer came quickly.

IT happened in the second exhibition match of that afternoon's meet. My kids were EVERYWHERE. We didn't have enough space for them to sit on our bench, so I instructed the 8th graders to gather the smaller kids around the mat, and NOT let them wander around. Besides, several of the little guys were going to wrestle in that meet, and I wanted them to watch and try to learn how the wrestling moves were being performed by the better wrestlers. However, the lesson of THAT day would be on sportsmanship..... and what THAT meant to their coach....ME!

I had a small 5th grade wrestler from Wilhelm going for us during that second match. He was relatively new to the school and came to us with a chip on his shoulder, TRYING to act like a street-tough kid, even though he was only in the 5th grade. Discipline wasn't in his vocabulary, most of the time at school, but I was glad he was giving the sport of wrestling a chance to become a legitimate outlet for his aggression.

And he WAS aggressive, pinning his over-matched opponent in the first period of the match. Remember, MY message was to shake hands with the opposing wrestler, go shake hands with the opposing coach, then come back to me and tell me all about it. To make matters more interesting, we were wrestling a school from a rather wealthy part of the Valley, and they weren't sure they even WANTED to come to our steadily-growing tough neighborhood and wrestle with mean kids.

After the pin ended the match, MY kid jumped to his feet, bent over his vanquished opponent, and started to tell him how he was lucky he (my guy) didn't have time to REALLY take care of him. Poor sportsmanship 101.

I EXPLODED off the bench. I screamed at my punk wrestler, which startled the referee as well as everyone else in the room, "Get on the stage RIGHT NOW!" We wrestled in the cafeteria, but also had an all-purpose stage, where plays and concerts took place. And we ALWAYS had the curtain closed during our wrestling meets.

I looked into the crowded stands, and saw this 'tough guy's father. "I need to see YOU, TOO," I bellowed. I was obviously furious, and my comment to Dad WAS rude, (I apologized later to the father) but both the wrestler and his dad went immediately onto the stage, behind the curtain. The drop of a pin could be heard while the three of us moved out of sight of the other people in the room.

I started my rant, telling the offensive kid and his dad about MY expectations for sportsmanship at Wilhelm. The auditorium stayed dead silent the entire time I was reading them the riot act. I finished by telling the boy, "You will go back out there, go find your opponent and apologize for your poor behavior. THEN, you will go apologize to their coach. THEN you will apologize to the audience for acting like a bully. DO YOU UNDERSTAND?"

Now the boy, who was only a fifth grader, mind you, started to have tears come down his cheeks. He didn't want to be humiliated in front of everybody....but, he KNEW he had made a mistake.

"Do YOU have any questions, Dad?" I asked the kid's dad.

"No, Sir, you said it all," and then he looked at his son and told him he backed me 100%.

My ill-mannered wrestler, seeing his dad agreed with me, did what was asked. He then sat sheepishly with the team for the rest of the meet. The other wrestlers displayed great sportsmanship for the rest of the matches. In fact, I don't remember EVER having that issue with my wrestlers during the rest of my coaching career. It DID help that I found an outstanding assistant coach for my next six years, and HE believed in good sportsmanship, too.

As for the scolded fifth grader wrestler, he finished the school year, but like many, MANY families, he and his family moved after just one year at Wilhelm.

While Wilhelm and DeWitt wrestlers never again showed poor sportsmanship in front of me, there WAS an incident that occurred during the 1991-'92 season, by students from another school. The team I had that year was the best team I ever coached in wrestling, and you will hear more about them later. BUT, they were also the target of poor sportsmanship AT an opponent's schools. The incident actually happened AFTER the match was over.

I could NEVER get enough uniforms for all the members of my teams, and, quite honestly, we LOOKED like a bunch of ruffians from the Inner City, especially to teams from other districts who had money to clothe their teams with class. We had FOUR different kinds of uniforms, in THREE different colors. And we didn't have enough uniforms, for all our kids. So several of them wore tee shirts and shorts, but they were ALL proud to represent the Brighton wrestling team.

On my 1991-'92 wrestling team, we had a LOT of very good wrestlers....so many good athletes, in fact, that there were times when opposing teams couldn't win more than three or four matches (including exhibition matches) in a meet. Even the meets where we had fifty or SIXTY match-ups, we dominated practically EVERY one of them.

One night, after we had traveled to and thrashed an opposing team, I gathered my sixty-plus wrestlers, and headed them to the door. Outside was our bus, and the driver was waiting for us. So were about eight or nine HIGH SCHOOL wrestlers, who had gone to that particular school, and were MORE than angry at the beating Wilhelm wrestlers put on the kids of their former school. I lead my guys outside, and I heard one of the 'brave' high school 'tough guys' yell, "We want to talk to you boys over here!"

They were just a few feet behind the bus, in the darkness, and it was easy to see that trouble was brewing. My guys were hardened Inner City, even gang-type kids, who NEVER walked away from a challenge. And my best wrestlers were my biggest kids. They started to immediately head toward the group of high school kids, AND there were more kids standing not far behind THOSE high school students, as well.

I quickly jumped in front of my lead wrestler, and told him to stop. My wrestlers were bunching up, ready to charge after those kids, and it didn't MATTER that they were older, my guys showed NO fear. Thankfully, my wrestlers did as I asked and stopped. I turned to face the vigilante group behind the bus, and spoke loudly enough for EVERYONE to hear. "First, you will have to come into the light by the bus so we can see who you are. Then, while my wrestlers are boarding the bus, if you make a move on them, I will grab at least ONE of you, and hold you until the police come. IF any of the rest of you attack me, I will fight with you, and I promise some of you will have a problem….and I may not even be able to stop MY kids from coming off the bus and helping me hold you until the authorities get here. This will NOT end well for you, any of you in your group. If that is what you want, then come forward….if not, go HOME. My wrestlers beat the wrestlers from this school fair and square, and you, wanting to act like thugs, doesn't speak very well of this nice neighborhood. Won't your parents be proud of you when they have to pick you up at the police station?"

Immediately, racial and ethnic slurs were hurled our way. But I kept watch as the rest of my team boarded the bus, and none of my kids retaliated in any way. We enjoyed our trip back to campus, and my wrestlers seemed to forget about what had happened. They were used to hearing slurs aimed at them, but were glad they didn't have to defend themselves. We got a nice apology letter from the principal of the opposing school the next day, which ALSO indicated that the 'leaders' of the group who antagonized us, were being 'dealt with,' whatever that meant.

Sportsmanship WAS important, and I tried very hard to instill that into EVERY athlete I coached. I couldn't control their behavior when I wasn't living in their neighborhoods, but while they were with me, we worked on acting like civilized people, and I feel certain they learned to make decisions and seek actions, based on knowing the consequences they chose, OFF the mat, too.

There were times when PARENTS got 'overly involved' with my wrestling team, though, like Jeremiah Alberhasky's mom.

Jeremiah was a pretty good wrestler, and a leader on one of my teams in the late '70's. He was an 8th grader, and had a brother in the 5th grade, who would become the first HIGH SCHOOL champion Wilhelm produced in wrestling.

Jeremiah's mother never missed any of her sons' matches, during Jere's 8th grade year, and was ALWAYS quite zealous, even though she was pregnant with a future Alberhasky wrestler, whom I'd eventually coach, too. I remember her being eight months pregnant when she....let's say.....got VERY involved with one of Jeremiah's matches.

A well-coached opposing team had come to our school to wrestle, on that fateful day. They weren't really a very STRONG team, but had some good individual wrestlers. Jeremiah Alberhasky was undefeated at the time, winning his first four matches, and the opponent he would face had not beaten anybody yet.

The meet had us winning five of the first seven matches, when young Mr. Alberhasky took to the mat. Jeremiah LOOKED the part of a wrestler. He was fairly muscular, and was shadow-wrestling just prior to his match. His opponent looked rather dumpy, with a small gut, and he was just standing by the mat, watching Jeremiah warm up.

The two wrestlers were called to the mat, they shook hands, and the match started. Alberhasky IMMEDIATELY tackled his opponent with a double-leg take down. He released his opponent, then took him down two more times, rather handily. He was at the edge of the mat, when he tried a fourth takedown, using something I had never seen him try before. He was keeping his hand behind his opponent's neck after going to his knee, AND trying to pick up the kid's leg, which is a wrestling no-no for beginning wrestlers.. But, when Jeremiah tried to reach across his opponent's body FOR that leg, he slipped and ended up falling right onto his OWN back.

His opponent fell on top of him, and Jeremiah just lay there, seemingly just content to keep his shoulder raised and avoid NOT getting pinned.

Mother Alberhasky freaked out. She was at the top of the bleachers, and eight months pregnant or not, Jeremiah's mom came flying down those bleachers through a pretty thick crowd of people. She went right to the edge of the mat, where Jeremiah was lying. She actually got on her hands and knees, right ONTO the mat, though ever so slightly, but enough to look her son in the eyes. The referee looked up at her with a surprised look of his own. Mrs. Alberhasky hollered, "Jeremiah, you get off your back RIGHT NOW!"

One second later, Jeremiah, using tremendous strength, not only had gotten off his back, but did so in a way that he flipped his opponent onto HIS back. The ref was in perfect position to see both shoulders flat on the mat, and called a pin for Jeremiah, JUST before the time had run out on the clock.

Mom was sitting up on her knees when the pin occurred, and waited for her son to not only get the pin, but to help HER get to her feet before he went to the center of the mat to shake hands with his opponent.

Both the referee, a fellow who had done a few of our earlier matches, and the opposing coach, looked at me after Jeremiah's hand was raised in victory, and I could tell they wanted me to tell them what just happened. I simply threw my hands in the air as I shrugged my shoulders, and we all watched as Mrs. Alberhasky headed slowly back to the top of the bleachers.

7

Coaching at DeWitt

While coaching at Wilhelm was fun, and all our teams were competitive where EVER we competed, in most of our sporting events, we were decided underdogs. We liked to be on the 'big stage' competing with bigger schools, but winning was difficult for us. Not ENOUGH star athletes. Quite simply, a few other coaches in Brighton District, and I, had talked about what our teams could do if we had half, again, as many students to choose from. Steve and Jerry Randolph had taken a COMBINED basketball team to tournaments where that was allowed, AND they had done quite well. As for myself, I KNOW that both Cahill and Pfister schools had many athletes who didn't come out for wrestling. I had seen some of them in soccer, basketball, and track....athletic-looking with speed and coordination. I just wished I could get some of the OTHER school's star athletes (I had a few, so it wasn't a complete shutout) interested in wrestling.

In the late 1980's, rumors started that Brighton was considering placing ALL its junior high students in one school by themselves. Population had been growing, and the neighborhood schools would need to expand THEIR classrooms in order to accommodate the sudden burst of students entering our district. There was thought given to adding portable rooms to campuses, expanding class sizes, adding rooms to several of the established buildings. SOMETHING had to be done by the start of the 1990-1991 school year. With coaches leading the way, it seemed like a school solely for the older kids was the answer. Busses would simply pick-up and take home the junior high students from the furthest reaches of the neighborhoods, and ATHLETIC teams would surely be enhanced.

Naturally, ALL teachers in Brighton were polled. Several of the lower-grade teachers thought that discipline could be better controlled if the older, more street-wise kids weren't on the same campus with the younger students. However, many of the veteran 7th and 8th grade teachers saw trouble multiplying for them if all the thirteen and fourteen-year-old kids were on one campus. They argued that students from one neighborhood school might not get along with students from a long-time rival school....at least for the first few years. They pleaded with the decision makers to keep the older kids in their OWN neighborhoods, where discipline would be easier for teachers AND administrators alike. I saw where the discipline might bother a lot of teachers, but I was willing to trade THAT problem for the chance to be a super-star athletic school.

I believe, and I can't be sure on this, that it was discovered that it would be more COST effective to build a new school for younger kids, while housing ALL the older kids of Brighton in their own new school. So, DeWitt Middle School was built for junior high-aged students. The completion date of DeWitt would be for the start of the '90-'91 school campaign. I was delighted!

Sadly, problems arose from the very beginning of the project. The teachers, who would be teaching at DeWitt, were asked to submit a wish list of what THEY thought the new school should include on its campus....to better facilitate a better education for the students, of course. Anyone with half a brain could see that IF everything teachers wanted was PUT into the new school, it might well become the most expensive grade school ever built in America. BUT, there were several 'WISHES' that the Brighton School Board agreed to try and get.

However, as the school got deeper and deeper toward completion, the construction prices of THIS, and plans for THAT, were getting WAY too expensive to be considered. MANY of the 'wish list' items were scrapped. The campus design would end up being beautiful, and mostly functional, but several of the 'extras' would NOT make the final cut. For instance, Alex Fenstemaker had REALLY hoped for a well-functioning theater building, complete with lighting and sound systems. What resulted was that DeWitt had NO theater of any kind. Any Drama productions would have to be produced on the all-purpose cafeteria stage as it always had been. Alex decided to retire. An elaborate gymnasium WAS planned....maybe a weight room, a separate wrestling room....perhaps dressing rooms. None of those 'wish' items came to fruition.

DeWitt would end up having an all-purpose gymnasium, too, ATTACHED to the all-purpose cafeteria. That would turn out to be one busy, and noisy building.

The beautiful campus turned out to be literally divided into fourths. First, the west side of the campus was dedicated to working strictly with 7th graders, and the east side of the campus would house only 8th graders. Those were the designated areas for the five core classes to be taught. The division was thought to be the true middle school concept. However, the separation of students didn't stop with just east and west side locations.

While all 300 DeWitt 7th grade students were on the west side of school, THEY were divided into half. A hundred and fifty kids would be assigned to occupy the southern end of the west side of the campus, and one hundred and fifty seventh graders would occupy the northern half. The same was done with the 8th graders on the east side of school.

In essence, there were truly FOUR different groups of children occupying a single campus. Each 'fourth' of the student body would have its own set of 'core' teachers....assigned to teach only THEIR students the following classes: math, science, English, reading, and history. By this method, there would be NO co-mingling with students from the other three teams during the majority of the day. Lunch and special classes had students mingling. BUT, when core classes were in session, all four sections of students were isolated. It was like having four different schools on one campus. I really only got to KNOW my own 150 students, other than when I was coaching, of course. Yet, I, and all the core teachers, had to deal with EVERY 7th and 8th grader before school started, during lunches and after school, exactly when discipline was at its worst. Working with junior high students we DIDN'T know became a true nightmare.

While core teachers had specific students assigned to them, the 'special' teachers: music, art, P.E., shop, band, Special Education, etc., got only a smattering of students from EACH of the four teams of kids. I thought them to have it roughest when it came to discipline.

Between the two grade levels, however, a nice amphitheater had been built....big grassy and tiered area, with a cement stage with roof included. So THAT separation helped with problems of a disciplinary nature, at least DURING class time. But, as you will read, separation and distance would NOT be the answer for stopping discipline problems completely. Not on DeWitt's campus.... not by a long shot.

EACH separate core team of teachers had one hour scheduled for them to meet together each day. That gave the 'teams' time to discuss problems, OR highlights, of the 150 kids students assigned, strictly, to them. I would like to be able to say those 'team' meetings were a 'peaceful' time of the day, but that wasn't ALWAYS the case. Before I get into core team meetings, let's deal with OTHER issues teachers faced at the start of DeWitt's 1st year of existence..

Yes, the school was set to open for the 1990-1991 school year, and ALL the construction was to be finished. Quite frankly that didn't happen. There were two MAJOR problems on opening day. Plans called for DeWitt to be built on the former Pfister campus, with Pfister students having to attend two of the other Brighton schools, which were located not ALL that far away.

On opening day, however, Pfister had NOT yet been demolished. It couldn't, as on opening day, DeWitt didn't have a finished cafeteria OR gymnasium. The junior high students needed to have lunch at Pfister....with the still present Pfister kids. Demolition of Pfister Elementary wouldn't take place until we were all on Christmas vacation.

A second problem arose as there was NO playground for DeWitt students. With Pfister still in existence, and the smaller children getting to use their OWN playground, the DeWitt kids ONLY had its own amphitheater to 'loiter' around before school and during lunches.

The DeWitt gymnasium/cafeteria building would NOT be completed until half its first year was over. P.E. classes were held inside the library during DeWitt's 1st semester. Exercise was done in a library, for crying out loud! Jerry Randolph was NOT happy.

Since DeWitt's cafeteria wasn't finished, and there were still kids attending Pfister, those of us teachers who had classes just prior to lunch, had to walk our junior high students to the Pfister cafeteria, and sit with them while they ate. Fortunately, the younger kids were in class at that time.

Since the DeWitt students were restricted to spending their time in the amphitheater during ALL free time, there was NO separation between grade levels or core teams before school started, after school ended, nor during lunch. Stopping fights was the primary function of teachers having duties at those times, and we ALWAYS seemed to have duties!

It wasn't until the 2nd semester began, when both the gym and cafeteria were ready to be used by the students of the new school, that SOME of the craziness was lessened. Pfister Elementary was finally torn down so our students actually had a playground. It didn't stop the 'quarreling' amongst our kids completely, but it DID mean that DeWitt students could FINALLY get some separation from each other.

Discipline problems were non-ending, however, and coaches were finding poor attitudes being carried with the students onto the various teams, as well.

When basketball and wrestling seasons began, Steve Lipinski's b-ball team got to work out in the gym, naturally, and MY wrestling team got to use the cafeteria for practice. That meant that my wrestlers had to fold up lunch tables so our wrestling mat could be put into place. Then, after practice, the wrestlers had to roll up and store the mat, and put the tables back up for the next day's breakfast. That was exactly the same procedure I had at Wilhelm. I didn't complain about the accommodations, though. I was just excited to have ALL the junior high students available at one school, and I was excited to recruit as many athletes as possible to join the DeWitt wresting team.

Steve was excited about having a great basketball team, too, but that was short-lived.

Lipinski and I were on the same core team, which was great, except when it came to finding athletes for the sports teams. We basically had our 150 students, but we wanted to have a single junior high school so we could see MORE than just the athletes we taught. Steve noticed that ALL of the kids he coached, while at Wilhelm, were on the other core team, so he was set with them. There was NOT, however, a lot of potential from the returnees, so he hustled the boys on our team of students. And there were several 'new' kids who had moved into our district. Steve watched them in pick-up games at lunch, and noticed that a few had some very good potential on the court, but he also noticed that those same 'potentials' displayed poor attitudes if NOT getting what they wanted during the 'pick-up' games.

That was a shame since Coach Lipinski was all about basics and conditioning. He had so MUCH knowledge of the game that he enjoyed having his players practicing all the time. Steve's message, therefore, to his teams EVERY year was simple, 'We want to be better prepared technically and better conditioned than our opponents for EVERY game.'

This is a philosophy that worked well at his former school, especially considering he hardly EVER had a kid who was six-feet tall. His teams just executed better than most, AND they were toughest in the 4th quarter, when the other team was wearing down physically.

How delighted Steve was, when, on his first day of practice at DeWitt. He had THREE tall kids show up for his basketball team.... all of them measuring in the 6'2"-6'4" range. And, according to the coach, when I talked him the day after his first practice, he had one smaller athlete who displayed ball-handling wizardry with dribbling and passing skills. PLUS, that smaller athlete seemed to be a natural floor general, always encouraging his teammates throughout the beginning warm-up drills. According to what he told me, Lipinski was delighted at what he saw during the first half hour of practice.

However, while working on the fundamentals necessary for ALL basketball players, his tallest player stopped in the middle of one of the skills. "Coach, when do we get to play basketball? We KNOW how to do these things you are having us do here."

"Son," Lipinski said calmly, "I know most of you know how to do these, but I want you to do them better than anyone else on the other teams. AND, we have LOTS of basics that we have to master.

So, we will practice these simple skills a lot, at the beginning of EVERY practice, until you don't have to think about what it takes to do them well....you'll just have them engrained in your memory. We'll be working on LOTS of different skills, THEN we will play in game situations."

"Coach, Coach, Coach," the tall kid said. "You mean we have to do this kind of stuff EVERY day? I think we would get better by just PLAYING basketball, like we do in the 'hood.' I have no trouble with ANY of the guys I play....EVER!"

"Young man," Steve continued, "this is not street ball. The teams you will be playing ALL practice their skills. None of them just goes out and starts to play games."

"And we're gonna do this EVERY practice?" the big kid asked with disgust in his voice.

"Yes," was Lipinski's response to the question.

"I can't do this, Man. I'm gonna go play with my boys," and with that, the tallest player Coach Lipinski EVER had come out for one of his teams, was gone.

Steve looked at the rest of his team, then asked, "Anyone else think practicing the basic skills is a waste of time. We're going to play a lot of games, but we need to be sharp in all facets of the game, that's why we practice every day."

"Coach," one of the OTHER tall kids asked, "when you say we are going to practice EVERY day, what does that mean?"

"It means, I will have practice every day I can, AND we may even have a couple of practices on Saturdays, if we need them."

"Coach, I have a girlfriend, and she didn't even want me to come OUT for this team. I HAVE to be with her SOME days after school, or I will lose her….and I don't want to lose her."

"You will not lose her. She will be proud of you when you are a STAR on the school team," the coach said with much encouragement.

"I can't be practicin' all the time," and with that, a SECOND big kid walked out of the gym. Steve and the rest of the 8th grade basketball candidates just looked at his departure in amazement.

"Anyone else?" Lipinski asked and sounding a bit annoyed after seeing two defections before the first practice was half-way finished.

Nobody said a word, and practice continued.

Coach Lipinski's teams were always known for their fine conditioning, but there was a reason for that….Lipinski WORKED on conditioning a lot, always ending his practices with a well-known basketball conditioning drill called SUICIDES!

This drill had an easy concept, but when players are pushed by their coach, they get VERY tired, and Steve pushed. But that is why his players always seemed inexhaustible during games.

For the drill, players line up at one end of the basketball court, on the baseline. When the whistle blows everybody hustles to the free throw line, bends down and touches the line, than races back to the baseline. They quickly turn, go touch the top of the key, then back...then run hard to the half-court line, then the top of the key at the other basket, then the far free throw line, and finish up by racing to the opposite base line, touching it and racing back. Every time they go OUT to touch a line, they race back to the start. They run as hard as they possibly can throughout the 'suicide,' and the players are ALWAYS exhausted after each completion of the exercise. Like I said, GREAT conditioning drill.

Players knew they had to run at the end of each practice, so Steve would use incentives to get the players to run harder. He, generally, liked to run three suicides every practice, but his players did NOT like to run three. SO, on their first suicide, the coach would tell his players, "The first two finishers do NOT have to run any more suicides today." It became an all-out sprint by everybody during that first suicide. He would then give the same promise for the second suicide, which resulted in more sprinting. With four players watching from the sideline, Lipinski 'pushed' the remaining players, whose tongues were usually hanging out, until all had finished the third suicide.

BUT, Coach Lipinski made NO such offer for the first practice with the DeWitt players. He didn't say anything, just had them get on the line saying, "We are going to run a suicide."

When his players finished that FIRST difficult exercise, they practically collapsed on the floor, making comments like: "Oh, Man, that was tough," "That was a killer," and the ever popular, "I NEVER want to do THAT again." Music to the coach's ears.

"Go get a small drink of water," Steve said to his exhausted boys, then get back on the line. We are running another suicide tonight."

The boys started grumbling rather loudly, BUT they all lined up for a second go at the conditioning drill. Steve then gave his incentive, telling the players that there would be a third suicide, BUT the first two finishers of the second run would be excused.

Some of the boys were hustling, trying to impress their coach. Some were really out of shape, but were bound and determined to finish. Others LOOKED like they were in pain. Steve was finding out who REALLY wanted to play on the school basketball team. All finished the second suicide….well, ALMOST every one.

Coach Lipinski's outstanding ball handler, the future leader of his team, was running in the middle of the pack, during that second run, holding on to his side to indicate he was hurting. When the team's 'leader' reached the opposite base line, he never came back. The doors, leading in and out of the gym, were at that that far end of the gym, and the young 8th grader, didn't look back. He continued right through the doors, and his days of playing basketball for DeWitt were over.

The coach lost two of his three tall players, AND his projected team leader, after only ONE practice. There would be a few more defections, and the team ended up NOT being very talented. When I talked to Steve one day, toward the end of the basketball season, he confided in me that he was finished coaching at DeWitt….and he was….one year and done.

Wrestling was different, however. I had a VERY capable assistant coach for my last four years at Wilhelm. His name was Clint Waterston, and he had been a fairly good wrestler for me at my former school. He wrestled throughout high school, and the sport became a passion of his. Clint brought that passion to Wilhelm, and the wrestlers all really liked him. He was strong in fundamentals, and helped a great deal with disciplining when I asked him to do so. He asked if he could help me at DeWitt, and I couldn't say 'yes' fast enough.

I didn't have very many good 8th graders, from Wilhelm, who went to DeWitt, and there weren't many 8th grade boys, from Pfister or Cahill, who were interested in trying the sport, but I DID have a VERY strong bunch of 7th graders from Wilhelm, who came to the new school. They would become the nucleus of my team for the 1990-91 season. We actually finished in the top twenty at the State Championships that year. And it was that group of 7th grade kids who made Wilhelm's wrestling reputation take off.

Something 'different' did occur at the end of DeWitt's first wrestling season, however. I was approached by a 7th grade girl who asked me why I didn't have any girls on the team. Title 9 was big, and she thought I was discriminating by not letting girls at DeWitt join the team. I told her that if she had come to me when the season was happening, I would have let her join. That comment ended her claim of discrimination, and I told her to come out during the 1991-'92 season. I finished MY comments by explaining TWO things to her. First, I was only coaching ONE team....not a separate girls' team, and a separate boys' team....ONE team. Secondly, if she was to wrestle, she would be required to do everything the boys did, AND she would be wrestling AGAINST the boys. I, once again, reiterated my earlier statement, telling her, "I will be coaching just ONE wrestling team, and it is the DeWitt wrestling team. Be on it, don't be on it, your choice."

Isabelle Vasquez told me she could do ANYTHING boys could do, and then I watched her walk away. "See you next year," I said, LIKING that kind of attitude.

Isabelle came out for the team, worked as hard as anyone, but never got a match against another team. She DID, however, go on to high school, and earn three, or is it four, Varsity letters in wrestling. She, apparently, was the only kid in her high school who could make the lowest weight, (98 lbs.) any of her years in school.

While Isabelle broke the gender gap for our school, she wasn't the only girl to come out for my team. A 7th grader, named Sonia Morales, ALSO, came out. She was short and stout. I don't want to embarrass her, if she is reading this, but she had the look of a bowling ball to me....quite round. BUT, she was the nicest person! She had to wrestle heavyweight because of her size, and I already had one VERY good heavyweight, a Native American kid, who looked like he had no neck. Looking at him from behind, it just looked like his head was directly attached to his back. I also had a pretty good 2nd team heavyweight, as well. My third team heavyweight reminded me of the Pillsbury doughboy....he giggled a lot when you touched him in the belly. ALL of them could beat Sonia in their matches, however. Still, I DID have two female wrestlers on that team.

There came a day that Sonia WASN'T expecting, however. NONE of us expected it. Sonia Morales got a wrestling match against a kid from another school.

The season was coming to an end. My team, that year, was the best I ever had, or would ever have. And when I say my team, I mean from the starters to the reserves, I had a vast depth of talent. I used to count every single match we had, in all of our meets, toward the final team scores. Having that knowledge, ALL the DeWitt wrestlers wanted to contribute to the team total. My wrestlers (with my encouragement) had come to realize that we were ONE team, win or lose. In dual meets therefore, both 1st team wrestlers and exhibition wrestlers composed the final score of the meets. The DeWitt team developed a one-for-all, all-for-one attitude. And THAT was the team concept I loved!

We had a home meet the night Sonia wrestled. I will tell you that, not only were we UNdefeated at that point of our season, we were winning by legendary margins. We were beating teams by scores like 82-0, and 113-3. Believe me….DeWitt had a VERY good team that year!

On 'Sonia's night' we were wrestling a team out of a VERY rich part of Phoenix. Their school district did not sponsor a wrestling program, but the coaches of that particular school (along with the support of the parents) decided to have a sort of 'wrestling club.' Transportation was provided by the parents, and EVERY parent took pride in getting his/her wrestler to the 'away' meets. There were no busses coming to our school that night, just many, MANY family cars.

THIS team could boast an undefeated team, too, when they arrived at DeWitt, and had nearly as many wrestlers as DeWitt. Over sixty wrestlers, and their families, came to wrestle our Inner City school. Since our reputation was very well known amongst our students, there were many DeWitt supporters in the gym, too, rooting us on during the evening. With our 'home' support, and all the opposing wrestlers having been driven by parents, our bleachers were so full we had to have areas where stragglers could stand and watch without obstructing the views of the people in the bleachers. That night may have been the biggest crowd to ever see our team wrestle.

The difference of both teams' wrestling attire and equipment was startling to me. The wealthy team had, not only all the same uniforms, but matching warm-ups as well. Everybody from the wealthy school looked cloned. They brought with them VERY expensive, well, EVERYTHING....same fancy wrestling shoes, same state-of-the-art headgear....same EVERYTHING! That team had a LOT of financial support.

We looked like the rag-tag street urchins that the other team thought we were....several different-colored uniforms, with each style being different from the others. DeWitt wrestlers who DIDN'T get a uniform had to wear plain shorts and tee shirts. Maybe six or seven of my wrestlers had wrestling shoes, and that was it. At least all my kids had shoes, (wrestling or tennis shoes) as no one was allowed to wrestle bare-footed. It really looked like a classic rich versus NOT rich scenario. But like I have said, we had a LOT of good wrestlers that year.

As the other team entered, I noticed a tall, but not too heavy, kid. Everybody on the DeWitt team assumed that he would be their heavyweight. He was a good 6'4" tall, and had a little paunch. My heavyweight star, we'll call him Marine because, well, with no neck he LOOKED like he could have been a marine, came running over to me. "I'm going to tear that guy apart," he grumbled.

I told him to settle down, and ALL of my wrestlers relinquished the mat so the other team could warm up. Waterston took command, while I went to a quiet place, with the opposing coach, to set up matches for the evening.

After we identified who would be wrestling first team, we decided to have as many 'extra' matches as possible. His FIRST WORDS were, "I have four heavyweights."

I looked at him, with a smile, and replied, "I have four heavyweights, too. My fourth teamer is a girl, though. Do you have a wrestler who wouldn't mind wrestling a girl?"

"My #4 heavyweight is a pansy, he can't beat ANYONE over 150 lbs, and he would LOVE to have a match with someone.... ANYONE!"

"Which boy is he?" I enquired because I KNEW Sonia would want to know. I also knew that after I would show her who the opponent was, she would want to use the restroom immediately. Her bladder was kind of skittish when she was nervous on MOST days, so I could imagine what it would be like after telling her she had a wrestling match.

"Did you notice my tall wrestler?" I was asked.

"That kid? He's your FOURTH team heavyweight?" I responded in disbelief.

"Can't beat his own shadow. Trust me, the only thing intimidating about him is his size. Do you want the match?"

And with that, Sonia would be the first girl to have a wrestling match in DeWitt history. To top it off, she was going to be the first exhibition match of the day, as well.

I entered the gym and called all my wrestlers around me. "OK, we will have about fifty matches today, and Sonia, you have the first one."

Her face turned white, her eyes widened until I thought they were going to pop out of her head. "I'm going to wrestle, and I have to be first?" she said while some of the boys were patting her on the back. "Which boy is he?"

"You see that tall kid over there?" I said while pointing toward the 6'4' wrestler.

"Oh, no, Coach, he is too beeg. I can't beat HEEM," she said in her delightful Mexican accent.

"He is supposed to be the easiest big kid on their team. EVERYONE on his team can beat him, according to his coach. Besides, YOU wrestle with the toughest junior high heavyweights in the state every day. Just wrestle THAT guy like you have learned from OUR tough heavyweights, and you will give him everything he can handle. Do you want the match, or not?"

Sonia nodded affirmatively, and asked, "Coach, I got to pee first?" She was gone in a flash, and with that, my whole team loosened up, as I gave the other wrestlers their matches.

The referee, Slim Jim Portman, was an old friend of my team. He had refereed MOST of our matches, both home and away. He centered himself in the middle of the mat, and said, "Let's GO!"

I sent Sonia out, and she sprinted to the center of the mat to wait for her opponent. Slim Jim looked at me with a bewildered look, and I just smiled.

The big opponent ambled out to meet Sonia, kind of with a sheepish, maybe embarrassed, look on his face.

The audience had already become rowdy. NOBODY could believe we had a girl going to wrestle that giant, and they were vocal about it.

My wrestler was all business, and had a very serious look on her face. Then Slim Jim had them shake hands. Sonia WAS a good head shorter than the big guy, so she reached UP to shake hands. The whistle blew and the match began. Sonia immediately threw her right hand upward, cupping her hand behind her opponent's head.

The big fellow looked almost bashful, as he lazily moved HIS hand to cup Sonia's head. Instantly, my heavyweight snatched that lazy arm reach with her left arm, yanked it down while moving her RIGHT arm around his head, pulling him down toward her level. She got hold of his head AND shoulder and executed a beautiful headlock, dropping him to the mat like a sack of flour. Sonia proceeded to pick up his elbow while grinding her heels into the mat and arching her back. She was determined to get a pin, and had her opponent on his back, and her headlock was tight.

However, the big guy had long arms, and was forcing his own shoulder OFF the mat with everything he had. The noise in the gym was deafening, and from where I was watching, it looked SEVERAL times like Sonia had earned that pin. I kept hollering "That's a pin, Ref!"

For his part, Slim Jim held up his thumb and index finger, showing me the kid's shoulder was a half inch OFF the mat. The period was over, and Sonia had a 5-0 lead, BUT she hadn't pinned this big fellow.

In wrestling there are three possible periods, and in junior high EACH wrestling period was one minute in length. In dual meets, it is pre-determined which wrestler has the 'choice' on how he/she wants to start the SECOND period. Sonia was given that choice and looked at me. I told her to start back on her feet. (the 'down' and top' positions were her other options) I ALSO mentioned that the big fellow knew he was behind and might take the match more seriously. "Keep inside his arms, Sonia," I yelled. "Keep circling. Do NOT let him get inside YOUR arms, or he will be able to muscle you down."

The two wrestlers parried and circled, but neither could get a takedown. Second period over….still 5-0 in favor of Sonia. The boy took the 'down' position to start the third, and last, period of their match. This required HIM to get on his hands and knees, with Sonia JUST behind him, and to one side. She had one knee down with her one hand on his elbow, and the other hand reaching around TRYING to touch the big guy's belly button. Sonia had NO chance of reaching all the way around, but she extended her arm as far as she could.

Slim Jim gave the wrestle signal, and immediately the big guy did a 'Switch' move which allowed him to completely reverse the positions, as he went around her, putting her underneath him.

Sonia went to her belly with a thud. The guy knew what he was doing and he looked to hit the girl with a half-nelson, a move that is usually fatal to junior high wrestlers with inexperience. As luck would have it, however, MY team worked on how to NOT allow the half-nelson to take place....elbows in, get to the hip nearest the opponent, and move into him while your head is high....keeping your belly facing the mat while trying to step over your opponent with your nearside leg. Complicated, maybe, but Sonia knew what to do.

That big guy was becoming exasperated. He couldn't quite get his hand completely around Sonia's neck on the one side. Then, seeing her OPPOSITE elbow up in the air to help her push herself into him, he leaped to her OTHER side to try and get a half-nelson on THAT side. She would tuck THAT elbow, switch her weight to the new hip, and begin pushing into him once more. The crowd was in a near frenzy, by this time.

Suddenly, the big wrestler GOT a niche under Sonia's near-side elbow and cupped his hand around her neck. There were just SECONDS left in the match, and with a mighty push, that big moose rolled Sonia onto her back....JUST as the time expired.

Slim Jim DIDN'T call a pin, but IMMEDIATELY went to the scorer's table to see IF time had gone out, or did the girl go flat on her back BEFORE time went out. Since he didn't slap the mat and CALL a pin, I had a good feeling. But I didn't know what Slim Jim might do.

When he returned to the center of the mat, there was not a sound in the building. Slim Jim had his combatants shake hands, then he raised SONIA'S hand in victory....a 5-2 decision.

Pandemonium broke out! Our fans were yelling, "We have the toughest girls in the city," The fans from the other district were yelling, "I can't BELIEVE our big guy lost to a girl!"

EVERYONE was on their feet screaming something....except for one lady, who was quietly sitting on the bleachers with her head buried in her hands. I believed that woman to be the mother of the losing wrestler, and then I had a cruel thought.....what if she went somewhere, and someone asked her if her son played sports. She would answer 'wrestling,' but would she say, 'He wrestled yesterday and lost...to a girl." Now THAT was a cruel thought.

Two things here. First, DeWitt only lost three matches that night, while winning well over forty....nearly fifty matches. Secondly, Sonia's dad moved the family before the next school year. She BEGGED him to let her stay in Brighton District with a friend....at least through the wrestling season, but he told her 'No.'

I had a few more female wrestlers in the next couple of years, but none of them won a match. Sonia would have been the LAST girl I could have guessed would win a match for the team....especially against such a large opponent. But she holds a special place in my heart, and I will NEVER get that match out of my mind.

Sonia's victory was a little jewel for the wrestling team of the 1991-'92 season. It drew a lot of interest for the wrestling program, and that team's success would sustain the sport for the next few years at DeWitt. But the stress of coaching wrestling in the Inner City, even as good a team as I had that year, was beginning to take a heavy toll on me. And that was never more evident than when we competed in the State Wrestling Tournament in March of the 1992 year. The stress started BEFORE the tourney even got underway, too.

I had some real junior high studs, that year, as I have mentioned. But with just two weeks before that year's STATE meet, I was told that TWO of my 'stars' would be ineligible to participate…. my heavyweight, AND my undefeated 133 lb. wrestler. BOTH were over the age cut-off date for their 15th birthday….Marine by just THREE days, and the team's legitimate 133-pound star, by five days. I sent in a petition for a waiver, and got rejected. Those two guys were dejected, and I felt terrible for them.

As stunned as we all were at the news, I knew that both their replacements were pretty good, especially the 2nd team heavyweight. We would STILL enter a strong team, and THAT gave me a good feeling about DeWitt's chances of winning the State title.

Two events happened, before the tournament, however, which kind of dinged my confidence.

For one, with the team's star heavyweight out of the tourney, his replacement began to shine in the practice room. He looked good, and I felt confident in his doing well, possibly even scoring major points for the team. Sickeningly, however, with TWO days remaining until we were to go to State, my heavyweight 'replacement' got ill. His family told the school nurse that he had a fever and would NOT be in school for the remaining two days of the week, and THAT meant he would not be going to the tournament!

I had to replace HIM with my third-team heavy, and he, as I have mentioned, was a giggler, not a tough wrestler like the two guys he replaced. I was pretty sure I couldn't expect him to get many, if any, points for the team at State. Unfortunately, I was correct, as my replacement's replacement lost both his matches. Going from entering a second seed (as I figured out Marine would have been) to a nice kid who just wanted to BE on a wrestling team, was a major set-back to the team's goal of winning the coveted State team trophy. An aside here, my 133 lb. wrestler would have ALSO been the #2 seed. HIS replacement would only win ONE match for the team, so the team suffered major point loss. What can I say, rules are rules, but 3 and 5 days too old was tough to take.

An equally disappointing occurrence came when Clint Waterston told me he HAD to be out of town the weekend the tournament was being held. I really wasn't listening to his reason, I only heard that he wouldn't be with us. The fact is, in big tournaments there are several wrestling mats having action at the same time. Chances are good that a team could have more than one wrestler WRESTLING at the same time. When that occurred in the 1992 State tournament, I had no choice but to send a couple of 8th graders to sit in the corner to coach a teammate, while I was coaching on a separate mat with another wrestler. The team, and especially I, missed Clint not being with us that weekend.

Losing two top wrestlers could destroy any team's thought about being the best team in a sport. However, DeWitt had a plethora of talent still available for the 1992 State Wrestling Tournament.

No one on THAT team was better than Sergio Hernandez. He was the undisputed TOP star on DeWitt's wrestling team. He would have been the star of the 1991 team, too, but, at THAT state tourney, he made a mistake in the quarterfinals that devastated him and me. Simply said, he was controlling his opponent, tried to do a move NEITHER of us had ever seen, and he ended up, not only on his back, but in a tight Cradle. He was pinned, and settled for 3rd in State.

When the '91-'92 campaign began, Sergio was dedicating himself to NOT make any move he hadn't already perfected. I had him on my wrestling team since he was in the 4th grade, and, while he wasn't the smartest kid I ever coached, he could execute several moves, that other kids couldn't stop. It helped that he was man-strong, and had a stare that could scare an adult male. He wrestled at 154 lbs, and he looked MUCH older than his 14 years indicated him to be. In his 8th grade year, he was simply the best junior high wrestler in the state of Arizona, no matter the weight division.

He was undefeated, AND un-scored upon during his last season. He went into the State tournament with a winning reputation that every junior high coach knew about. He was so dominating that there wasn't a coach attending the tournament who DIDN'T expect him to be crowned 154 lb.champion....every coach, that is, except one.

In DeWitt's next-to-last dual meet, that year, I took my team to wrestle a team from the West Valley. They didn't have a particularly great team, and my wrestlers destroyed them, like they had every other team that year. They DID, however, have one wrestler that their coach assured me was the best wrestler HE had ever seen in Arizona. His kid was a California transfer, who had gone unde-feated his 7th grade year, and won a few tough California tourna-ments. The coach HAD heard of Hernandez, but was convinced HIS wrestler was better. As for the kid, himself, it is true that he was just as muscular as Sergio. His bravado must have been shaken as he continually walked around on his side of the gym in a haugh-ty manner, flexing his muscles while making angry sounds, staring across the mat at our team....doing his best to intimidate Sergio, trying to indicate to MY guy just how 'tough' he was.

Didn't work, however, as my DeWitt 154 pounder was pretty dom-inating. Nothing flashy, just controlling, as he beat the California transplant 4-0. That victory got the Westside coach very quiet, for the rest of the DUAL meet. But I heard from him again....at the Arizona State Junior High Wrestling Tournament.

As was the usual custom, at State, coaches were called into a room, prior to the start of the tourney. There were 61 head coaches present, and we were meeting to discover whose wres-tlers received tournament seeds, AND to ask any questions that needed to be answered.We rolled through the first several weight divisions without many whimpers or comments on pairings of any kind. Things were moving along smoothly until we got to the 154 lb. division. THAT'S when things started to get a little heated.... and the 'beef' was coming from that very same Westside coach whose team had wrestled MY team two-and-a-half weeks prior to State. "Why is my wrestler seeded #4?" the suddenly irritated coach said, while rising to his feet so he would be recognized as having something to say. "He has ONLY lost to Hernandez, and I think THAT was a fluke."

"Coach," the leader of the meeting interrupted, "the seeds were based on records, and in THIS division, the numbers 1 through 3 are ALL undefeated. Your kid has a loss."

"My kid SHOULDN'T have lost to the DeWitt kid, AND we have been working on what he needed to correct ever since. He will beat Sergio Hernandez this time around, I guarantee it!"

"Coach," the leader said, while TRYING to move the meeting along, "your kid has to beat EVERYONE he wrestles, in order to be crowned champion. He will get his chance at Hernandez, I'm pretty sure."

"I'm not saying he WOULDN'T beat everyone he faces....he will. MY objection is that he will face Hernandez in the semi-finals and NOT the Finals. This will be the best Finals match all tournament, and it would mean a lot to MY wrestler to beat Hernandez in the Finals, ON the center mat."

"The changes of seedings are just not done, Coach, can we PLEASE move on?"

"I just think this is SO unfair, and I think the process needs to be changed so that the best TWO wrestlers, in a weight division, get to wrestle in the limelight of the Finals!"

It was about to get loud and unruly, as other coaches were getting anxious to get on with the meeting. It became obvious that the bickering by the Westside coach was going to delay the start of the tournament. Suddenly, OTHER coaches were 'kindly' asking the objecting coach to, 'Please sit down and be quiet, so the proceedings can commence.'

Finally, ONE coach stood up, raised his right arm HIGH into the air so he could be recognized by the leader, and said, in a loud voice. "WAIT....EVERYBODY, WAIT! MY kid is in the OTHER bracket. He is NOT a seeded wrestler, and probably doesn't DESERVE to be one. BUT, if this annoying delay can be ended by having my wrestler switch brackets, I'll do it. Have this coach's kid switch brackets with my kid, than we can get on with our business. BESIDES, my kid would LOVE to be seeded fourth."

A general agreement was reached quickly, and the upset coach, from the far western part of Maricopa County, seemed satisfied.

Sergio Hernandez won the championship match with a 6-0 score, and the other coach just shrugged his shoulders when the bout was over.

How did Sergio do in high school? He didn't wrestle. He had an older brother, who had ALSO gone to Wilhelm, but was three years older than Sergio. The brother was on DeWitt's wrestling team, but was more interested in gang activity, so wasn't a serious wrestler. Manny, the brother, didn't want to have baby brother wrestle during Sergio's 8th grade year, but I intervened on the younger Hernandez's behalf, and Manny didn't pressure his younger brother during the season.

However, Manny wanted his brother to join the gang full time, and to do so, he got Sergio to get into a fight, on the high school grounds, during the second week of Sergio's freshman year. Word got to me that it was a 'jump-in' beating, which was tradition to join any gang. Sergio was kicked out of school for a short time, but Manny refused to let his brother return to high school ever again. I had heard that Sergio's family had moved to one of Phoenix's western suburbs. Then, many years later, I heard that someone named Sergio Hernandez was killed in a gang-style encounter.... on the western side of town. I don't know if it was DeWitt's star wrestler who died, but the man killed was 29 years old, which is EXACTLY the age MY Sergio Hernandez would have been that year.

I had already been retired for a couple of years, by then, but I wasn't surprised with the news....just sad. Sergio's fate was not THAT uncommon as a few of the other kids I knew, during my 32 years in education, suffered similar, sad endings.

I feel obligated to tell you MORE about the 1991-'92 State Wrestling Tournament. Losing two top wrestlers to the age cutoff, and crowning the school's best wrestler as champion, does NOT tell the whole story of the kids on that team. In fact, the make-up of the rest of the team is kind of a microcosm of the kids I taught at DeWitt my last ten years in the classroom.

Though DeWitt's wrestling team finished second that year at State, I believe I had the best team in the tournament, and our team SHOULD have been State champions, if three OTHER missteps hadn't occurred during the two-day tourney.

By the end of the first day of wrestling DeWitt found itself the leader in points Yep, we were in first place, and I had SIX wrestlers who went 2-0 that first day, and another three who had won their first individual wrestle-back rounds, which kept them all alive in the tournament. I am going to tell you about a huge upset, which one of my wrestlers pulled off that first night, too, but that story will come later. Now will be told the three horror stories that

KILLED DeWitt's chances of being Arizona's junior high wrestling champions in 1992....and I feel my blood pressure rising as I remember them.

I had a 98 lb.wrestler, who was undefeated for the year, and was given a three-seed at the State tournament. He wasn't an affiliated gang member, but thought himself a tough guy, anyway, (that's right....only 98 pounds) and seemed to get into more than his share of trouble, both in the classroom and on the campus.

He had wrestled for me during his 7th grade year, where he did pretty well. At the time of the tournament, during his 8th grade campaign, he had won every one of his matches, even though several of them were close scores. He WAS undefeated, at the time of the seedings, and that earned him his high ranking. The team and I were counting on him to earn a lot of team points over the two-day event. He was 2-0 when the smoke cleared after the first day of the tournament.

I gathered the troops, that Friday evening, just as soon as our last match was over, and told them, "Be here at 8:00 tomorrow to warm up and get ready for the day." I finished the evening with positive energy saying, "We have a chance to win this whole thing, and that means that EVERYONE needs to wrestle the very best he can, in each match. Now let's get DeWitt its first EVER championship team!"

My guys were tired, but several of them perked up and left the gymnasium with many positive thoughts, and even making comments about us being #1.

The next morning I had a team meeting exactly at 8:00 a.m. "Where is Jamaal Blue?" I inquired, as I did NOT see him with the other wrestlers.

"We stopped by his house to pick him up," one of the other wrestlers said, "But he never came out of his house. He was supposed to be waiting outside, so we assumed he found another way to the meet."

This was NOT the way I wanted to start the day, as I wanted to focus on my team becoming state champs....not trying to round up all my wrestlers. I asked the father of one of my kids to PLEASE take his other son (who was in 7th grade and not on the tournament team) and go to Jamaal's home to get him. I was irritated, but knew it would do me no good to get upset at a wrestler who was late getting to the tournament.

Upon the dad's return, I learned there was NOBODY at the Blue residence. At that point I didn't know whether to be upset or worried. He was a tough enough guy, but the tournament location was a little over five miles from our neighborhood, and I knew there were a LOT of tough guys between DeWitt, and the high school where the tournament was being held. PLUS, he would be exhausted if he DID walk all that way to wrestle.

Eventually, Jamaal Blue's bout was called, but with him STILL not in the gym, he had to forfeit the match. There was no news of any trouble near the tournament that morning, so I hoped he had stayed at a friend's home and would be driven to the tournament in time to, at least, wrestle in the consolation rounds.

An hour, or so, passed, and Jamaal Blue still had not shown up. Suddenly, he was called to wrestle in his first consolation match. When he forfeited THAT match he was eliminated from the tournament. He could no longer help the team, and that bothered me, but I was MORE worried that something may have happened to him, so my stress level was VERY high.

At noon, of that Saturday, I was on a mat, coaching one of my remaining wrestlers in a match, when I happened to look at the entrance to the building. There, dressed in a DeWitt wrestling uniform, and carrying a large bag over his should, was Jamaal Blue. My stress level may have subsided a bit, but my anger was steadily growing.

I went to where the DeWitt team had set up their area in the gym, and asked Jamaal to come over to talk to me. "Where you been, Blue?" I said trying NOT to sound as unhappy as I really was.

"Stayed at my girlfriend's last night. My family was visiting my aunt yesterday, and I didn't want to stay home alone."

"What time did I ask everyone to meet me here today?"

"Eight o'clock, but I thought I would come early," Jamaal said, thinking I would buy that excuse.

"You thought the whole rest of the tournament would be held AFTER eight at night today, did you?" I gave him a stern look, and he smiled, while lowering his head to look at his feet. He knew he had been caught in a lie.

"Nooooo," and he shrugged his shoulders while still looking at the floor. "She didn't want me to leave her so early, so I stayed a while longer than I should have, that's all."

"What's in the bag?" I asked, referring to the big bag he had with him.

"My street clothes,"

"Go change and come back to see me." When he returned I took his singlet and warm-up, and told him to sit up in the bleachers with all the fans. He was NOT to sit with the rest of the team. He looked a little confused, but complied. I had essentially kicked him off the team, and he was NOT given a wrestling certificate at our school's year-end sports assembly. From the tournament on, the only time I talked to Jamaal was in my English class, where he was a student. His 'desire' to be with his girlfriend cost OUR tournament team many valuable points....points we needed if we were to become state champs. So, as far as I was concerned, I just didn't care to be around him outside of the classroom.

I DID have one side event with him, however, which occurred just a few weeks after the State Wrestling Tournament concluded.... but it was NOT related to athletics. It had to do with Jamaal Blue's character.

Steve Lipinski and I were exiting the cafeteria, one day, when we noticed a large crowd of students, apparently cheering on two combatants in a school fight. We hustled to the area and several students disappeared immediately. However, there was a 7th grade teacher in the area already, and he was in full motion trying to stop the two kids rolling around on the ground.

The teacher was PHYSICALLY on the ground in his attempt to break the two students away from each other. Suddenly, out of the small pack that was still watching, ran Jamaal Blue. He raced toward the teacher's position and KICKED that 7th grade teacher in the ribs, TWICE! Then Blue took off like a scalded dog, and Steve and I got to the teacher to help quell the disturbance. The teacher was grabbing his side, and Steve told him we saw the kid who kicked him, and would disclose the culprit when the current mess was settled.

The injured teacher decided to sue Jamaal, to compensate his pain, PLUS a charge of assault was apparently slapped on Jamaal Blue, too.

A few weeks later, I was called to the school's office where an attorney was waiting to talk to me. I gathered that he was a Public Defender, didn't know for sure, representing the Blue family in the assault matter. I was invited into, what was laughably called, the teachers' lounge, and four pictures, of current DeWitt students, were laid out on the big work table in the room. "Mr. Stein," the attorney asked with all seriousness, "do you see a student here, who has SINCE been accused of kicking a teacher, during one particular lunch period at this school?"

I nodded my head, and pointed to Jamaal Blue's photo. "These kids look very much alike," the attorney continued, "How can you be absolutely POSITIVE that this is the student accused of that act?"

"His name is Jamaal Blue. He has been in my English class all year, and was on my wrestling team." I pointed to a second picture, "This is his cousin Willie, who ALSO was on the wrestling team. And both these students (and I named them) are in my 8th grade

English class, too. PLUS, I was within twenty feet of Jamaal when he kicked that teacher, and when he saw me, he tried to hide his face while running away. But, I SAW him just as clearly as I see you right now. And HE knows I saw him, too."

"I won't be calling on you as a character witness, Mr. Stein. Thank-you for your time," He left, and I went back to my classroom. I WASN'T summoned to appear in court by either him or the prosecuting attorney.

Steve Lipinski, however, our Civics teacher, volunteered to testify at the trial. Jamaal was found guilty and faced some sort of punishment, but, to be honest with you, I forget what that punishment was. In truth there were a lot of our students having trouble, both at school AND out of it. Jamaal wanted to be known as a thug, and he proved he was. I have never heard anything about him since the 8th grade, and that is fine by me.

NOW, back to the wrestling tournament, and two OTHER reasons why I think we lost the Championship Trophy.

A more subtle mishap occurred in the tournament's 108 lb. weight division. Our representative was Ephraim Aguilar. He and his fraternal twin brother were new to Brighton District, and both were athletic. His brother was a bit smaller than E, as we called Ephraim, but he couldn't beat E or my regular 108 pound wrestler. The second twin WAS a good second team wrestler, which helped us immensely during our dual meet season, but DeWitt could only go with one Aguilar in the State tourney....Ephraim.

E and his brother had very good seasons, especially considering it was the first season in the sport of wrestling for both boys. They were naturals, and helped us collect big scores in duals, as BOTH were 'pinners,' which meant they liked to PIN their opponents, not just beat them by decisions. Ephraim had a VERY good record, when he went to State. He had lost just one match throughout the regular season, (finishing second in another tournament) which earned him a fourth-seed at State.

He was wrestling in the quarterfinals, that Saturday, and a victory would not only move him toward an important semi-final match, but his advancement points would have given the DeWitt team enough points to WIN the State. (which I calculated AFTER the tournament was over) I knew we needed his victory, especially after the Jamaal Blue selfish gesture of not showing up for his matches. I just didn't realize HOW much E would mean, point-wise, until the whole show was over.

In his quarterfinal match, E had gotten a first period take-down, and turned his opponent over onto his back, slightly, in the second period, to get a two-point near-fall reward. Aguilar was ahead by a 4 to 0 margin entering the last wrestling period. His decision, IN that third period, was to take the 'down' position. He never looked at me for what I wanted him to choose. But I kept the faith.

ALL I had told my wrestlers, in the practices prior to the State, was for them to get to their feet, (from the 'down' position) then fight to get away. I emphasized again and again, do NOT try anything fancy when the other guy is on the 'top' position....just get to your feet and get away.

E had already proven he could get a takedown, AND could control his opponent when on top. Why he chose the bottom position,

I have NO idea, but I had to stay positive. I began to holler, "GET TO YOUR FEET, E....GET TO YOUR FEET ON THE WHISTLE!"

But....surprise....he DIDN'T try to get to his feet! He tried to get a 'Switch,' which would allow him to reverse the position of both wrestlers, allowing E to end up on top, and his opponent on the bottom. When Aguilar sat out, and reached back toward the other wrestler's leg, the opponent simply let go of the waist hold he had and came OVER E's shoulder, dropping my kid flat onto his back.

Ephraim was straining to not get pinned, and EVENTUALLY, got to his belly. But, he was exhausted, and just lay there. He was ahead 4-3, (the opponent getting a three-point near-fall call in his favor) but E couldn't get to his knees, let alone onto his feet.

The other wrestler got, what's called a double arm-bar, on Aguilar, and as time was running out, turned Ephraim a SECOND time. The opponent only got a two-point near-fall count, but it was enough for him to send E to the consolation matches....Aguilar lost 5-4.

I wanted to ask him what he was thinking, but I was being called to another mat to coach another DeWitt wrestler. Ephraim Aguilar was a very sensitive kid, and he got down on himself pretty badly. He wouldn't listen to anybody, trying to encourage him and help him get back together psychologically. He lost ANOTHER close match in his first consolation round, and was out of the tournament. His departure was a HUGE reason DeWitt didn't win the tournament. The Aguilar family moved away during the summer. Transiency was SUCH a big player in the school's athletic successes and failures. I never heard another word about either twin again.

The last 'blow' my team suffered in its attempt to be declared wrestling champions, came in a 78 lb. semi-final match.

My wrestler was Christopher Cortez. He was an 8th grade student, whose home situation was similar to Sergio Hernandez.... older brother a gang member, who didn't like that little brother wanted to wrestle instead of join the local gang. The difference between the two students was that Sergio and Chris lived in different neighborhoods, and each was 'affiliated' with different gangs. However, the two 8th graders were friends at school.

Christopher had lost a tough semi-final match when he was in 7th grade, and ended up finishing 3rd in his weight division.... the same result as Sergio had, and BOTH were aiming to become State champions in 1992.

Cortez was a little guy. In 7th grade he was in the 72-pound division. He was a 78-pound wrestler for his 8th grade campaign, but he suffered a loss earlier in the season. For THAT match, Chris was ill but convinced me he was fine, so I let him wrestle. However, he was NOT fine, having very little strength, and lost a tight bout. That single loss got him a 4th-seed at State, so he had to wrestle the #1 seed in the Semi's.

His opponent was the DEFENDING 78-lb champion, wrestling for a Native American reservation team from Northern Arizona. Two things here....one, this team was a COMBINED team, comprising of two different reservation boarding schools.

I didn't believe combining more than one school, to form a singular team, had ever been allowed before, so THAT seemed a bit unfair to me.

However, in 1992, BOTH Native American schools complained that NEITHER could field a full wrestling roster. They indicated that neither would be entering the State tourney UNLESS they were allowed to enter as ONE team. From what I heard, the Native American community would spend the money to enter the tournament, ONLY if they had a possibility of winning a team championship. Essentially, I thought they were entering an all-star team.

BUT, the State powers to be, wanting as many teams as possible competing, caved in to the reservation's 'request.' I just have to think that losing money from two schools was a major factor in the decision, so State officials gave in….my opinion, only.

It should be noted, however, that there were still two OTHER reservation teams, from two different boarding schools, who were ALSO entered into the 1992 tournament, which gave the Northern Arizona reservation boarding schools two school teams AND one all-star team.

As for the all-star team, BOTH teams had several very good wrestlers, and as luck would have it, those really good wrestlers just happened to cover the weaknesses of the other team. The 'combined' team became a heavy favorite to win the championship, and many of the coaches (me included) questioned the 'all-star' decision, though those discussions were just amongst ourselves. Coaches had no input because we weren't invited to have input. Didn't matter what coaches thought, the decision had been made by SOMEONE, so the matter was closed.

The second 'thing' I had on my mind (just before the start of Chris' match)....how does a kid, an EIGHTH grade kid NOT gain any weight between his 7th and 8th grade years? But, there he was, a year AFTER winning the 78-lb crown, going for it again. I was tense before the match even got started.

The match lived up to its billing as BOTH wrestlers were aggressive in the first period....attack, counter-wrestle....it was an exciting first period, but no score.

For the second round, the reservation opponent, who had come closest to getting a take-down in the first period, chose neutral, so the wrestlers were back on their feet. RIGHT at the end of the period, the opponent got hold of Chris' right leg and was maneuvering around my wrestler.

Chris was still on his feet, and threw a defensive move, called a 'Whizzer' on his foe.

The wrestlers were on the edge of the mat, and the reservation wrestler was moving to get around Chris, though both of them were STILL on their feet, AND Chris still had a pretty good Whizzer.

As the time expired, the referee called a two-point takedown, for Chris's opponent. I about went ballistic. I screamed, "HOW CAN THAT BE A TAKEDOWN? MY WRESTLER WAS NEVER ON THE GROUND AND THE OTHER GUY WAS OUT OF BOUNDS WHEN YOU MADE THE CALL!"

The referee raced toward me, and while putting his finger up toward my face, said in a VERY distressed way, "IT WAS A TAKEDOWN, AND IF YOU SAY ONE MORE WORD, YOU WILL

BE OUTTA HERE!" He seemed as angry as I was, but I had no choice. I was the team's lone coach that day, so I HAD to shut my mouth, or be kicked out of the tournament....and that means outside of the building.

I called one of my 8th graders over to sit in the coach's corner with me. "I can't say anything more this match," I told my 8th grader in a calm voice. "But, when I tell YOU to say something, you scream out exactly what I tell you."

Chris Cortez chose the bottom position for the start of the last period, and as he was a master at getting to his feet, he escaped in two seconds flat. From that moment on, the opponent was engaging Chris, but backing off the mat. Immediately, I had my co-coaching 8th grader start to yell, "He's STALLING, ref! He's backing OFF the mat!"

The referee never looked in my direction, but kept allowing the backward movement. Chris was attacking, attacking, ATTACKING, and the kid from the reservation was parrying EVERYTHING while continuing to back away.

FINALLY, with five seconds to go in the entire match, the ref gave the kid from the Northern Arizona a stalling WARNING! The match ended quickly, and Chris lost 2-1. Cortez never said a word to me, when he came back after the match. My blood pressure was sky-high, and I wanted to yell at EVERYBODY....but stayed quiet. Chris walked dejectedly to the team area. I walked with him and put my hand on his shoulder. He looked up at me, nodded that he knew how upset I was, too, then got dressed in his warm-ups.

Chris Cortez finished 3rd in his weight division for the second consecutive year, BUT him losing that semifinal match cost us valuable advancement points, and contributed to our NOT becoming State champions!

At the end of the tournament I went home and couldn't sleep the entire night. I couldn't shake the events that contributed to us finishing second in the final standings. We lost the Champion's trophy to….damn it….the reservation all-star team. I kept thinking about how my team lost two really good wrestlers, BEFORE the tournament….losing them BOTH to a grand total of eight days for being too old between them. I thought about Jamaal Blue and HIS selfish act of being late to the Saturday wrestling session. I thought about Ephraim Aguilar's NOT thinking about winning but of his own personal glory in wanting to pin his opponent….losing to his own ego. And I wanted to cry when I thought about the way Christopher Cortez lost. It was one of the worst nights of sleep I could remember since I had been in Vietnam.

As an aside to Chris….he visited me at DeWitt five years after he graduated from 8th grade. Apparently HIS brother didn't let Chris attend school at all after 8th grade, not even ONE DAY of high school. But, Chris came to tell me he was thinking of going back to school. He was tired of the gang life, and had actually gotten beaten up to get OUT of the gang. "Coach," he asked rather shyly, "I want to start wrestling again. Do you think they will let me wrestle this year?'

"How old are you, Chris?" I asked hestitantly.

"Nineteen."

"Sorry, Chris," I quietly uttered, as I put my hand on his shoulder. "You're a year too old."

Tears began to well up in young Cortez's eyes, and he quickly turned so I wouldn't notice a former gang member cry. He left without a word, and I could see him wiping his eyes as he left. I remembered his last hurrah for wrestling glory in the 8th grade, and I, TOO, got tears in my eyes. The gang life didn't allow for nice junior high kids to have a successful childhood, and I felt very badly for him. Never heard from Christopher Cortez again....and so it went....the streets had swallowed up another one of my ex-students.

The 1991-'92 season had its downs, but along with the championship won by Sergio Hernandez, there were two OTHER stories from that tournament that were positive, and I do NOT want to end me telling you about that wonderful wrestling year on a sad note.

Besides the two Aguilar twins moving into the district, another athletic kid moved in from California. Omar Sentman was his name, and he was tall, thin, and quite strong, even if he didn't LOOK all that muscular. He was a natural basketball player, really, but with Steve Lipinski NOT coaching at DeWitt anymore, I pressed the kid to join the wrestling team. It wasn't easy to persuade him but some of the popular mat maid cheerleaders convinced him that wrestling had become THE sport at DeWitt. I think the girls just wanted to see him in a wrestling singlet, which was simply just a tight-fitting unitard.

Omar had one BIG problem, other than he had never wrestled before. He weighed 149 lbs., which put him in Sergio Hernandez's weight division. There was NO way Omar could beat Sergio that year. My next lower weight division was 145 lbs. but I didn't allow my kids to lose more than TWO pounds, let alone four pounds. (Ruben Cordova was the lone exception in my career) However, my team did NOT have a very good wrestler at the 167 lb. division, which was the wrestling weight between 154 lbs. and heavyweight, and, since both my good heavyweights weighed more that 210 lbs., Omar would have to fill the bill.

Omar Sentman was a natural all-around athlete, and having him work extensively with Hernandez proved very valuable. When he wasn't working out with Sergio I had him work out with my tough 145-lb. wrestler. Those practices worked, as Omar won his first two dual matches, then finished second in his first tournament of the year, to a two-year undefeated wrestler from a mining town in Eastern Arizona. The championship match wasn't all THAT close, but Omar was so new, I was happy he did as well as he did. He won his next twelve matches and had a record of 16-1 when he went to State in the 167-lb. division. Omar got a third-seed for the tournament, which I thought was great testimony to his desire to win ALL his matches.

He won a thriller against the #2 seed, in his semi-final match at State, then faced that same wrestler, from the mining community, who had given Omar his only loss up to that point. And WHAT a match it was. Sentman was giving away a lot of weight, since the 'champ' was a SOLID 167 pounds. Even with the nearly 18-pound difference, and falling behind 3-2 late in the last round, Omar was working on turning his opponent to his back when time ran out. Omar finished second, BUT, when the champion came to shake my hand, he said, "That is the toughest kid I've EVER faced"....a real compliment to my young wrestler.

Like so many before him and those who would come after him, Omar graduated and I never heard a single word more about him, either.

The MOST pleasant surprise I got all day came to me by way of the team's 145-lb. wrestler, whom I mentioned had worked out with Omar AND Sergio. His name was Kerry Gibbs, and he was one of only a handful of non-ethnic wrestlers on my team. He was raised by a single mom, who was struggling to make ends meet. I believe I had heard that Kerry lived in a trailer court at one time, but his mom, who had recently gotten a better-paying new job, either rented or bought a home in the Brighton area when Kerry began the 7th grade.

He was kind of an angry kid, always seemed to be mad at something or someone. Since Kerry was a minority member on the team, he didn't make many friends....didn't TRY very hard at it, either, but he didn't take any 'crap' from anyone. Gibbs was a scrapper, and because of his quick temper, and surly disposition, he had gotten into a few smaller scraps around campus. I was always worried about his temper setting him off....even for trivial matters. He used wrestling as an outlet for his anger....controlled aggression as I saw it. He DID know that fighting on school grounds could get him a five or ten-day suspension from school, so during the season, he kept his cool....mostly.

Gibbs LOVED wrestling, and was VERY coachable. His 7th grade wrestling campaign was just fair, as he was new to the sport.

After that first season he wanted to improve and improve vastly, so he worked on increasing his strength before his 8th grade year. He looked quite a bit more muscular when the 1991-'92 season began.

Unfortunately, Kerry Gibbs got injured during one of the early practices. He was desperate to wrestle, so he shrugged off the pain, and easily won the 145-lb. classification on DeWitt's team. In BOTH his first two dual matches, however, the injury was bothersome, causing him to lose both bouts to just 'decent' wrestlers. Even though he was angry with me, I made him sit out of EVERYTHING for almost three weeks....no practicing even. He spent practice time conditioning, which had nothing to do with his injured shoulder, and his stamina increased quite a bit.

The lay-off helped him immensely, and he went on a tear for his last ten matches....winning them all, and pretty handily, too, I must admit.

It is important to note, here, that for the week prior to State, my team worked exclusively on something, I call 'tournament wrestling.' The boys worked again, and again, and AGAIN, on double-leg takedowns. It was attack, attack, attack, when they were on their feet. My guys worked HARD at getting to their opponent's legs. I would tell them, "If you can only get one leg, keep working on getting that second leg. Get that takedown. Hustle, hustle, HUSTLE....keep the pressure on and GET TO THOSE LEGS." Nobody was better at the double-leg takedown than Gibbs.

The team also worked on a hard riding technique, which consisted of flattening the opponent and getting an arm-bar, (or a double arm-bar, if possible) while looking to sink in a half-nelson. The objective was to keep MY wrestler's weight from getting too high, where a reversal could result. I had SEVEN wrestlers who were very adept at doing that, and Kerry Gibbs was one of them.

Finally, we worked CONSTANTLY on quickly getting to the feet when put in the 'down' position....no fancy stuff....no resting, trying to figure out what to do....just get on the feet as soon as the referee begins action, and THEN, get away. With the escape achieved, my wrestlers could attack the double-leg combos, again. Kerry had rather short legs for his build, and hopping to his feet was his specialty. In that ONE week he became a take-down machine, and an escape artist....AND he was tireless!

On the first night of the State tournament, Kerry Gibbs had to wrestle the #1 seed in his second, and final, bout of the opening night. The opposition 'star' wrestler was a member of that infamous all-star reservation team....and a kid who brought in a 27-0 record into the tournament.

Kerry was ALWAYS a nervous kid before any of his matches, and he always seemed to ask the same question, "Is this kid any good?"

My stock answer was always the same, too, "I don't know," I'd often begin, "I haven't wrestled him. You do YOUR best, then come back and let me know how good he is." I then said to my 145-lb wrestler, "Kerry, you are good at 'tournament wrestling,' really good, so just use what you have been practicing all week, NO fancy stuff!"

Gibbs BEAT the #1 kid 7-0, with THREE take-downs and an escape, and after shaking hands with both the opposing wrestler and his coach, he came back to me. He was scratching the top of his head, looking a little bewildered. "Well," I started, though I had a HUGE smile on my face, "was he any good?"

"Yeah, he was a pretty good wrestler," was the non-chalant answer Kerry gave me.

"He was ranked #1, so you know what that means?" Gibbs kind of screwed up his face into a frown, and shook his head negatively, "That means that YOU are #1 now." I said with great pride in MY voice.

His eyes opened very wide, and with an equally wide smile, looked at me and said, "Oh, YEAH, that means that I should be #1 now, doesn't it?" I nodded, patted him on the back of his shoulder, then went to coach another match. Kerry was VERY good when his confidence was up, and it couldn't have been higher after beating the reservation wrestler.

Kerry Gibbs WON the State 145-lb. weight class, and started a WONDERFUL streak for me, sitting in the corner of championship matches. I watched THREE consecutive boys from DeWitt wrestle for their respective weight championship bouts….Gibbs, who became the champion at 145 lbs…..Hernandez, the champion at 154 lbs.….and Sentman, who ended up being a hard-fighting second-place finisher at 167 lbs. I was proud!

I had SO many things on my mind when I tried to sleep the night after the tournament ended….reasons why we did well but DIDN'T win the tournament….my outstanding upper-weight championship matches being SO good. But I couldn't shake the saddest moment of them all, the look in Chris Cortez's eyes when he realized he could NOT wrestle for the title. The 1992 wrestling team was MY best ever!

As you probably realize, I get VERY excited about me getting to coach wrestling for 22 years. While I had junior high State champions, and kids who went on to be high school State champions, I also had many OTHER outstanding kids go through my room. I remember a special wrestler, who I believe, was the best of them ALL....Simeon Jefferson.

Sim was another Los Angeles transplant, and was every bit as gang-oriented as Curtis White was when the former student moved into the Wilhelm neighborhood fifteen years, or so, earlier. Shorter than Curtis, and more stockily built, Sim had the strength of a dock worker, especially in his legs. At 5' 8" tall, he could 'slam' a basketball, as he demonstrated for me one day.

Simeon was VERY intelligent, too, and represented DeWitt in the Sectional Spelling Bee during his one year in our school.

As far as having wrestling skills, he had no previous experience, but had ALL the intangibles that I looked for in a wrestler. He was the quickest wrestler I ever had....lightening quick reflexes and moved like a striking rattlesnake when he went to execute a move. EVERYTHING was explosive in his repertoire. He was hard to get off balance, and never seemed to tire....which didn't surprise me as he pinned most of his opponents in the first period.

I knew when I saw him wrestle in the school's first tournament that year, that I had a bonafide champion-caliber wrestling candidate....and he had only been to FOUR wrestling practices before the tournament took place. He had three matches, for that tournament, but his championship match was the toughest he would have ALL year.

Jefferson's Finals match (at 154 lbs.) went into overtime, with Sim getting the victory by getting a sudden takedown on his opponent. The kid he beat was the TOP wrestler on his Tempe, AZ team....a kid who had started wrestling when he was six years of age, and had lost only three times in his last 50-something matches. (according to his coach)

As the season progressed nicely, so did Simeon. He was not only a star in wrestling; he was a charismatic leader on the 8th grade Beta Team. (which was MY team of core teachers) He chose to lead by example, not only in the classroom, but around the campus, as well. It's not that he STOPPED a great deal of trouble, he just chose to not BE one of those problems.....and other kids followed his lead. DeWitt had MANY discipline problems, especially the first three years, so having a calming force, amongst the students, was very welcome.

Simeon, however, seemed to get ill more than the average student, and he missed half the wrestling season due to illness. He WAS 11-0, however, when State rolled around, and had had a GREAT week of practice just prior to the opening Friday night tournament matches.

I was excited when I got to school, and I couldn't wait to showcase Simeon. Plus, I had a few more kids who showed promise of a good State finish. I expected DeWitt to be a challenger for the championship once again. As I got to my classroom, I saw

Simeon sitting outside my doorway. His faced looked green in color. "Coach, Stein," he said slowly and seemingly in pain, "I don't think I can wrestle today."

I got him to his feet, and he walked, unaided, to the nurse's office. She took his temperature, and there was none, so I asked her if she could keep him with her all day. I ALSO told her that if other teachers would ask about him, I would appreciate it if she told them Sim was not feeling well and would be lying down for awhile. I wasn't sure if he would be able to wrestle in State, but as long as he was at school, I was hoping for a miracle recovery, and he couldn't have THAT if he was traipsing around from class to class all day.

Since he had brought his wrestling gear, I picked him up in the nurse's office after school, and told him I would take him to the high school where the meet was being held. If he felt he COULDN'T wrestle, then he wouldn't have to. He told me his mom would be at the tourney, and that she had gone to work before he woke up, therefore, she didn't realize he wasn't feeling well.

Since Brighton District didn't provide us with transportation for the State Wrestling Tournament, and I wanted to try to keep him as calm and comfortable as I could before he wrestled, I decided that he would ride with me to the tournament. I crammed all the other State wrestlers into a few more parent cars, and we headed to the meet.

When we arrived at the host school, all my wrestlers made weight without a problem, and I took Simeon outside to rest under a shade tree. I told him I would have someone come get him before his match, but if he didn't feel good enough to wrestle he should just send the messenger in to tell me.

At the appropriate time, I sent a kid out to get him. In came Simeon to wrestle, where he commenced to pin his opponent within 30 seconds of the first round, then back outside he went, where HE promptly lay back down.

I DID see his mother in the stands, and told her that Sim wasn't feeling too well but if it was alright with her I would appreciate it if he was allowed to have one more match that evening.... it would be his last of the night. I told her he was resting outside, and if she wanted to talk to him, and take him home, I would be all right with that. She looked at me and said, "My boy really likes you, Coach, and you been real good to him this year. You want him to wrestle, then I'm OK wit it. I can take him home after the match, right? He don't have to ride wit the other boys back to school, do he?"

"No, he can leave right after the next match. But, Mom, if you think he is all right tomorrow morning, I'd love to have him here to wrestle. I feel that he could end up as the junior high champion, in the state of Arizona, in his weight division." I said and I saw her just nod a couple of times before I headed back onto the floor.

About an hour later, Simeon was summoned once more, with the same quick pin, and immediate exit outside. I hurried out to see him, and he admitted that he had thrown up after the first match, which I didn't know at the time, but DIDN'T want to go home. I sent him to the bleachers to be with his mom, and they left for their home immediately.

Not surprisingly, Simeon Jefferson was a no-show for the second day. One of his friends had stopped by to pick him up and get him to the tournament, but his mom told the 'friend' to tell ME that he had a fever and would not be wrestling. I understood but was sad for him, the team, and me.

The Finals, at 154 lbs., matched a kid off the reservation, with a Paradise Valley wrestler, whom Simeon had pinned in DeWitt's last dual meet of the year. The Native Amercian wrestler won 4-2, but the match was boring. I KNEW Jefferson would have been State champion if he had had the opportunity to wrestle EITHER kid.

Simeon returned to school, two days later, and seemed fit as a fiddle. "My mom said I had a 24-hour bug, Coach, and I feel great today!" I bit my tongue, believing that I would have had back-to-back 154 lb. champions....Hernandez then Jefferson, only to have a ONE-DAY illness stop the dream. Simeon Jefferson and HIS mom moved after that year at DeWitt, and once again, I never heard what happened to one of my star wrestlers.

Two years after Jefferson graduated, I had a VERY interesting kid come into DeWitt. Not that he was a star in wrestling because he only came out, for the team, during his 8th grade year. He was a roughneck who was 'asked' to leave his former district for discipline reasons. I didn't ask about his previous problems, but I liked his aggressive behavior in wrestling, after I talked him into coming out for the team. His name was Robert Sutton, and that kid was a man in kid's clothing, I swear. He had man strength, and could have really hurt someone's hand, when he shook hands, if he wanted to.

He was pretty smart, too, learning the wrestling moves quickly, and actually finished sixth in the 167 lb. division at State that year. My team did well, too, ending up 7th amongst the sixty-some teams, but the real story was Robert, and an incident that occurred two weeks after wrestling season finished.

Sutton was one of my homeroom students, whose family lived just three blocks from school. He lived with his hard-working mom and a younger sister, in a tiny shack of a house, situated right near an abandoned bowling alley.

The morning after the 'incident,' Robert Sutton came wandering into homeroom earlier than the other kids. He appeared to be in a lot of genuine pain. "What's wrong, Robert?" I inquired as he gingerly sat down in his homeroom seat.

"Had some problems last night, Coach." Yeah, a LOT of the wrestlers called me coach even though I was their English teacher, too. He continued, "Ginny (his sister) and I were watching TV, with the lights off like we usually do, and I hear someone at the front door. I get up to see who it is, and the doorknob was being jiggled like someone was trying to get in. I open the door quick-like, and there is this guy, using a knife, trying to jimmy the lock on the door, and at the same time he is trying to open it by turning the handle."

"What? Who was it?" I asked almost not believing him.

"It was an older man….looked like he might be homeless. When he saw me, after I opened the door, he took off running."

"Did you call the police?" I asked, upset that somebody was breaking into homes around the DeWitt neighborhood....and into one of my student's house to boot.

"Naw, I CHASED him," my young 14-year-old student said with some discomfort as he was painfully squirming in his chair.

"You chased a man who was holding a knife?" I said, while shaking my head in disbelief he would do something like that.

"Caught up with him, too, when he couldn't get over the neighbor's fence. I went to grab him when he started swinging that big knife at me. I wasn't wearing a shirt, and he got me three times....like Zorro, making a big 'Z' on my chest," Then he opened his shirt so I could see his wounds. "I had to back off so he ran away. My sister called 9-1-1 and I went to the Emergency Room. Got over a hundred stitches put in, and I'm sore as hell today."

"My mom didn't want me to come to school today, but I had to tell my story to everybody, didn't I?" And Robert got quiet.

"What did your mom have to say about all this?" I asked while looking the knife wounds, and the multitude of stitches.

"She told me to stop chasing people with weapons in their hands," Sutton said with another little grimace of pain coming across his face.

"I hope you learned your lesson, Robert," I said trying to back his mother's advice up with some encouragement of my own.

"I told her that the NEXT time a guy comes to the door with a knife, I will get a knife, too, and THEN go after him." I sat there just shaking my head. This was DEFINITELY the type of kid who was moving into our district, and that was upsetting to me.

In 1996, I had my last coaching year in wrestling. The talent pool was getting shaky due to lack of experience, though; I STILL had several willing participants. I was just plain getting tired of the long days teaching and then coaching. However, I ALMOST went out with one last champion, at least in MY mind I would have gone out having coached one more DeWitt champion. Well, here's the story.

Wrestling season was just around the corner, in October of 1996, and all the talk around the school was about the up-coming basketball and wrestling seasons. I was teaching one of my morning classes, when in walks a giant of a person. He was standing 6'4" and looked to weigh two-sixty or better. However, that big person just walked into the class and plopped himself down in a chair in the back of the room. "How can I help you?" I queried, as now EVERYBODY had turned around to see who the huge person was.

"I think I am supposed to be in your class," was his answer, and he was TRULY slouching down in his chair as much as possible at that point.

I had thought it was a father who entered, when I first saw him. He brought me his schedule, then went back to his seat in the rear of the room. Every other student in the room knew EXACTLY what my next words were going to be. "Have you ever wrestled before?" I asked with obvious enthusiasm.

"Naw, I hate the sport. It's all fake anyway."

"Not the wrestling that is done at THIS school," I said emphatically, but didn't say any more on the subject, at the time, as I had to get back to the classroom task for the day.

He was only thirteen, just HUGE for his age, AND he wasn't fat. Broad shoulders and muscular arms, he looked like a longshoreman, I swear. I EVENTUALLY convinced him to try DeWitt's wrestling program, and mentioned that if he didn't like it, he could quit. He came out on the first day of practice. I was pleased.

His ego was thoroughly massaged as I taught HIM, and him alone, the Bear-Hug hold and throw, which is how I wanted him to start every one of his matches that year. Simple stuff that I KNEW he would like to do. To 'massage' his ego even further, I even 'let' him take ME down....once. But I also knew that if he ever DID get a good solid Bear-Hug on me, he likely COULD have taken me down whether I wanted him to or not. He was, hands down, the strongest kid I ever had out for wrestling....and he was ONLY thirteen! He was going to be my NEXT State champion....or so I thought at the time.

I was SO EXCITED the day of our first meet! It was a home match, against a pretty good, high-quality team from the Westside of Phoenix. I couldn't WAIT to unveil my heavyweight prodigy. I had already told Steve Lipinski, and any teacher who would listen, that the big kid would be State champion.

When I arrived at school that Monday of our first meet, the secretary called me over. "Mr. Stein," she started and I INSTANTLY heard doom in her voice," You won't have your heavyweight wrestler tonight, or ANY night, for the rest of the season. He and his brother were removed from DeWitt's campus last Friday, and told they will not be allowed to come back to this school."

"What happened?" I said, more in shock than anything else.

"You didn't have practice last Friday, did you?" the secretary said rather non-chalantly.

"No, we took Friday OFF! WHAT HAPPENED?" I was getting annoyed at having it take so long to give me bad news.

"His 7th grade brother got into an argument with one of our little Mexican gangs at the bus stop last Friday, and when they came after him he yelled for BIG brother to help. The five gang members decided to attack your wrestler first, but he proceeded to pick them up, one by one, and start throwing them in front of the school busses. The busses weren't MOVING, but that didn't stop him from hurling them into the bus paths.

"My State champion.....SHOOT!" I said, seething with anger. I calmed down a touch, then asked respectfully, "Are you SURE he will not be back? I am grooming him to be this school's heavyweight wrestling champion at State, you know, so I NEED to get him back here soon."

"No, he won't return. His mother was told to find another school. Seems like a couple of days LAST week they had trouble by extorting kids out of their lunch money. There weren't any charges brought, and they paid back the money they took. But the boys were warned to keep their noses clean, or they couldn't go here any more.

They had had trouble at their last school, too, and were just staying with some friend's of the mom, near Cahill School, until they could move somewhere permanent. Sorry, Abe, they're done at DeWitt."

Even though I heard the story, and should have said 'Good riddance,' all I could mutter was, "I just don't want to face him wrestling for ANOTHER school,"

Coaching….ESPECIALLY coaching wrestling, was a big part of my happiness in Brighton District. I enjoyed teaching at Wilhelm, too, but the discipline at THAT school began waning with the passing of the years. Once I got to DeWitt, discipline had gotten so bad, that I started to count the days when I could retire. Teaching had become a JOB to me, and that bothered me.

8

CALIFORNIA TRIPPING

WHILE I DIDN'T ever feel I needed help with discipline in my classes, during my first year as an 8th grade teacher at Wilhelm, I received BONUS help anyway. It was called the California Trip.

My best friend Steve Lipinski had been asked by a teacher friend of his, Perry Langdon, to INVITE the best 8th graders in Wilhelm, to join Perry and HIS 8th grade class for a weekend in California. Mr. Langdon was using the trip as a reward for his kids for having a wonderful year in school. He and another teacher friend had been doing the California 'reward' with THEIR students for a few years, but they had a problem every year. If they took just one bus they had too many kids wanting to go, with not enough seats on just the one bus. Deserving kids would, sadly, be left behind. On the other hand, if they booked TWO busses, they were definitely able to get all deserving students to go, but had trouble filling the second bus. Langdon's buddy teacher, Russ Allenby, was a crusty OLDER teacher, who just wanted to take his kids to California, so filling two busses was left for Perry Landon to do; thus the invitation to Steve.

Langdon's plan was to go to Disneyland, leaving at midnight one Friday evening toward the end of the school year, travel to Disneyland to spend the day, THEN ride to San Diego after Disney, where everyone would check into a hotel. A short time AFTER check-in, everyone would go to an amusement park for several hours before returning to spend the night in their rooms. Then on Sunday, the group would visit the famous San Diego Zoo for a good portion of the day, arriving in Phoenix around ten at night.

By filling busses, the price was reasonable for students, generally. If busses were NOT filled, the kids would have to pay more for the trip. The expenses for chaperones were paid for, but that seemed fair, since all the kids had to do was go have fun. The adults were 'on duty' for nearly the 48-hour excursion.

When Steve found out that the trip was 'invitation only,' and he didn't have to invite ALL the 8th graders in Wilhelm, he saw a wonderful opportunity for 'deserving' Wilhelm students to have a great year-end adventure with friends.

Also, all information between Perry and Steve was done on the phone, or at meeting places, so neither school district got directly involved. What Perry did was use the up-coming trip like a dangling carrot. He would constantly remind his kids, all year long, that BOTH grades and behavior were going to be the deciding factors as to which kids were invited, and which weren't.

Perry Langdon happened to work in an economically-challenged school at the time of his invite to Steve. The 'incentive' speech worked wonders, and Langdon had quite a few students who 'shaped up' in order to get the invitation. Most of his kids saved money from the beginning of the year in HOPES they got invited.

Wilhelm had many, MANY students who could afford to go, and they were well-behaved kids, too. The problem Steve encountered was the fact that he had SO many kids to invite that he was forced to accept students on a first-come, first-serve basis. Wilhelm could not only help Perry's school fill a bus, it could fill its OWN bus, too.

In 1975, when I got my teaching position in the 8th grade, Steve asked if I minded helping him chaperone the many, many Wilhelm kids. I loved that invitation, and accompanied Steve AND Perry for over twenty more years.

It was obvious that Perry knew his 'dangling carrot' idea would work. Steve and I did the same thing with our students, and I credit the California Trip with helping keep both discipline AND grades in check for many students throughout the years.

As time passed, however, the District's economic demise made it apparent that Wilhelm students were struggling to get enough money for such an expensive trip. Perry Langdon was constantly working to find GREAT deals to save money on busses, hotels, and many of the parks, over the years, so money was NOT a serious problem for our students, most of the time.

Sadly, however, Wilhelm was getting more and more students who didn't qualify, behaviorally. Therefore, Steve and I were having fewer and fewer kids, we felt, earning eligibility for the invitation. Though we struggled some years, we always managed to get enough students to fill the 'Wilhelm' busses.

On one trip, however, in the early '80's, we needed to invite my fiancé Katherine's school, to insure we had the quota needed to go to California. What had happened was simple, Steve and I needed eight more students to help fill the second bus. That was our situation with only four days remaining until the scheduled trip was to take place. When I mentioned the dilemma to Katherine she told me she had several 'good' kids in her school, and she was sure she could find enough students for the trip. Two days later, she presented me with checks and notarized permission slips from EXACTLY eight of her best students. Katherine would be one of two female chaperones, too.

Steve and I welcomed her, and her students, BUT, on the day of the trip, we were presented with another conundrum.

Maxwell Riggins was the Wilhelm student body president. He had good grades, was a good athlete, and may have been the most popular kid in the 8th grade that year. He had HAD a problem getting his money, though, which meant he DIDN'T have his money by the time we filled the bus with eight kids from Katherine's school.

Max came running into my classroom, the Friday of that trip. He had a check and his notarized permission slip in hand. "Mr. Stein!" he cried out as he entered, "my grandmother gave me some extra birthday money, and now I can go to California."

I looked at my student and in an apologetic tone I said, "Maxwell, the invitations were NOT coming in well enough for us to fill the two busses, so I invited my fiancé's school to join us, and she had JUST enough students respond so that we now have filled BOTH busses. I'm so sorry."

Max slumped at the shoulders and looked absolutely crestfall-
en. "But, Mr. Stein, I have been saving all year to go, and I KNEW
my grandmother would come through for me, and she did last
night. I really, REALLY want to go. Maybe I can take somebody's
place," and with that his face brightened up.

"I can't tell the other school to cut one of their students. If I
did that, they might ALL decide that was unfair, then we would be
seven students short, and costs would have to rise. Let me show
you the Wilhelm roster, and YOU decide who can't go from our
school."

He knew he couldn't do that, and he turned to walk out of the
room. "Max," I blurted out, "I DO have a suggestion, though. A
few years ago we had one student who got ill and never showed up
at the mall at midnight. We left without her and ended up having
an extra seat on the bus. Every other trip, however, we have filled
our busses, so the odds against us having an extra seat again are
huge. BUT, if you still want to try, then pack your bag, have your
money and your notarized slip with you, and meet us at the mall
parking lot tonight at 11:30. We leave promptly at midnight, and
who knows, maybe someone WON'T show, and you'll be ready to
claim the seat. At the worst, all you and your parents will lose is a
little sleep. And MAYBE some of your friends will feel sorry for you
and get you a gift from one of the California parks."

"Yeah, I might do that, but Mr. Stein, I really, really, REALLY
want to go!" and Max began to mope as he turned and headed to
the door.

"See you in class, Maxwell, AND at the busses tonight," I said
while preparing for the start of the school day.

And the day seemed to drag by. Those students going on the trip were electric with anticipation. They could NOT focus on the work at hand, and each of them seemed to be looking at the clock constantly. Max stayed quiet, for the most part, except to tell his friends what HIS plans would be for the weekend....he didn't say a word about going to the mall where the busses were leaving.

Steve and I got to the mall parking lot early, as was our custom, and NOT to our surprise there were at least eight or nine students (and parents) already there waiting for the busses to arrive. Maxwell Riggins had not yet arrived. The busses arrived within a half hour as did most of the Wilhelm students.

Max got there, but he was one of the last of ANY student to get there, and many of his friends ran to him to find out why he was there. He said he just wanted to wish them all a good trip, and everybody was amazed what a good friend he was.

Katherine had all HER students ready to go. In fact, ALL signed up students from Wilhelm were there, too, but Max decided to do what he said he would do and see everybody off while wishing them a great trip.

I stood by the steps leading up and into our big, beautiful bus, and called out the names, starting with those who signed up first. I got into the list Katherine had given me, and the first four students bounded onto the bus when their names were called. BUT, when I called student #5, from Katherine's school, the young girl got ON the first step of the bus, turned around, and upon seeing her mom weeping a bit because her daughter would be leaving for the weekend, said, "Mom, I CAN'T leave you for the entire weekend!"

With that, she scampered OFF the bus, and Maxwell Riggins, who was standing just behind all the parents, shot his hand in the air, with check in hand, and shouted, "I'll go!" He had just become the luckiest kid in Arizona. (according to him) My fiancé's student DID get her money returned during the week after we returned.

Katherine was impressed with the students from my school, as I was with hers. However, just before bed-check, which was done to make sure students were all in their rooms for the evening, I remember talking to my fiance in the hallway, and Kathrine was saying SOMETHING about how nice and how intelligent the students from Wilhelm were. Suddenly, a door opened up down the hallway, and two girls from Wilhelm came running, in what seemed to be a panic, toward us two teachers. "Mr. Stein, Mr. Stein," they began to yell, "We have a FIRE in our room!"

Without any questions being asked, the four of us were then running QUICKLY toward the girls' mini-suite room. Upon entering, it was easy to see that there was smoke wafting from the stove's oven door. I choked on a LARGE dose of smoke as I opened the oven door. The problem was easy to spot. The girls had had a pizza delivered, but it had turned cold just prior to them deciding to eat it. So they made the decision to warm it up in the oven. The problem was that they DIDN'T take it out of the box, and naturally, the box caught fire.

Using a hand towel, I extricated the container from the oven, and flung it into the sink, turning on the water to douse the flames. Problem solved.

After a discussion on what SHOULD have been done, Katherine and I left the room. "Well, at least I think your kids are NICE," she said as a little smile came across her face.

A strict rule that both Lipinski and I had was....IF you go to California, you MUST show up for school the following school day....Monday. Wilhelm was kind enough to OK the trip, but they did NOT want to lose revenue which was based on daily attendance. In fact, the California kids were so good about getting to school following each trip, that the attendance at school was HIGHER for the 'return Monday' then on a normal Monday.

Max got to school, as did all but one student who really WAS sick....legitimately. I never had a kid thank me as much as Maxwell did. He beamed all that Monday, and sought both Steve and me out, on several occasions, to thank us personally for letting him go on the California Trip. The truth was, if the girl had NOT opted out of going, Riggins wouldn't have gotten to go. He really owed HER a huge thank-you.

The change to DeWitt was a mixed bag, as far as the California Trip was involved. On the one hand, there were nearly three times more students in the 8th grade, BUT, there were so many discipline problems, and kids whose grades were poor, that finding enough kids to invite seemed like a problem for us, at first.

I have mentioned that DeWitt had four distinctive 'teams' of students. The 7th grade was divided in two separate teams, called the Alpha Team and Beta Team. Not surprisingly, the 8th grade was also divided into two teams called Alpha and Beta.

Steve and I were teachers of the 8th grade Beta Team, and had practically NOTHING to do with the students from Alpha Team. We knew some of them from sports, and other 'extra' clubs around school, but what we DIDN'T know were the grades or behaviors of the majority of Alpha Team students.

Sam Armstrong, with whom I worked for sixteen years at Wilhelm, was the Alpha Team science teacher. He didn't realize that Steve and I were still planning on going to California, but news spread quickly, on Alpha, that Beta was getting invitations to go on a year-end trip, and Sam came to see us.

Sam indicated that the Alpha Team had MANY good students, a fact that Steve and I knew very well. (the DIFFERENCE between Alpha and Beta students will be embellished a little later in the book) His point was well-taken, and because we knew we might have a problem filling our bus with just Beta Team kids, AND because we trusted Sam and ALL the Alpha Team teachers for that matter, we agreed to have a talk with Alpha students and give them the low-down on the trip. We DID highlight, however, that ANY Alpha Team kid who was getting an invitation, would be highly scrutinized by both Steve and myself, as we needed ALL the Alpha teachers to verify that those 'invitees' would be 100% trustworthy.....500 miles away from home for the weekend....WITHOUT their parents or any Alpha teachers being on the trip.

Steve and I had NO problem with Alpha Team students on any of our consequent trips, per se, so that worked out really well for ALL 8th grade students at DeWitt. We definitely had enough students to fill our Brighton bus, AND help fill the second bus, which Perry Langdon could barely get HALF full as the years waned.

We had ONE problem with one Alpha Team student, however, that occurred during one of the last years Steve and I went to California.

Ironically, if was the EXACT problem faced by Maxwell Riggins during HIS California adventure at Wilhelm, some ten years, or so, earlier.

While filling the DeWitt bus wasn't all that hard, and was usually accomplished a few days before we all headed to California, one of the veteran Alpha Team teachers came to see us about a situation that concerned her. She mentioned that Alpha had an extraordinary student whose family had been struggling financially, so it looked like the young lady would have to miss the California Trip that year. BUT, the girl had gotten, for her early graduation gift from her grandmother, enough money to cover California expenses. The Alpha teacher KNEW that Steve and I were headed on the trip that very night, but wanted us to hear about this student.

The young lady was the consensus #1 student on the Alpha Team, 'Ask any student or teacher,' we were told. On and on the Alpha teacher went, and I have to admit, this kid sounded great. BUT, we had the buses filled, and they had been filled for a few days already. I told the teacher to send the girl to see me during lunch, and I would give her some long-shot options that actually worked one year, and the girl could decide if what I said had any merit.

The girl WAS a sweetheart....courteous; polite, attentive....she most surely would have been a wonderful addition to have on the trip. When I finished the Maxwell Riggins story she completely understood where I was coming from, (like I said, a very mature girl) and told me that if there was even a ONE-in-a-million shot that she could be on the bus, she would take it. She desperately wanted to spend a 'vacation' with her friends, ESPECIALLY since she had never been out of Phoenix before, let alone Arizona.

Friday night, her family, and we're talking Mom, Dad, and two smaller siblings, got her to the mall. I called off all the names of those students already accepted for the trip, and every student boarded when called. As the busses began pulling out of the parking lot, I saw that wonderful Alpha Team student waving and smiling at her friends. However, she would NOT be accompanying them for the weekend. I would have gladly given up MY seat to her, I felt so badly for her, but we were required to have enough chaperones for the students, so it was necessary I go. I just looked at her and felt VERY sorry for her.

That young lady actually came to see me the following Monday and thanked me for allowing her to go to the mall and be a replacement if one was necessary. While the California Trips were ALL successful and fun, I felt badly that we couldn't take EVERY deserving student every year.

While I had mentioned that we USUALLY had no problems with our own students, one did occur with OTHER students during one of my early trips.

In fact, during the FIRST year I joined the group, there was a glitch in plans from the get-go. That is when Perry Langdon asked STEVE to make room for four 'extra' students that he had invited from another school, and there was a problem almost immediately. Here's what happened.

Perry and Russ had had SOME problem getting enough kids to fill their bus the previous years, and knew that Steve would help, but Perry also knew that Lipinski would rather take one full bus of Wilhelm students instead of sending a couple kids to ride with HIS kids. Langdon, wanted to make SURE he had enough students to fill his bus, however, so in the spring of 1976 he asked ANOTHER teacher friend, from a different school, if there were reliable students in HIS school who could be invited. Nothing had been heard from the 'new' friend, except he handed the material out.

Within one week of the trip, Langdon and Allenby DID get enough response from THEIR kids that they filled every seat on the bus with their own students, so they seemed happy.

Then, with three days to go before California, the new teacher 'contact' got back to Perry, saying he had collected money from four of HIS students, and they were excited about going on the weekend adventure. The friend expressed how grateful he was to Langford for inviting him and his kids.

Problem....it became apparent that Perry had overbooked his and Allenby's bus, which put him in a real bind. That's when he turned to Steve Lipinski for help.

The solution meant that OUR student quota had to be lessened by four kids. Steve Lipinski was a bit upset, as you can imagine, as Wilhelm could likely get MORE than enough interested students to occupy our own bus, and we had three days to do so. Steve DID realize, however, that Wilhelm was brought onto the California Trip in order for Langdon to have space for any overload of HIS students. Still, there was never any conversation that OUR bus would be the dumping place for a hodgepodge of kids from other schools.

Fortunately, at the time of the 'overload' the Wilhelm bus had not yet been completely filled, so Lipinski simply stopped accepting Wilhelm students when there were four seats remaining. Perry PROMISED, that Wilhelm would never again be asked to take 'strangers,' on our bus, and with embarrassment being averted, the two busses headed to Disneyland at midnight on a beautiful Friday night.

We had asked that the first pair of seats behind the bus driver be saved for the four NEW kids. Those seats also happened to placed right across the aisle from Steve and me. Steve had a very good reason for having the kids from the other school sit across from us, too. We were, apparently, taking two sets of boyfriends with girlfriends. Steve noticed how 'chummy' they were in the parking lot, and there was NO way he would allow them to think they were going to get to 'neck' while on the bus. After all, we had talked extensively, to OUR students about the proper behavior expected over the next two days. Since we hadn't had an opportunity to 'invite' these two boys and two girls, and explain the rules, we would have to watch them and correct their behavior, if necessary.

It was also easy to see that, since these four kids came from an exclusive private school, they saw themselves as being entitled.... yes, even in 1976, there were several young people who thought of themselves deserving to have everything without expecting to have to work to get anything. Quite simply, they thought this was going to be a weekend of doing whatever they liked, and they WERE quite haughty in their mannerism, too....not acknowledging other students who said 'Hi' to them....wanting to play their music loudly, to the point it was bothering those of us around them....pretending not to hear either Steve or me when we gave them directions. They really just believed that they were on the bus all by themselves and didn't want to recognize that there were other people on board.... like I said, very snobbish.

Just as the bus got over the Arizona/California border, it was time for the bus drivers to take a break. We stopped at a fast food restaurant and everyone got off the bus. Students used the restrooms, got a quick bite to eat, or just stretched. Half hour later we had everybody board again. However, when our bus driver came aboard and went to sit down, he froze. "What is THIS?" he said in a very loud voice.

The four strangers tried to hide laughter, but it was obvious they did something. "Who poured water on my seat?" the driver said, and he turned toward Steve and me. "I'm not going ANYWHERE until this mess is cleaned up!" And with that he stormed off the bus.

He was headed to talk with Perry and Russ, the two teachers who signed the contract with the bus company. Steve immediately got up, and asked the Wilhelm students to get off, but asked the four strangers to stay. Gawkers were looking at the small puddle of water, still soaking into the driver's seat, then looking at the four new kids.

Once off the bus, Steve said to the brats, "We can do this one of two ways. Either you four get this seat COMPLETELY dry so we can continue, or Mr. Stein and I will dry it, call your parents and have them come get you at this restaurant, and give you back your money. Your choice."

"It was just a joke," one of the boys said, but NOT smiling.

"Did it look like the bus driver was laughing at it?" I chimed in.

The two girls whipped into action, using their clothes to sop up the water, and some sort of battery-powered fan to dry the seat. It took them fifteen to twenty minutes before they asked if it was 'good enough?'

"You," Steve said as he pointed to one of the boys, "sit in the seat." He had wheat-colored short pants on, and if there was still any wetness at ALL on the seat it would have shown up on his shorts. It was dry, so Steve went out to get the kids back onto the bus.

When we were full again, the bus driver came on, followed by ornery Russ Allenby. THEN the driver ran his hand over the seat, and said, "It still feels wet to me."

Allenby, brushed the smaller man aside, and felt the seat himself. "This seat is not wet at ALL," and then Russ commenced to raise his voice for all to hear. "You are NOT the pilot of a 747, you are a bus driver, whom we commissioned to take us on a two-day California trip. Get your ass in this seat, and let's get going. We are already behind schedule!" And with that, the big guy left the bus, and the little guy, STILL grumbling under his breath, got into HIS seat, and we were off to Disneyland.

Ten minutes down the road, Wilhelm's best athlete yelled to us from the back of the bus, "Mr. Lipinski, would you please sent those four guests of ours back here. We want to talk to them."

"Just stay where you are. The only ones YOU will talk to is Mr. Stein or me. Now get some sleep." It was after three in the morning, and, believe it or not, there were NO problems from the 'entitled' students for the rest of the trip.

I WANT to tell you there were no more problems, of any kind, on my virgin trip, but that would be a lie.

Betsy Unger was invited to go that year. I knew she had a sour attitude, (if you remember, she was the girl who threw the relay baton to the ground out of frustration, which likely kept Wilhelm's 'star' track athlete, Esther McCloud, from becoming the State track meet MVP) but she was allowed to go. It seems that Esther, herself, went to Mr. Lipinski, and promised that she would be with

— 257 —

Betsy every minute of the trip. She also claimed that she and Betsy were best friends, and Esther would make sure her friend stayed in line. Steve bought that, and Betsy was invited.

We all enjoyed Disneyland, checked into a nice hotel, then enjoyed Knott's Berry Farm. It was a fun first day in California. The following day we woke the kids early, and ate breakfast before heading to San Diego. Our plan was to first go to the ocean for a short swim, change clothes in the beach dressing rooms, then head off to the San Diego Zoo for the rest of the day. We would arrive back in Phoenix around midnight.

Our stay at the ocean was to be short. Most of OUR students had never seen the ocean before, so we thought we would give them the experience of getting INTO the water...especially since the zoo didn't open until mid-morning.

The kids that wanted to get into the water went to the changing rooms near the beach, and got into their bathing suits....and we're talking about half the students did so.

Meanwhile, we saw a red flag warning by the shore. After talking to the lifeguards we discovered that THAT part of the beach was having particularly rough under-currents, which had been knocking people down and dragging them under water out to sea. We were advised to inform our kids that it was dangerous to venture into the water any higher than their knees, EVEN if they were good swimmers.

We chaperons gathered the 'swimmers' around us, and implored them, in VERY strong terms, that they NOT go into water past their knee height.

All the kids seemed to love just getting wet. The water was cold, too, which was a deterrent to going deeper than the knee. At least by standing in the water, they could tell their families that they had gone 'into' the ocean.

Suddenly, kids came running up to Steve and me, yelling, "Betsy was swept out to the deep part of the ocean!" We ran to where they pointed.

Sure enough, we saw a lifeguard charging into the water. Then we saw Betsy Unger waving her hand frantically. She was nearly SIXTY feet out to sea. When she was returned to the shore, she was blue in color and coughing up water. She was just cold, so the blue was NOT a breathing problem, and she was coughing because she had just swallowed a lot of water. She lay on the warming sand, covered with towels as the guard talked to her. Naturally, everybody on OUR trip surrounded Betsy and the guard. She was embarrassed, but explained what happened.

Betsy stated that because she could hardly feel the water on her when it was just coming up to her knees, she decided to see how it would feel if she went into water up to her WAIST. WOOOOSH! She was sucked out to sea with a strong riptide, ALL sixty feet under water; resulting in her taking in a lot of sea water.

Steve and I couldn't yell at her because we felt lucky that she was still with us. After we got Betsy to her feet, the students changed into dry clothes, and the two busses left the ocean and headed to the zoo. The rest of THAT journey was just fine, and everyone showed up for school the next day, including Betsy Unger. BUT, she remained as defiant as she was when she had thrown the baton to the ground at the State track meet. She didn't think she did anything wrong, therefore, she never apologized to either chaperone, or any kid, either, for being so foolish by not following directions.

Trips to the ocean were never that much fun, and we only made three side-trips to get close to it. During the 1977 trip, the riptides gave us a break, so kids headed into the ocean to swim. However, I had a DIFFERENT kind of experience with one female student. She was a very nice girl, of Apache descent, and had never seen an ocean before that trip. She stared and stared out at the water. She seemed to LOVE looking at the ocean. I approached her and asked why she wasn't going into the water. "Jaws is out there," she proclaimed in fear, "and I don't want him to get me." That movie had, apparently, had a profound effect on her, and she was VERY frightened to try the water. I could sense, however, that she really WANTED to get into the water, she was just afraid of the legend of a giant, mechanical shark lurking about.

After a few minutes of discussion, I finally said, "I'll go with you." She looked at me, with some fear in her eyes, but took my outstretched hand, and we walked slowly into the water. Her head on a swivel the entire walk as she searched left, right, and forward, looking for her animal of terror, and making nervous 'oooh' sounds until we stopped.

When we got to HER waist high mark, I dunked myself down under the water. I encouraged my 8th grader to do the same. She did, and came up smiling. She declared she was no longer afraid to be in the water. I, on the other hand, announced I was leaving the water, as it was too cold for me.

That girl stayed in, and stayed in, and STAYED in. After many calls to our students to exit the water (we needed to get to the San Diego Zoo) that girl simply looked at us and grinned. "I like it here," she would exclaim after each demand that she exit the water. Only when we threatened her with having to sit on the bus with Mr. Lipinski and the bus driver, while the rest of the kids went into the zoo, did she come out of the ocean. The trip was another success, though, but HER ocean story was a highlight, and she couldn't tell enough people how much she liked the ocean.

The last time we went to the beach, we went to a busy San Diego beach with a boardwalk on it. While the kids swam, and Steve and I kept watch on them at the shoreline, Russ and Perry were setting up four grills, which they had brought. Their idea, to save the students some money, was to grill hamburgers, have the kids changed from the ocean and finished eating BY 10:30 that morning, then head to the zoo.

The chaperones were simply trying to save the students a bit of money, so they wouldn't have to spend so much time AND money eating in the San Diego Zoo. Theoretically, that would allow the students more time to see exhibits and shows. I couldn't believe that Russ actually wanted the students to eat burgers at nine-thirty in the morning. However, the plan became a bust for two OTHER reasons.

First, the grills couldn't hold enough burger patties, which made the time necessary for students to eat go MUCH more slowly than anticipated. THEN, on more than one occasion, I could hear Russ cursing at the top of his lungs, as surfer-type kids would skate past the just-finished-grilled burgers, and take one or two of them for THEIR lunch. We didn't leave the beach until AFTER 11:00 that day. The zoo was still fun, though.

Perry and Steve had already discussed the fact that going to the beach was NOT an effective way of using our time, and the 'burger fiasco' was the last straw. In fact, THAT trip was the last time Russ Allenby went to California with Perry, Steve and me.

Steve and I always talked over the kids we wanted to invite on that special trip. USUALLY, if one of us vetoed a kid, for any reason, that kid wouldn't be invited.

We decided to try to go to San Diego first after Russ wasn't chaperoning. Our plan was to go to Sea World during the daylight, and to Balboa Park at night. We would stay in a nice hotel, near Balboa, Saturday evening. We would go to Disneyland Sunday morning.

The plan was great, and the hotel Perry found for us was magnificent. Getting into Sea World, when it first opened, was great, too. The sun and sea air tuckered our students out, or so we chaperones hoped because we were tired as all get out. Our plan was to get settled into the hotel, rest for a few hours, then go at night to a nearby amusement park to ride on some of their thrilling rides. The kids were to order pizzas for the room, or go to a nearby fast food restaurant for take-out, and we would chaperone at the restaurant. Once back in the hotel, however, we asked for the students to stay put in their OWN rooms until we were ready to go to the amusement park. When the kids were all back at the hotel, Perry, Steve and I went to a nearby restaurant for OUR dinner. When we finished eating, we headed back for a short rest before we would all head to our second attraction.

We got onto the elevator, and pushed the button for floor seven, a floor which was almost entirely occupied by the people from our trip. Suddenly, a U.S. Marine hopped on with us, and he, TOO, pushed the 7th Floor button.

The elevator started to move, when Perry asked the marine, "You staying on the 7th floor?"

"No, Sir," was his curt answer.

"WE three are staying there, but I am wondering why you would be going to THAT floor. We have brought 100 students with us and, pretty much occupy the entire floor."

The Marine looked at us and said plainly, "There are two girls on a balcony telling everyone below them that there's a party on the 7th floor. I was going to check it out."

"I apologize," Perry continued with some seriousness in his voice, "but those girls are part of our group, and I want to inform you that they are all 13 and 14 years of age. Unless you are looking to have problems involving fourteen-year-old children, I suggest you take this elevator right back down to the bottom."

With that, we departed on the 7th floor, and the Marine went back down.

Steve and I went to the room where we told the girls were being obnoxious with invitations to people on the ground. Lipinski and I had HAD a serious debate about allowing ONE of the girls to go on the trip. We felt that the second girl would be fine if she didn't have her friend along. I argued that putting them together might be like striking a match to gasoline, and I was definitely against letting the more troublesome girl go on the trip. But, somehow, 'Matches' sweet-talked Steve into believing that she would be 'good as gold,' in California….BOTH girls claimed that statement. My best friend was convinced they would be great on the trip, so I reluctantly gave in. Boy, was STEVE wrong!

The girls had simply been shouting down, at the top of their lungs, encouraging any fellow they saw, to come visit them for a party. Steve lost his temper, a bit. "You know," he said, showing some disappointment, "I TRUSTED you. You promised me you would behave, and I overrode Mr. Stein, here, who had some reservations about letting you both go. (sure, make ME the bad guy, Steve) And the first chance you get, you cause some trouble."

Lipinski had put a guilt trip on the girls, and they apologized. However, the damage had already been done, so we demanded that EVERY Wilhelm student be restricted to their rooms for the remainder of the time BEFORE going to the park. They were also required to stay in their rooms after we returned from the amusement park, too. Lipinski announced that if there was any more trouble from ANYBODY, for the rest of that day or night, those involved would be sitting on the bus during our entire stay in Disneyland. Steve explained that, "If necessary, we two chaperones will alternate sitting on that bus WITH the problem kids, and that would make us VERY unhappy." We had no more problems, and the trip ended JUST fine, but those two girls were NOT very popular the rest of the time in California.

We actually only went to the San Diego Zoo three times, too, as it wasn't nearly as exciting as the amusement parks. The students did say they enjoyed seeing the animals, though. The time moved so slowly there, that the chaperones realized that other attractions held greater appeal for 8th graders....three times, no more.

One NOT so fun memory at the zoo for Steve and me, however, was the day he and I were riding the zoo's tram. We enjoyed being able to relax on the transportation. Our thought was to let the kids run hard and get out a lot of their pent-up energy, but we didn't have that kind of energy, so we rode the slow-moving tram. I was starting to doze, feeling VERY relaxed, when suddenly the tram driver stopped her transport abruptly, and shouted, "Hey, quit poking a stick at that animal!"

Steve and I looked to where her wrath was being leveled and, surprisingly, saw one of OUR students, with a longish stick in hand, trying to awaken a sleeping leopard. The beast had curled itself against the bars of his cage and fallen asleep. The student couldn't quite reach the sleeping animal, thankfully, and it was VERY embarrassing to have one of the Wilhelm students causing controversy. In fact, Steve and I debated which one of us allowed that wannabe trouble-maker to be invited. We BOTH talked to him later, and he was no more problem.

It was during my second California Trip, that Steve decided to pull a prank on the really great group of kids we invited that year.

As we arrived at the San Diego Zoo, and just before exiting the bus, Steve made an announcement to the kids, "If you are looking to start this trip off by having an interesting experience," Lipinski began, "I want to suggest you ALL head to the gorilla habitat. They have a male gorilla that LOVES to have audiences come see him. He is an entertainer, especially when groups get him going. He seems to enjoy it most when he sees people laughing in his direction. He will do tricks. And the louder the laughter, even pointing your fingers at him, the more he will entertain you. That SHOULD be your first stop today."

Steve barely got off the bus when the stampede began, and ALL the students headed to the gorilla enclosure. He and I followed to watch the show.

There were two viewing areas at the gorilla site, one up above, and one pretty close to the large cage itself. The kids FLOCKED to get as close to the male gorilla as possible. Steve and I.....we watched the show from above. We wanted to get a REALLY nice view of the proceedings.

And the students were relentless. They laughed long and hard, trying to get the animal's attention.....and he was a huge gorilla, to boot.

And attention they got. The large mammal started pacing back and forth in his cage, going faster and faster, continually looking at the students. It seemed to me; as he was picking up his pace, he was getting more and more irritated, and NOT enjoying the loud laughter. Since the kids were told that their attention would get him to do tricks, THEIR antics and laughter was getting more animated, too.

Finally, in what seemed to be a fit of anger, that big, male gorilla stopped, reached down, and took hold of a HUGE pile of his own feces. At THAT sight, the students in the front row knew the jig was up, and they turned and started to try and run, practically trampling anybody who was standing behind them. BUT, too late, for that VERY angry animal flung poop at them with such ferocity that Steve and I could hear pieces of the crap hitting student after student. Fronts, backs, MANY students were hit, but fortunately, NO one was hit in the head.

When the 'dirty' deed was finished, and students were bemoaning the fact that they had gorilla feces dotting their clothing, they looked up at us. Naturally, we were laughing, too, but not at the gorilla. "We're going to get you, Mr. Lipinski!" they all started vowing, as we turned and walked away. There WAS a not-so-light odor in the bus as we went to the hotel, but it was just a memory of the zoo for ALL of us to cherish.

We never really had any major problems with either our kids OR Perry's kids. Though, one night, I had an interesting encounter with one of HIS students.

When we stayed at motels, we usually had all the boys, both Langdon's and ours, occupying one single floor of a large motel, with the girls occupying a second floor. The motel, on this particular trip, had ALL its entrances opening up to the parking lot. There was a railed walkway outside the rooms. It was easy for a chaperone, standing at one end of the walkway, to keep watch of an entire floor.

Perry, Steve, and I took the room at the far end of the row of boys' rooms, so we only had to sit outside OUR room to get a perfect view of the entire floor.

I happened to be on 'duty' at midnight, when the door of the room NEXT to ours slowly opened. As the door opened outwardly, it blocked the view to anything to the right....which happened to be where the male chaperones' room was. I watched intently as a young man, from Langdon's school, came out of his room, slowly and quietly closed the door behind him, while staring down the entire floor. But he NEVER looked to his right to see if there were any chaperones outside.

Once he was standing alone on the walkway, he started to move as quietly as possible toward the steps. It was obvious that he was heading toward the stairs, so he could go down one floor and visit his girlfriend. I was, JUST as quietly, walking behind him, and that kid never looked back to see if someone was following him. JUST as he hit the steps, I said, rather casually, "Going somewhere?"

The startled kid turned quickly, and upon seeing me standing there, started to yawn and stretch, "Naw, I just came out for a little fresh air, is all," He was very cool about being caught trying to sneak down to see the girls.

"Not a problem, young man. But you're going to have to get all your fresh air at Disneyland tomorrow. If you remember, we told ALL students that nobody was allowed out of the rooms until we wake you in the morning. Would you like me to wake Mr. Langdon and have him explain that to you again?"

"No," was his sullen answer, and he hung his head down while walking back to his room. No more problems THAT night.

That motel was a special one for me and Steve because of ONE entertaining event. There was a pizza restaurant's parking lot right next to the motel's parking lot, and BOTH lots were easily seen from our balcony. When we stayed at that motel we allowed our kids to go to the pizza place, order pizza, then take it back to their rooms. The chaperones let it be known that there was a 'last call' to get their pizzas, and to 'be back' in their rooms before we made bed checks. Once again, ALL students were heavily advised, that once the pizzas got to the rooms, they were NOT to exit those rooms until the chaperones woke them in the morning.

Like I mentioned, from our balcony, Steve and I could watch our kids coming back from the restaurant, as well as any other 'goings-on' that occurred in BOTH the restaurant and motel parking lots. Our perch was perfect for witnessing ANYTHING that was happening below us.

One year, after we made sure our students were set for the night, Steve and I were on the balcony enjoying a few moments of conversation, just before I went in to sleep for an hour. There occurred, however, an event that makes me STILL laugh today.

The incident was about bully behavior, and ALL the good things that can happen to them. It did NOT involve any students on our trip, but it is worth retelling to anyone who likes to see 'bad guys' get their just desserts.

A Volkswagon Beetle pulled into the restaurant's lot, and found a place to park pretty close to where Steve and I were standing. Three older teenagers emerged and headed to get a pizza. There was a tall kid, and two shorter ones, but it was the big guy who did ALL the talking....loudly....and all the way to the restaurant. We just observed, and when they were gone, Steve began regaling me of tales of his 'good old days,' when he was driving the exact same model of Beetle around Northern Arizona University.

We visited for a long time, long enough to see those same three fellas emerge after they had eaten. One again, the tall guy was constantly talking, AND he was loud, once again. He certainly appeared to us to be a loud-mouthed braggard in ADDITION to being a non-stop talking machine. But to his credit, his pals were listening intently.

The talker's appearance seemed a little 'different,' to Steve and me, too. He had very tall boots for a guy, (practically up to his knees) and there were several feathers hanging from the tops of the boots. He wore a strange-looking hat, as well, which ALSO had a couple of feathers hanging from it.

The parking lot had gotten very full, and there was one vehicle circling, trying to find a spot to park. Since the VW was back toward where Steve and I were standing, 'Feather' and his two little buddies exited the pizza joint and were slowly headed our way.

One smallish truck had just come onto the lot and began circling, too. As it passed by the slow-moving teens, a smallish young man sitting in the bed of the truck, began staring at Feather's attire.

This caused the oddly-dressed kid to stop walking, and look BACK at the smallish little fella in the truck bed. Not, seemingly able to control his mouth, he bellowed, "What YOU looking at?" And the tone definitely sounded like it might come from any bully trying to use a bit of intimidation, on ANY playground, at any school in America.

"I'm looking at you. You LOOK like a faggot," said the occupant in the back of the truck. His response had a more insulting tone to it, as opposed to sounding intimidating. He CERTAINLY didn't show any fear of the three boys who were heading to their car. And the truck kept moving slowly, still trying to find a parking place.

Feather and his 'boys' just stared at the truck for a few seconds, then began walking toward their car again. One of the smaller guys happened to notice that the truck found a parking spot, not far from the entrance of the restaurant. Suddenly, our comical-looking bully stopped walking and said, in full bravado, to his buddies, "Hey, just a minute. since that truck found a parking place, what say we go see that asshole in the back, and let him know we DON'T like his big mouth?" And with that, the three fellows turned and started to walk with a purpose toward the truck.

The kid in the back of the vehicle jumped to the ground, and the driver got out, too. Our three 'heroes' began moving a little bit more quickly toward the two kids from the truck, when SUDDENLY, the rider who had been sitting in the PASSENGER-side of the truck got out....and he was BIG. We're talking Paul Bunyon big, or he could have blotted out the image of the moon, if we saw him from ground level big....this guy was HUGE!

Seeing Feather and his friends moving toward them, the three TRUCK occupants suddenly became more interested in going to pummel the on-coming trio than wanting to eat pizza. The three VW antagonists, now seeing the big guy and his buddies coming toward THEM, stopped on a dime.

'Bigfoot' and his buddies were moving slowly, but surely, toward the VW trio. Feather, now realizing HE was about to be devoured, said, but only loudly enough for his buddies to hear (though Steve and I heard it, too), "Get back to the car....Get back to the car!"

As Goliath and HIS two buddies kept coming, the VW boys reached their car. One little guy was the driver, and the second smaller kid was TRYING to get into the back seat, but he was moving too slowly. "HURRY!" Feather suddenly began shouting, as the other three guys were gaining ground on their location. Feather yelled at the top of his lungs, "GET IN THERE!' then he proceeded to shove his 'friend' into the back seat, while he, himself, DIVED into the front seat. He didn't even have his door CLOSED when the VW driver PEELED backwards, swung around, almost sending Feather back onto the pavement, and tore out of that area like the car was on fire.

The huge kid, moved toward the car, as it was speeding from the parking lot and right past them, closed his fist, and BANGED the roof of the little car. There WAS a dent there, too, but that VW flew into traffic as fast as the driver could get it to go.

Steve and I were laughing so hard, I thought I might not be able to catch my breath. As for the three truck inhabitants, they were laughing, too, as they turned and headed toward the restaurant for something to eat. Now THAT was fun to watch.

There are hundreds more stories that I could tell about the California Trip, each one more entertaining than the last. It was, however, just a part of the 8th grade experience, and for Steve Lipinski and me, it was special. It helped us with discipline in our classrooms, helped our students make better choices about behavior throughout the year, helped children work for better grades to qualify for the trip, and helped solidify friendships, across the various social groups in our school. The administration recognized the 'good' that the California Trip created, so they allowed us to go about our business in dealing with all aspects of the trip. I enjoyed it very much, each and every year, because chaperones got to go for free, AND I have always been a big kid at heart. As long as we had wonderful kids on the trip, (which was why it was invite only) the theme parks and I were a match. Thanks, Steve, for getting me involved.

9

THE FALL BEGINS

FROM DAY ONE, DeWitt appeared to be a pariah to normal education, as I interpreted it. Construction was mis-managed. Administrative leadership was discombobulated. Teachers were thrown into the fray on a wing and a prayer. I don't know about the Alpha teams, for both the 7th and 8th graders, but the Beta teams faced a student population that could have starred in any juvenile delinquent movie ever written. Let me explain the first girl in my homeroom, who was LESS than cooperative.

I don't know what school she had attended prior to DeWitt. I'm not sure anyone did. And she wasn't a loud, boisterous child, as long as you didn't bother her in any way. But she gave an air of toughness that no other student wanted to test. It's NOT that other girls didn't try to befriend her….at first. But every attempt at 'warmth' shown her was met with a scowl and a stare that one BOY described as 'down-right scary.'

Teachers didn't fare much better with this girl. (name forgotten on purpose, for sure….don't want her to come look me up)

She would do the minimum on ANYTHING school-oriented at best. She was not looking for trouble with the teachers, for which I was grateful.

Then came a day in early October when my homeroom had an incident. The tardy bell hadn't rung yet, and I was working on shuffling papers at my desk, when I heard a disturbing noise. Big Girl (did I tell you she was a rather large individual) had slammed her desk against the wall behind her, and with clenched fists and a look of hate on her face, proceeded to cross the room....right toward a group of girls who had, apparently, said something that was un-kind toward the on-coming combatant.

"HEY!" I yelled at the top of my lungs as I moved quickly to intercept her path toward the four terrified girls, "YOU AND ME.... OUTSIDE....RIGHT NOW!"

Big Girl looked at me, then at the girls who were looking to run somewhere, then she stormed outside.

Before I left the room, I asked the, suddenly, VERY nervous girls what happened, and one of them indicated that they were just laughing....but NOT at her.

I really wasn't listening, though, as I hustled outside to my irate 8th grader. She was just standing there, arms folded, still peering inside the room at the four girls, and giving the look of hate that would be intimidating to ANY person, let alone girls her age. "Look, I don't know what you think those immature girls were laughing at, but they just told me it had NOTHING to do with you. I want to believe them. What I DON'T want is any trouble in my classroom. You now have a choice. Stay out here, but you can't wander anywhere else because then I'll be forced to come get you and take you to the office. OR you can come inside, wait for the bell, and go to your first hour class, peacefully. You decide." I was looking at her JUST as intently as she still was the girls in the room.

Without a word, Big Girl walked back into the classroom, sat down, stared at her own desk with that non-ending glare she had, and waited for the bell which sent students to their 1st hour classes. I watched as all my students went about their business AND to their classes. Disaster averted....for the time being.

Generally, this girl was not a problem in most classrooms....with the exception of one Beta Team teacher, who butted heads with the student all the time. When THAT happened in the teacher's class, I was 'lucky' enough to have the kid sent back to MY room, where she would sit out the rest of that class period. Sadly for me, I got her three times a day on many, many occasions....Homeroom, Language Arts, and the harried teacher's class.

Big Girl didn't last long at DeWitt, however. On Halloween night, she and an older female friend of hers were roaming the streets far from their 'turf,' when they discovered an old man just sitting in his dilapidated truck. Tired of walking, Big Girl simply opened the truck door and dragged the scrawny old man from his truck. The girls jumped into the truck and drove off down the road to do some 'joy riding.' Girls from the 'hood' just wanting to have fun, I guess.

The Beta teachers were told of this 'adventure' in our meeting the next day, and, to a person, we all sighed with relief when told she would NOT be returning to DeWitt.

Big Girl was just the tip of the iceberg, so to speak. Our team of students was littered with 'bad seeds.' We did not know about a 'special' discipline peculiarity on the two 8th grade teams until Steve Lipinski and I went to Alpha team to pitch the California Trip, that first year of DeWitt's existence.. It was shortly AFTER the Alpha students heard about our year-end reward that Beta Team called for a special meeting with our principal, Mr. Howard Boyd, to find out how it was decided which team was assigned which students at the beginning of the year.

Oh, Beta had a number of good students. That was not the issue. But, according to Mr. Boyd, the WORST of the trouble-makers, and a majority of the OTHER difficult kids, were assigned to us because WE had been 'chosen for the job' due to our strong disciplinary backgrounds. Then the Beta Team regaled our principal with some of the 'war stories' we endured since the beginning of the year. He just nodded as we spoke.

"Listen," Boyd said, trying to defend the vast differences in student body make-up, "I wasn't REALLY aware of the extremeness in behavioral differences between teams, as I didn't make student team assignments." The five of us Beta teachers just looked incredulously at each other. He knew, or why did he talk about us getting so many 'trouble-makers' because of our 'backgrounds.' That weasel knew. He was just looking for a way to deflect responsibility, as far as we were concerned. "And I admit it DOES look like the numbers were a bit skewed more than they should have been."

"You mean SCREWED don't you?" chimed in Steve Lipinski, with some anger, I might add.

"The teachers on Alpha Team are just not as aggressive on discipline as you five, so the committee decided what students go to what teams accordingly."

"Who was ON the committee deciding that?" Grace Armbruster blurted out, "The teachers on Alpha Team?"

"A committee of teachers, yes, and a couple of administrators. I am sorry that none of you were included," Boyd continued, seeming annoyed that his leadership was being challenged. "I have to tell you that the student populations have been divided for next year already, BUT, we will definitely make some specific changes two years down the road. Let me assure you, whatever help you need from me, let me know, and I will get it for you. This first year was rough for you, I understand, but it will be better next year, you'll see."

Howard Boyd was more politician than principal, as he was constantly OFF campus. So we five teachers knew HE didn't get to see the daily discipline problems that plagued both the 7th grade Beta teachers and the 8th grade Beta teachers during those first two years of DeWitt's existence. And, yes, the 'divide' of students was VERY similar the second year to what it was the first year.

Boyd was gone from the school with the start of the third year, as were three 'senior' teachers from Alpha Team 8th grade, and one 'senior' member from Alpha Team 7th grade. The third year was when the teams, of BOTH grades, started seeing better dispersion of behavior problems.

Did Boyd ever help us? He tried, once, in his second year.

Both 7th grade Beta and 8th grade Beta continued to struggle with discipline during the school's second year of existence. With our principal wandering, who knows where, but definitely being off campus, the assistant principal, bless her heart, was being overwhelmed with students needing some 'straightening out.'

A behavioral 'specialist' was brought to the school, by Principal Boyd, as a gesture of good will toward us Beta teachers. This fellow was to show us HOW to deal with students with bad attitudes, or students who were just plain incorrigible.

The 8th grade was selected to be first to observe the 'expert' in action. We were told to have two of our students, with mis-behaving tendencies, come to a Beta Team meeting. That is where we would be able to witness proper techniques to be used when dealing with troublesome adolescents.

First, we brought in Fernando Avila. He wasn't a 'tough guy' per se, he just didn't want to do anything in anybody's classroom. He even refused to acknowledge the teachers when they tried to help him. He would just stare at the adults, and when they went about OTHER business, he would open his omnipresent notebook and draw....and he was a VERY good artist.

When Fernando entered our meeting room, the behavioral specialist (we'll call him Mr. X because I forgot his name) asked our student to take a seat. Young Avila looked at his five core teachers, shrugged his shoulders, sat down, and immediately began to open his notebook so he could begin drawing.

"I'm sorry, Fernando," Mr. X began, "I need you to close your book, put your pencil away, so you and I can have a little chat."

Silently, the kid followed directions.

"Your teachers have been telling me that you are, basically, non-responsive in their classes," Mr. X stated. Fifteen to twenty seconds of silence followed. "Do you know what non-responsive means?" Another fifteen to twenty seconds of silence went by. "It means that you do not want to work in their classes, AND you don't want to tell them how they can help you."

Fernando just stared at our expert, with a definite bored expression on his face, but he never uttered a single word.

"Perhaps there is ONE teacher here whose class you enjoy, but are afraid to let other students see you liking it. Is there one, or more, classes that you might participate in if you weren't worried how your classmates might react to your getting involved in class?"

Again, Fernando sat quietly, staring at Mr. X, with absolutely no expression on his face.

"Can you tell me what the teachers can do to make you feel more comfortable in class?"

More silence and staring.

"What are you thinking right now, Fernando?"

When Avila picked up his pencil and began to open his notebook again, our behavioralist said, "All right, young man, you can return to your class now."

As the student left the 'team room' Steve Lapinski said, "See you tomorrow, Fernando."

The kid stopped for a second, turned his head around to address his teachers, and said quietly, "Yep."

"Some students are impossible to work with after just one meeting," Mr. X stated with conviction. "I would have to see him several more times before I could get him to act positively in a classroom setting."

As an aside here, the five of us 'core' teachers got SOME work from Fernando during the school year. But he did as little as possible, and it wasn't quality work. His mother was equally frustrated by his 'don't care' attitude, and just before the end of our school year, Mom shipped him off to HER father, who lived in California. With Fernando not qualifying for promotion from DeWitt, we five teachers recommended to his mom that her dad have him do another year of 8th grade. I never heard what happened, but MY guess is that Grandpa enrolled him in a California high school....hopefully with a great art department.

For Morton, Steve, Ginger, Grace and me, Fernando was just a warm-up. He was no real behavioral challenge in the classroom. He was just 'different.' We wanted Mr. X to feel our PAIN....to experience a girl who was our most behaviorally-challenged student that year. This was a kid who took each of us teachers to the brink of total frustration each and every day. Her name was Sunshine Fiske....but a ray of light and warmth she wasn't!

Sunshine was a very smart girl. SO smart that we wondered why she wasn't tracked with the gifted students on the Alpha team. Oh, yeah, she was a behavior problem, and Alpha didn't get many of those during DeWitt's second year as a school.

She was a physically beautiful girl, too, who had a delightful personality when she felt like it. But those moments were few and far in between. I wanted to think of her as being bi-polar, but she was 'nasty' most of the time, with the 'good' Sunshine only appearing as a fleeting moment in everybody's life.

She lured in boyfriend after boyfriend. But like the Black Widow spider, after a boy showed her any REAL attention, she grew tired of him and would unceremoniously dump each guy using hateful and humiliating words.

I prayed every day for the 'charmer' in her to show up for my class because she could be 'hell on wheels' when she was angry....and, sadly, that was her usual behavior in the classroom.

She REALLY didn't enjoy being in the classroom setting. What she enjoyed was being the center of attention, which wasn't always possible in a room where learning had to take place. She would grumpily come into the classroom, plop herself in her seat, and wait for someone to 'tick her off,' as she would say. Unfortunately, that someone was most often the teacher.

We 8ᵗʰ grade Beta Team educators could hardly WAIT to see how Mr. X would deal with Ms Fiske.

When Sunshine entered our meeting room, she got a smirk on her face. She knew she was going to be the center of attention for sure, and that seemed to make her happy....temporarily.

"I'm Mr. X," our guest said with a broad smile, while extending his hand. "Please have a seat."

Sunshine ignored his hand, as well as him, dropping heavily onto her chair, while looking quizzically at her five teachers. She maintained that impish smirk on her face.

Mr. X continued. "Your teachers, here, tell me that sometimes you show...."

"Who the hell is this guy?" interrupted Sunshine while addressing us as a group. Suddenly, she lost the smirk, got a very dark look about her, raised her voice, and practically shouted. "I don't know what you all want from me, and I don't care." She pointed at the stranger in the room and continued. "I don't like this...whoever he is, and now I DON'T want to be in here anymore!"

She rose to her feet, and gave an ugly scowl to Mr. X, as he stared at her incredulously. "OK, you can go back to class now," he said in a quiet tone. Sunshine left quickly, without getting her 'pass' signed, which was a typical Sunshine Fiske thing to do. We five teachers just looked at the 'expert,' to see his reaction.

"Students need to show a willingness to work with you," X said while rising, gathering his belongings, and readying himself to leave our room. "That young lady was no where near where she needed to be for me to show you how to interact with her in the classroom. You needed to tell me more about those kids instead of just 'they have problems in the classroom.'"

He was gone in a flash, and we realized we had set him up for failure. But that guy never really ASKED for a detailed description of out students' classroom behaviors, either. He had just indicated that he was going to show us techniques on 'how to deal with students who had difficulty in the classroom.'

Neither Fernando nor Sunshine was typical of our ornery students. They represented some of the worst behaviors that we had to face, that year AND the previous year, for sure. In fact, they were extremes. Fernando needed to be in an art school, NOT an educational setting where he wasn't going to be successful. And Sunshine....we all decided that she needed to be in an institution for mentally-challenged kids. She was a clear and present danger to herself and others at DeWitt.

Yet, we had to deal with her....and Fernando....and every other troubled kid who walked onto DeWitt's campus. Our patience and resources were limited, that is for sure. It would have taken MUCH of our team-meeting time to prepare Boyd's expert for the students he was about to face.

Maybe we WANTED to see him fail, I don't know. But the fact was that Beta Team had LOTS of students with issues inside and outside the classroom. No 'one time' meeting with a behavior expert was going to give us, even remotely, enough ammunition to be successful with many of the students we were getting at DeWitt.

We were, also, beginning to hear rumors that teachers' pay was going to start being tied to student ACHIEVEMENT in the classroom, too. The Beta teams, at DeWitt, would be in big trouble if THAT ever came to fruition. That I knew for a fact.

Before DeWitt's second school year ended, before the third year began, meaning the Alpha team would have to start taking ITS share of trouble-makers, I decided to look into the possibility of teaching in another district. I knew I had ten more years remaining in education before Arizona's qualification parameters would make me eligible for retirement. I decided to check out what OTHER schools were around, where I might wish to teach for those last ten years.

DeWitt certainly had its share of misfits, that's for certain. Sadly, I had also seen WILHELM students beginning to slack off, in both achievement and attitude, during the last few years I was working at my former neighborhood school. Maybe this happens as a normal transition for ANY district, when decades-long established families move out of their areas, and tougher families move in. Seems logical to me.

I truly believe that by the time MY district had moved all its junior high students into one single school, Brighton had become a bona fide Inner City school district. Therefore, with nearly three times as many 7th and 8th grade students enrolled in DeWitt as had been enrolled in Wilhelm, Pfister, or Cahill, individually, the situation for me had become uncomfortable.

It had become perfectly clear to me, during my second year at DeWitt, that I was VERY disenchanted with MOST everything at that new school. I decided that I would actively seek a change of venue. I wanted to see if I could find another school in which to finish my career. I wanted out of Brighton!

I knew of a former counselor from Wilhelm who had made a successful move to a suburban school in the Phoenix area. When I called him for advice he was VERY excited to tell me about his school, and especially the principal assigned there. His news was particularly appealing as he told me his Peoria District had just finished building a new school, and was having interviews to staff that school. My counselor buddy and his principal would both be transferring to the new school, so I asked to have an interview set up for me. I was excited about the prospect of working at a different school....one that may not have NEARLY the problems that DeWitt had.

I went to the interview after DeWitt students were excused for the day, but apparently, the Peoria school was still in session, as classes THERE hadn't been dismissed yet. I was pleasantly surprised at how quiet the campus was. There was NO yelling.

You may be surprised that the first thing I mention was that I heard no yelling at the Peoria school. Truth is, at DeWitt, almost ANY time of day, there would be students out and about, so it wasn't unusual to hear teachers yelling for kids to 'get to class,' or asking 'where are you going?' Sometimes....no....a LOT of times, students would be getting passes (usually to use the bathroom) just to meet up with friends who ALSO had passes, and those kids ALWAYS seemed to be shouting when walking together. To me, there was WAY too much LOUD noise around DeWitt, even when classes were in session.

The Peoria school had SOME students get passes during class periods, too, I imagine. But, on that particular day I saw no student, nor heard any sound of voices. It was a pleasure just getting out of my car and being on that quiet campus.

The interview went very well, and the principal seemed delighted at my resume of activities in which I was involved throughout my 18 years of teaching....Student Council advisor, Junior National Honor Society advisor, etc. But mostly, he was VERY excited to hear about my coaching experiences, and wrestling just happened to be a sport near and dear to his heart. Apparently, HE wrestled somewhere in his lifetime, and he admired the individualistic value of the sport.

Things were going swimmingly, and I REALLY liked that principal. I was so excited that I might get to work with him in the near future.... but then I asked the normal question, "What will my salary look like?"

"First of all, Mr. Stein, let me tell you that, as much as I want you to be a part of my staff, this district works from within. That means we put the jobs out to the teachers already in the district to see who might be interested in going to a brand new school. Indications are that there are not many people interested in leaving their current schools, which bodes well for you. AND, because I have a say in hiring, I would certainly find a place for you on my staff. You are just what my school would be looking for. You have all the qualities of the kind of person I want to work with. I just needed to tell you what the situation is like in the Peoria District. I CAN tell you that right now it looks good for you to be joining me next year, but we have to wait to see what other district teachers decide to do for next year."

At that juncture, I was a little disappointed, but I understood the 'inner workings' of filling positions in districts. I was willing to risk quitting at Brighton for the chance to work in the Peoria District if it had leaders like the man who was interviewing me.

Then the other shoe dropped. "Mr. Stein, can I call you Abe?"

"Of course," I responded, appreciating the informality that my interview was taking.

"The bad news is that we can't honor your current professional level of pay. I would be forced to give you a reduced salary if you come on board. The absolute best I would be able to offer you would be Step-4 on our salary scale."

"Since I am at Step-18 in Brighton, what, exactly, would that mean to me?" I inquired, now not feeling so good about the situation.

"It is what it sounds like, Abe. You would have to start at the fourth-year pay grade. BUT, if you go to night school and take required classes that the district would be giving, you could leap forward quickly, and in, maybe five or six years, you could be at OUR Step-12 level, and the salary at Step-12 is comparable with what you are making now. Peoria's pay scale is much better that what yours is now."

I sat there is shock. I would have to go to night school again..... for several years....JUST to get back to where I currently was on my pay scale. "Sir," I said, now leaving the informality of the confer-ence, "I am being asked to forget fourteen years of dedicated ser-vice, and take a HUGE salary hit. I have already figured out that I may only need ten more years before I can reach retirement. If I worked for Peoria, and did all the schooling required during those five or six years, I would be left with only four or five years until I would be eligible to retire. I see that as a lot of work JUST to get to where I am now, in pay. I am working hard to save as much as possible so I CAN retire early. If I am hired here, saving retirement money would be VERY difficult."

"My wife and I are NOT in a position where I can take a giant step back in salary....not at this time in my career. I would LOVE to work in this district, and especially with you as a principal. But, as it stands, if you can't do anything to help my money situation, I will have to just look forward to ten more tough years in the inner-city, and then seek retirement."

There was nothing more to be said. He wanted me to work for him. I WANTED to work for him. But, according to him, the district policy was set in stone, so I left his office....a very sad person.

The students of the Peoria school were being dismissed as my interview concluded, so children were out of their classrooms, going about their business. I stopped to admire the fact that there was NO running, NO shouting, NO shoving to get onto the busses, and kids were acting civil to one another. This would have been a dream job, but I just couldn't sacrifice Katherine and me being forced to take a giant step backwards financially. We were just beginning to enjoy having enough money coming in to where we didn't have to worry about bills, AND we didn't owe anybody, anything. I liked that feeling, so I knew I would have to do the best I could in a very tough school environment. I was staying at DeWitt.

10

WHAT'S WITH ADMINISTRATORS?

THE PRINCIPAL IN the Peoria District was particularly nice, and that was a different feeling for me. While I had a FEW administrators that I got along with, the majority of them reminded me of most officers I had while in the military. The Peter Principal can take place in any profession, but with many officers AND school administrators, the level of inept ability to lead seemed to be magnified....at least in MY experience.

It almost seemed like GETTING to a leadership position was the goal. After that, being able to handle the responsibility was most difficult. I know that administrators had to deal with a lot.... legislature, school boards, demanding parents. I am well aware of that. But in the Brighton District, good administration people were few and far in between. And the one thing that I noticed most, few of them knew how to deal with teachers.

If a teacher didn't do EXACTLY what they were told by their bosses, they were often considered to be outcasts to the system, even persona non-gratis. The difference between military officers and school administrators, as far as I was concerned, was that in Vietnam, officers relied on sergeants to get the job done. And it didn't really matter how that job got done, as long as it DID get done. Sure, officers could get mighty upset if THEIR strategy was not followed, but when all was said and done, if the job had a good ending, everybody was satisfied. Education 'big wigs' were more arrogant about results.

Teachers were, and are, the sergeants of the education arena. Administrators get their strategies and ideas out to the teachers, and expect the teachers to get the work done. But, in my day, it often seemed that IF the administrators didn't have things done THEIR way, and their way ONLY, then the teacher was admonished and SOMETIMES thought to be a trouble-maker. Lighten up, administrators, there ARE ways, other than yours, to get the job done.

I was an instinctive teacher. I was NOT a straight-A student growing up. Teaching 'by the book' wasn't comfortable for me. My way of teaching was different than, say, Ginger Geiger, who WAS more of a by-the-book educator. She was very successful, but always seemed so high-strung, that if students didn't do things exactly the way she intended them, she would get flustered....even upset. For the most part, she listened to the administrators and did what they told her to do. She was happy. The administrators were happy. But the stress on her was immense, and there were many times when I thought she might be going to have a nervous breakdown. She was a great teacher, don't get me wrong, just different than I was, but we understood, and respected each other.

I taught six classes a day, and every class had its own make-up. My junior high kids weren't always sure how they wanted to behave.

They wanted to be treated like kids at times during each day, and then like adults at other times of the day. Man-child is what I called them. I heard comments like, 'Can I have some candy?' followed closely by a 'You can't talk to me that way' attitude. Multiply that times 150 students each day, and a teacher learns to adapt.

Ms Geiger relied on her strict regimen, and students WERE expected to follow it explicitly. She was known as a tough disciplinarian, and students didn't want to cross her because they understood they would have trouble with their parents and administrators if they didn't toe the line. It worked for her, but not me. I just couldn't follow strict guidelines.

Sure I was different, but I always KNEW what had to be done. And as long as I got the required work finished, which I always did, I was happy....and most of my year-end standardized test scores showed a nice increase in grade-level performances by the students I taught. And, after all, wasn't educational growth in the classroom the real objective for the year....not how they are gotten?

Several of the principals I worked with understood me and left me to MY ways of teaching. A kind of, 'if it ain't broke, don't fix it' philosophy. As long as I got good results, I was left alone, and that made me happy.

There were one or two adminstrators who wanted to bully me, and I expect OTHER 'instinctive teachers,' too, into doing what they (the bosses) wanted....which was using ONLY 'by the book,' methods of teaching. At the end of the year, however, when students' results improved by a year or two over the previous year, I felt justified in my methods and was pretty much left alone by everybody.

Truly, however, student achievement 'growth' was lower than administrators and I WANTED it would be. I kept adapting my teaching methods as the years went by, but the ever-increasing transient student influx, made GRADE level achievement less plausible, let alone higher standards. By the late '80's and throughout the '90's, all Brighton teachers had to face facts.... many students were coming into the District with less and less academic skills. What's worse is that those students were showing less INTEREST in becoming more highly educated members of society.

Principals, and other administrators, kept making demands that our students' skills be improved, but they had little idea of what teachers faced each day, and wouldn't have known unless they were actually IN the classrooms on a daily basis.It is NOT that District leaders weren't trying to improve student achievement.... they were. But, in my day, teachers had to do what was necessary just to maintain classroom INTEGRITY (discipline was a HUGE challenge for several of my peers) as well as educate their students. Most times goals COULDN'T be achieved simply by following administrator's demanded protocal.

I know Steve Lipinski was an instinctive teacher, and so was Grace Armstrong, for the most part. Actually, if she wasn't getting what she wanted from one or two students during a class, she would just send them to Steve's or my room, as a kind of timeout. She had no time for behavioral distractions, and that's how she got results. Grace had a successful intuitive teaching technique, for sure, but little patience for distractions by students; thus, sending troubling students to Steve or me was her answer.

While administrators left me alone, I don't remember getting any credit, (maybe one, which comes later in the book) from them, either. That wasn't nice.

Here's what I mean about no administrative plaudits. Early in my career, I wrote a play for the district. It was designed to help small kids be alert to something called, 'stranger danger.' I selected some popular characters, from a 'fantasy' play the Drama class did at Wilhelm, and made them heroes in MY play. The Drama students acted out, and even discussed, while staying in character, proper behavior little kids should take, when approached by a stranger.

I got permission to take my actors to Richland Elementary School, our nearby 'feeder school,' to perform for the kindergarten through second grade students.

The teachers at Richland, and the children, too, seemed to really enjoy the presentations, and discussions were held between my 8th grade actors, and the younger students, after each performance was finished. I thought that each time we performed; my actors did a great job. Even though both the teachers and students from the feeder school praised my actors' work, and we got letters of 'thanks,' we got absolutely NO feedback from an administrator. Not a single administrator came to see any of the four presentations, though they gave us permission to perform. I understand that Brighton District administrators DID get positive feedback from some of the attending teachers, but neither my students nor I heard a thing from Distict people.

I even got permission from MY principal to present the play, but he let me know that his MAJOR interest in the productions was having me get my kids safely across the two hundred yards separating the two schools. He never came, himself, to see us perform.

This play was written and presented to convey an important life lesson to our younger kids….and the 'stranger danger' topic was very big in those days, too. I can only guess that all the District administrators, and the principals of the two schools involved, had better things to do than witness my kids interacting with some of Brighton's younger kids. Sarcasm, anyone?

Heard from parents, who came to see us perform, too, and THEY thought what we did was an extraordinarily good thing. Bottom line….the actors got their well-deserved praise for a job well done, from parents, teachers, students and me, and that was great.

Getting recognition from bosses may seem a little petty, but lots of people crave that. I never really considered myself one of those people….not really. But I can't, during my ENTIRE 32 years working for Brighton, EVER remember having an administrator seek me out for anything positive that I had accomplished, while representing Brighton. Oh, there were the twenty year 'service apples' which all teachers got when finishing twenty years in the District. But that wasn't any project I did PERSONALLY.

The way I perceived administrators, in my day, was that they were not prone to giving credit unless THEY got credit, too. Lighten up, people in charge, being complimentary doesn't diminish a leader's power. It's a good thing, and we underlings enjoy getting a kind word from time to time.

I do, however, remember an incident, which occurred during my 9th year of teaching that kind of surprised me....but NOT in a positive way.

My best friend Steve Lipinski and I were having lunch with a former Wilhelm teacher who had become a Brighton District administrator. He had left the classroom in order to make good his college administrative degree. Turns out HE was the epitome of a Peter Principal failure....only lasted eight years at the District office.

Anyway, he was still a friend of Steve's, and we were enjoying lunch in a nice restaurant one day when there wasn't any school in session. The discussion we were having was about teachers being absent from school. Steve and I mentioned that we didn't enjoy taking days off from school because it took us three days to get our classrooms back in order. We explained that kids seemed to enjoy terrorizing some substitute teachers, and it was always a crapshoot as to who was running the classroom when a 'regular' teacher was absence.

Our administrator friend had been notorious for taking ALL his paid absence days, year after year, when a teacher. He also claimed to have zero problems getting right back into his subject material upon returning. Steve and I agreed that the kids in the Wilhelm District, during HIS day in the classroom, had strong backgrounds in their educational up-bringing, as those parents were sticklers for their sons and daughters getting the best grades. I told him he must have been a very good teacher to have had that kind of respect from his students. Steve then explained that he and I, too, were happy for the strong parental support....in the early seventies.

We THEN tried to explain, to the naive District administrator, that times were changing in the Wilhelm classrooms. By the early eighties his former school was NOT always getting the strong parental support that he remembered. We DID point out, though, that there were still parents pushing their kids toward getting a good education, but they had become fewer and fewer.

We tried to explain that there was the more prevalent 'live and let live' environment on the home front, and that the kids we taught were becoming more rebellious and powerful in their own homes. We argued that our parental base seemed to be allowing their children too much freedom, which was leading to less and less school work being done at home. Students were trying to continue the 'less work' trend in school classrooms, too, so teachers were working harder to get objectives met. Substitute teachers had NO chance of moving education forward, which required catching up to necessary.

The discussion ended with us telling the administrator that being absent from school was something we both tried to avoid. That is when Steve told the administrator that I, Abe Stein, 'Had not missed a single day of work during the nine years he has been in the District.' I was a little embarrassed to be recognized for that fact, but glad to have the compliment given to me by my friend.

The administrator, who had been drinking throughout lunch, looked at me through his alcohol-induced, bloodshot eyes, and asked, "You mean to sit there and tell me you haven't missed a single day of teaching since you came into the District?"

"That is correct," I said almost shyly, but still very proud of the fact.

The inebriated Brighton big shot chugged the last little bit of the drink he was holding, placed the glass on the table, looked at me with a deadpan expression, and clapped his hands, ever so slowly, three times. Then the sot ordered another drink.

I wasn't expecting a standing ovation, but to give me a 'mocking' hand clap was down-right disrespectful. If I hadn't felt valued by my superiors before that lunch, I certainly came to the realization that administrators and I were never going to be friends. And I was still teaching at Wilhelm at the time. My relationship with 'boss-types' got worse at DeWitt.

DeWitt's first principal, Howard Boyd, was a nebbish to me. He was hardly AT the school to show any leadership. And when he was there, he didn't seem to have time to talk to his teachers about any problems that they might be having. He was NOT a proficient leader. I was happy that he left alone in my classroom.

Suddenly he was gone from Brighton, and the District began having a 'nation-wide' search for his replacement. They brought in a tall, attractive, administrator from Pittsburg. She dispensed HER 'take-charge' attitude from the start. By that I mean to say that she expected EVERY teacher to do EXACTLY what she told them to do. And, folks, that is NOT the way to gain the respect of a senior staff of workers.

Missy Cornelius WAS a fashion plate. Everyday she looked like she had just walked off the pages of a fashion magazine. What's worse is that she thought there wasn't a man alive who DIDN'T want to sleep with her. Her ego was enormous, but sadly she, TOO, could have been the poster child of the Peter Principal.

I don't remember ONE meeting in which she accepted ANY advice from her staff members....on ANYTHING. Mostly, she just stated what SHE wanted done, regardless of what we teachers thought about the ideas. She didn't want to offend parents, or District administrators, but she sure had the knack of offending many of the DeWitt teachers....with her arrogance, if nothing else. She claimed she could teach ANYTHING to junior high students, and was willing to prove it. I couldn't resist the challenge.

I asked Cornelius to give a one-day lesson, to one of my classes, in poetry. She could use any style of poetry she wished, and I would take notes and teach my OTHER five classes the same lesson.

After a dissertation of how good a teacher she was, droning on and on for a good ten minutes, she agreed to teach my first hour class. It would HAVE to be my first hour class because she was too busy to teach in the middle of the day.

Oh, I wanted to give her my 4th-hour class in the worst way. It was the last class I had before lunch, and those kids, besides having the orneriest class make-up, personality-wise, of any of my classes, would have been a challenge to ANY teacher. Fortunately, I controlled the time when that particular class went to lunch, so I got the work from them that I needed.

My 1st-hour class had thirty-three people in it, including Aaron Holliday, of the famous Holliday brothers I told you about earlier. He was truly interested in getting good grades, so as to NOT disappoint his loving mom. AND he was the most popular kid on the Beta Team, so much so, that other students followed his lead in everything. Teaching my 1ˢᵗ-hour class would be a cinch for Missy Cornelius....at least that is what I thought.

Missy was charming, and bright-eyed, and VERY eager to do her lesson. However, she spent many, MANY minutes telling the class how skilled she was at teaching poetry....even telling the boys and girls about HER success in getting poems published. My kids were not impressed.

In fact, as SOON as Ms Cornelius turned her back to write on the chalkboard, (it was a white board and teachers used markers on it, not chalk....but I will ALWAYS refer to the boards as chalk boards) the class started to look around, and get busy writing notes to each other. Apparently, they had so much to tell each other, the note-writing became obsolete rather quickly, and they just started whispering to each other openly. For my part, I was busily taking notes off the board, so I could emulate the lesson for my other five classes that day.

I HAD warned Ms Cornelius that my students could be talkative, and she noticed them whispering, but she didn't seemed concerned. She kept smiling, writing on the board, and moving forward with her lesson. Even Aaron Holliday tried to get the students around him quiet....for a while. Then he gave up and got into the whispering conversations.

The whispering continued throughout her entire lesson, but good old Missy just kept plugging ahead. It was HER class, after all, and I was writing constantly so I could keep up with the note taking. I had told her I would teach the exact same lesson to my other five classes, but that would have been impossible if I had gotten involved with keeping the kids quiet, which definitely, would NOT have allowed me to take notes.

At times the class's whispering got so loud, that Cornelius was forced to raise HER voice, just to be heard. It was astonishing to me how she didn't ask the kids to quiet down....not even once.

She finished with a flurry, giving the students a homework assignment, which she made due the next day. She sounded exuberant about her work, and cheerily sent HER class to their 2nd-hour periods after the bell sounded to dismiss the students.

She left by just giving me a nod, which was fine with me. I had to study the notes I took, so as to emulate her instructions on that particular type of poetry before MY 2nd-hour English class.

When the 1st-hour class came in the next day, I asked them to turn in their assignments for Ms Cornelius. Comments like, 'We had homework?' and 'I couldn't understand what we did,' were plentiful. In fact, only ONE student did ANY work, and it was pitiful. I chewed them out for their inconsideration toward our guest, and went over the highlights of the lesson for them. I asked them to turn something in on the following day, and I took the one paper I received to Ms Cornelius at the end of the day.

"This is it?" Missy questioned while looking at the poor piece of work in front of her.

"Didn't you notice how much they were talking when you were instructing?" I queried.

"Mr. Stein," the principal said in a disdainful tone, "I ENCOURAGE discussion during the class. I believe it stimulates conversation, amongst the students, on the lesson being taught. That way, the students who understand what is going on, can help ME by telling the less-informed students how to get things done."

I wanted to ask her if she actually TAUGHT in an inner-city school in Pittsburg, but instead, I said, "I briefly went over your work with that class, and asked them to turn in their work tomorrow," and I left the office.

I didn't fare much better in MY five classes, either. I massaged student egos, I cajoled them, used Jewish guilt on them, but less than half of every class turned in ANY work. And it was terrible work. Why Missy Cornelius decided to use some Baroque-era style of poetry, (at least I THINK it was from an ancient era) I have no idea. The principal got less than ten papers turned in, and that was the end of her experiment to teach DeWitt students ANYTHING.

It didn't stop her from being a 'pain-in-the-ass' around the school and in teachers' meetings. Cornelius had poor communication skills with most of the teachers, and she stunk in the disciplinarian department. With her in charge, several of us 'senior' teachers were getting angry at her poor skills. Steve Lipinski wanted to help her, and the school out, with a program HE was looking to implement....called Student Court. Cornelius was not only hesitant about letting Steve do his project, she said she couldn't support him if the project bombed. There will be more about THAT program in a short while, but the writing was on the wall....DeWitt would be better off if Missy Cornelius was no longer principal.

Grace Armbruster, yes, Beta Team's own Grace, took it as a personal challenge to rid the school of Missy's poor leadership. When Grace got an idea to do something, she kind of became a bulldog....NEVER letting go until achieving her goal. As Cornelius' third year was coming to a close, (or was it her second year, and it just SEEMED like she had been with us forever) Grace found a personal connection of hers, who worked in a gentler, adjacent school district to Brighton. It seems that the 'friend's' district was conducting a search to replace a retiring principal. Grace worked VERY hard to let the neighboring district believe that Missy was the perfect fit for their educational system. Armstrong must have done a tremendous job of selling because when the next school year began, Missy Cornelius was history to DeWitt.

It should be noted, that under the leadership of Cornelius, there were two bomb scares at DeWitt, and Missy had TEACHERS explore rooms, looking for the bombs before the authorities got there. I think she would have been thinking of herself as a hero IF she had her teachers find a bomb. We teachers just thought she was crazy....but we didn't expect to find any bombs, either, so we searched.....found nothing.

Also, there was a rumor that a student had brought a gun onto campus, so Missy, using her less-than professional style, TOLD Steve Lipinski and me to "Go to the playground and see if that student actually brought a gun to school."

We didn't find anything, and I am not even certain she reported the incident to any authorities. She was reckless, but Steve and I did what she asked. Neither of us were worried, back then, but in today's society that kind of dangerous demand could spell real trouble for a regular classroom teacher.

All I know is that when Missy left DeWitt, things got a bit calmer around DeWitt. Never heard what happened at her NEW school, though.

Before she left Brighton, Ms Cornelius had developed a good rapport with a woman in the District office named Evelyn Snook. Evelyn was in charge of ALL academics in the Brighton, and was just about as arrogant as Missy, when it came to promoting herself as a leader. I didn't really have a run-in with her until she, TOO, decided to show ALL the teachers in our district just how good a teacher she was.

By this time in my career, I was getting pretty tired of braggadocios women claiming to know, better than most teachers, how to teach in the classroom. I'm not sure what she taught when she was a classroom teacher, but the feeling I got was that she hadn't taught higher than 6th grade, and I am pretty sure she had never taught in an inner-city classroom.

On one particular opening day 'teachers welcome' meeting, which was held in the Wilhelm cafeteria that year, Snook challenged ANY teacher to allow her to teach a lesson at any grade level. She offered to teach any subject material, as well. I kept wondering how THAT was going to be an incentive for regular classroom teachers to get charged up for the coming school year.... her telling them that she could show how skilled she was in the classroom. To top it off, she said she would teach a one-week thematic unit....ONE WEEK!

Other teachers seemed as turned off as I was about her challenge, and I never heard of anyone taking her up on her week-long boast. I was curious, though, so about six weeks into the new school year, I decided to see what she had.

Her deal with me was be the same as Cornelius's deal. She would teach my 1st hour English class, on ANY topic of her choice, and I would sit in the back of the room, observe and take notes, and simulate HER lesson for my other five classes during the day.

To this day, I can NOT remember what her thematic unit was about....some sort of writing lesson, I believe, but she was WAY over the kids' heads, and I was just confused at her method.

After the first-day lesson, I worked at adapting some of HER lesson into MY lesson for the day. But, when I tried to emulate her work, the kids seemed confused. Snook used terms that were WAY above the junior high level of comprehension, especially in an Inner City classroom. My students were still trying to move beyond their first-of-the-year skill levels, which were closer to 5th or 6th grade achievement, and I remember Evelyn's material being WAY advanced for DeWitt 8th graders.

Needless to say, her 1st-hour class seemed lost, almost from the beginning. Evelyn didn't even explain what she was doing in their classroom, or what her objectives were with them. She, literally, introduced herself, and got right into the material. It was as if she thought she was teaching a gifted class, and believe, me, this class had very few, if any, gifted students in it.

They were nice kids, and being the first class of the day, they were pretty calm, behavior-wise. But, they got bored within minutes of the start of Snook's lesson, so they started to look around at their friends. That is when the whispering began. Evelyn Snook could hear them, when she was writing on the board, and would turn around and stop what she was doing while looking around the classroom at the students. The students got quiet when that happened. But the administrator never said a word about the talking she heard.

I, on the other hand, was taking notes, and when she stopped to 'stare' at the kids, I stopped to see what was going on. THEN, she turned toward the board and started writing AND explaining at the same time, again. She chose to write and explain while writing, as opposed to writing, then turning to the class and explaining her work. It was like she didn't want to interact with the students, which I considered poor teaching technique.

Some kids took a few notes. Some kids doodled on paper. Some kids passed notes, and whispered about social 'happenings' going on around DeWitt.

Evelyn must have stopped to stare three or four times, but she NEVER asked if there were any questions, or tried to get her kids involved verbally in what she was doing. She REFUSED to stop her presentation. It seemed like she was on a mission, and while stopping to stare seemed to annoy her. My feeling was that Ms Snook wanted that lesson completed, come Hell or high water.

Her second day was similar, and maybe a bit more noisy than the first. And, at the end of that first day, she left my classroom without, so much, as saying good-bye. Yep, when the bell rang to excuse the students to their next classes, she packed up her things as quickly as possible, then vanished within seconds. I considered that rude because I had some questions about her lesson of the day....after all, I was to teach the material for the rest of the day.

Just after the start of Homeroom, on the third day of Evelyn Snook's 'thematic teaching,' she asked me to come outside for a minute. We hadn't even done the Pledge of Allegience yet and I needed to take role, get lunch counts, etc. But I accommodated her wish to see me. She talked to me during the Pledge, which I, as a veteran, thought was not only rude (again) but unpatriotic, as well.

"Mr. Stein," she began, "I noticed that you didn't help me, these past two days, but I will need your help today. Today is the crux of my whole week....the most important lesson I give."

"How was I supposed to help you the first TWO days, Ms Snook?" I queried.

"When the students got unruly, I expected YOU to get them back into order," the administrator said in a VERY condescending manner.

"How do you propose I do that, Ms Snook?" I said, trying NOT to seem too offended by her tone.

"They are talking when I am teaching, Mr. Stein. I don't WANT them to be talking, or doing ANYTHING that isn't lesson-oriented. Do you understand me now?"

Well, THAT just pissed me off. "Ms Snook," I said, maintaining SOME measure of decorum, but wanting her to know what the situation really entailed. "You offered to teach in my class, for a week. Now, ANY substitute teacher, getting into a new classroom, knows that he or she MUST establish control with the kids. Without THAT, there is no learning going to take place. Sure, I could keep interrupting your lesson while asking the students to be quiet and pay attention.

I could even scold a couple of them or remove them from your class. Who do YOU think they are going to be paying attention to if I do that….you, or me? If you want them to constantly be looking back at me, to see that I am looking at them, than two things happen. One, I don't get to listen to you, and, Ms Snook, I am doing what I can to get your lesson across to five more classes each day. Secondly, the students will be more concerned about whether I am watching them, than they will be about learning what you are trying to teach them. If you are worried about their behavior in the class, then tell them what you need from them in order for them to learn. This is not a team-teaching situation. YOU need to take charge, and allow me to learn from you, as well." And with that, I thought I got my point across, even if I WAS condescending to an administrator.

To say the class was a disaster that day, is an understatement. Evelyn, not only DIDN'T take control of the room, she barely looked back at the class. She just kept writing and talking, and erasing, and writing and talking some more.

"All right," she said, FINALLY turning to talk to her class, though there were just a couple of minutes left in the period, "I have given you enough good information on this topic. You are to write a 200-word essay on what you have learned. Be as detailed as you can be. I'm sorry, but I won't be back again on Thursday or Friday, so consider this your final instruction from me. Turn them in to Mr. Stein tomorrow."

The class AND I were confused by her statement. I wanted to talk to her about what just happened, but the dismissal bell rang, and she nearly beat the kids out of the door. She definitely looked upset to me.

Springing that news, at the last possible moment, was terribly un-professional, in my opinion. She could have been upset, that is a given, but not communicating that she was down-sizing her experience from five days to three, WITHOUT expressing that notion to the class and me before the class started, was just wrong. One of the worst teaching exhibitions I have ever seen.

The kids, naturally, turned nothing in. The main comment was, 'What was she teaching?' I couldn't start over with HER class, let alone continue with my other five classes. The lessons Snook wrote on the board were complicated and confusing to me, too.

Her thematic unit was definitely a flop as it was un-finished. She was mad, I get that, but to quit in mid-stream....embarrassing. Besides, I didn't believe that what she was teaching was appropriate for 8th graders in the Brighton District. It seemed more geared for advanced students, and my kids were still trying to grasp the basics of sentence structure, punctuation, and the like. All Evelyn Snook did was put me behind three days, in MY lesson plans. Teach anything at any grade level, my ass!

It wasn't the last I heard on her visitation. Seems like she bad-mouthed me to ANYONE who would listen....mostly other administrators, but anyone else who would listen, too. She kept claiming that I 'wouldn't help her control the students in class.'

I heard that an assistant principal at another school, as well as other teachers who had heard about the incident, defended my hypothesis that SHE needed to establish control of the students, NOT the observing teacher.

I really didn't care what was said, or wrote up on me to put into my file in the District office. Evelyn Snook left Brighton the very next year, and I didn't even care where she went. It's true that administrators, in general, and I did NOT always see eye-to-eye, and I only dealt with them when I had to. I absolutely knew what had to be done to reach AND teach my students. My teaching technique was intuitive, as I have mentioned, NOT highly structured. But for the most part, I got the majority of my students to learn the necessary basics, which would ultimately allow them to succeed in both school and life.

11

DISCIPLINE GETS HELP

DISCIPLINE IS, HAS always been, and will always be, a primary concern for teachers at any grade level. There are recommendations that veteran teachers pass down to rookies. There are classes on how to deal with the misbehaved. And there are experts in the field who can show you how it is done.....Mr. X being an exception in the case of students at DeWitt.

A teacher, ANY teacher, will not know how he/she will react until the 'crisis' is right in front of him/her. I had a student teacher who, literally, refused to stand in front of the students to give a lesson. She had LOTS of problems....had no speaking skills, was terrified of having people staring at her, and, as she claimed, was so scared of any misbehaving that she was afraid she might have 'an accident' if one would arise. She asked me NUMEROUS times how to handle trouble-makers. She even witnessed me dealing with situations, from time to time. But she was nearly comatose when I told her it was part of her curriculum to have to teach at least one lesson in front of the class.

She panicked, froze, and I didn't pass her on her practicum. She already had a good job working for the city, but loved children. Why she picked junior high-aged kids to teach was beyond me.

I thought that was the last I would see of her. BUT, in the '90's, with many school districts struggling to find teachers to fill their classrooms, Brighton hired her as a 7th grade teacher....placing her on the more discipline-challenged Beta Team. Rumor had it that she would bribe the students with candy, and other eats, if they would behave in class and do their work.

She wasn't alone in her use of unacceptable discipline techniques. DeWitt, which I considered a hell-hole during its first two years of existence, needed something to be done in developing a better discipline plan for our campus. It was 8th grade Beta Team member Steve Lipinski who came up with a great idea, a comcept where students would help the school by disciplining themselves. He MAY have heard of this method from somewhere, but he worked out his own specifications as to how it would work.

It has to be noted, that there was SOME sort of discipline being used at DeWitt, even from the start of that first year. No, it wasn't provided by Howard Boyd, he of the vanishing-when-needed act. Teachers could definitely NOT depend on him for support. Likely knowing of Boyd's vanishing act, the Brighton District did a smart thing. It asked the city of Phoenix to assign an SRO to be on DeWitt's campus. This meant our school would have a REAL police officer around to deal with extraordinary discipline situations. And we teachers were relieved to have help. Some of the officers were good, some not so good, but isn't that the way in any profession? At least we had a cop around, if we needed one, to handle criminal situations.

When DeWitt first opened, the school's BEST bet for discipline, however, lay with Mary Finnegan, who had been hired on as our vice-principal, and whose job it was to be the administrator in CHARGE of most of the discipline at DeWitt. She was fabulous! Most times during the day, there would be one or two students sitting outside her office, awaiting turns to plead their cases related to teacher misbehavior referrals. Mary was a defender of the teacher, having been one in her past, and students hated to see her, knowing there would be little chance of them being able to talk their way out of most situations.

But, Mary couldn't handle every problem, as teachers were sending her students for all KINDS of problems, including 'piddly' infractions like gum chewing, throwing trash on the ground, etc. She NEEDED to curb the tardiness, fights, and other REALLY anti-school infractions. And the Beta Team knew she wouldn't be around long if she didn't get some help.

Lipinski devised a system called the Student Court. While his concept was fairly simple, it was time-consuming. When Steve was ready to ask about starting up his project, he knew he would have to be able to teach Student Court as one of his Civics classes. And for the system to work, he would have to have the privilege of selecting top 8th graders, from both Alpha and Beta teams to serve as student judges., Also, Steve would be asking to bring a few 7th graders into his 8th grade class, so they could observe procedures and learn how the system worked, in order to create a foundation for the following year's class.

The objective of Student Court was to alleviate the school's principals from having to spend so much time on discipline issues. Mary Finnegan, in particular, was being bogged down with 'minor' infractions, which quite frankly was a waste of her time. The Court would take it upon itself to handle such offenses as littering, gum chewing, students using obscene language on campus, disrespect of one student toward another student, and EVEN disrespect of a student toward a teacher, in a few cases. Steve wanted his student judges to help clear the school of inappropriate behaviors, as best they could.

When most teachers heard about his idea, they loved it. So he approached Missy Cornelius, during her first year at DeWitt, and proposed his plan. She, however, wasn't so sure if Steve's idea was 'best for the school,' as she put it. "How successful can kids possibly be when trying to discipline their peers?" she asked Lipinski.

"The judges would be wearing black robes, which will give them the appropriate LOOK of judges who sit in most every court in the country. And judges' black robes are known by most American people to be symbols of respect. Just wearing them will set MY judges apart from offending students being brought into Court," Steve responded. "I won't be selecting weaklings to be judges, Missy, but kids who are not afraid to face their peers and dole out punishment....kids with strong character, who can not be bullied."

"Punishment?" Missy inquired, "How could they dole out punishment to other students?"

"Just like the courts downtown do, Missy. It's people facing consequences for their actions. Yes, my students are still only kids, and NOT learned law instructors turned real judges. BUT most of the students at DeWitt know right from wrong. My students, again, donning black robes giving them more respectability, will be able to dole out appropriate punishments....I'm certain of that. And I will be in the room to insure that proper respect is given."

"What offenses could kids rule on over other kids? What punishment could they dole out that the offenders would accept? This sounds like a farce to me. The tough kids will eat the judges up, and you will have riots in your class, Mr. Lipinski." And Ms Cornelius got up to leave the room to go....who knows, she just WASN'T going to accept Steve's idea.

"I can promise you I will NOT let the atmosphere of my court room be reduced to chaos. My judges will not just give the appearance of professionalism; they will HANDLE all cases with complete decorum. The student infractions my kids will deal with will include gum chewing, tardiness to class, being out of class WITHOUT a pass, cafeteria disruptions, littering, graffiti, bus violations, spitting, rock throwing, even kids jumping the fence at lunch, so they can leave the schoolgrounds to eat somewhere else. The judges will also be able to give appropriate consequences for reckless horseplay, trash talking which might eventually lead to fights, over-familiarization on grounds....things that would include inappropriate touching, or kissing, and even hugging on campus. DeWitt students know they are NOT allowed to do these things at school. But when they DO disregard any of those rules, my kids will be able deal with it appropriately."

Ms Cornelius had stopped to listen to Lipinski's soliloquy. "My judges will ALSO be able to handle obscene language on grounds, and disrespect toward adults on campus....especially toward teachers. My idea is to alleviate you, Mary and the SRO person from having to deal with so many, I'll call them, 'benign' behaviors, so you can deal with the more serious infractions."

"My court can really help EVERYBODY here at DeWitt. The only thing we would REALLY need, however, would be support from you. If we have an absolutely unruly student, that neither the judges nor I can handle in my classroom court set-up, I would need to know that I can get support from you and the front office backing us up 100%. Your total support would give my students the credence they need to follow through with the doling out of proper consequences to offenders." Then Steve finished his argument, and tried to read the perplexed look on his principal's face.

"How many judges did you say you needed for your court?" the principal queried, then she began tapping two fingers to her lips.

"I expect to have seven judges sitting on any case, while I will have seven other students acting as bailiffs, court scribes, record filers, or doing whatever else needs to be done to make it a functional courtroom setting. I don't mind increasing the class size for my other Civics classes, and I have talked to the rest of the Beta Team and they are behind this completely, even willing to increase each of THEIR class loads by a few students during that hour, if necessary." Steve answered with confidence that he had covered all the bases, and had given a strong case for his innovative class.

"Mr. Lipinski," Missy Cornelius started, "while the idea might SOUND fine to others, I can tell you as a former teacher myself, NO teacher willingly wants to increase class size. Having larger classes diminishes the learning environment. Your team is saying they will sacrifice, and they may even mean it, and you may be willing to increase your classes, too, but the learning process WILL be affected and that could possibly create more stress for you and your teammates. Also, how do the offending students, being asked to report to YOUR classroom, get to the court during that time period?"

"Bailiffs will seek them out in their individual classes for that hour, BUT no student will be gone for the entire hour. My bailiffs will get them to court and return them to class. We're talking three students a day out of class for just a third of their class period time…. that's all." Steve was getting a bit frustrated at Cornelius's lack of enthusiasm, but he knew she had to be given thorough details of the plan.

The principal, who was also exhibiting frustration with the conversation, said with some derision in her voice, "You're asking me to condone students being out of their learning environment, and that is a no-no in my book. I want you to know that. All right, Mr. Lipinski, tell me what kind of punishments your judges would be issuing."

"Hand-written apologies to any person offended will be a must, but they have to be written in an absolutely sincere tone. There will be other punishments given, too, like cleaning gum from the premises….off sidewalks, and from under student desks. This chore will be done during lunch; thus, students will be losing their free time. That would be a task the offending students would not enjoy doing often. And for those students using foul language, they will be called to my room during lunch, then they would make phone calls to their families, telling them exactly what they had said, and the circumstances surrounding it. Ms Cornelius, the punishments will be commensurate to the crime. Nobody will be picked on. All I want to try to do is make life easier around here, for teachers, students, and administration. Controlling behavior is a key, and this plan will work, if you give it a chance."

"Mr. Lipinski," the principal continued, speaking in an even more disagreeable tone, "you say you need MY support if you get a student your kids can't handle? I can tell you, right now, that I would have many more things, which would need attending, than to be 'on call' when you need me cleaning up a mess occurring in YOUR court. Ms Finnegan has a full slate of offenders to deal with, and the SRO has his hands full, too. THEN there is a question of what can legally be done BY students TO other students as far as discipline is concerned. It's just a quagmire. I can't accept the responsibility." And with that, Ms Cornelius abrunptly turned, wishing to leave Steve's classroom, where the meeting had taken place.

"Wait!" Lipinski implored, "What if I can get Mary Finnegan to accept the responsibility of working with consequences doled out by my judges? Can you allow the class to be a go if SHE is willing to back up Student Court?"

"She's a VERY busy person, Mr. Lipinski," The principal remarked in a rude tone.

"But, IF Mary accepts the responsibility, AND is willing to assist me with 'tough' cases, can YOU accept my plan?"

Ms Cornelius, showing great exasperation, both in voice and body movement, (think deep sigh here) looked at Steve and said, "If Mary Finnegan backs your plan, and takes the heat when parents start calling to complain about what is being done to their kids. AND, you don't interfere with the learning process of other teachers during that time, then I will turn a blind eye. I want it on record that I am NOT in favor of your Student Court."

Mary Finnegan was more than happy to welcome Steve's plan. She felt that ANY plan that could lighten her discipline load was a good thing. She rationalized that if SHE received a cantankerous kid, sent to her by the Court, then she would deal with it like any other behavior problem that comes to her, which meant she would be calling the parents to inform them of the consequences of the offender's behavior.

The 8th grade Beta Team was not surprised when Cornelius' chose to reject Steve's plan. We figured she wouldn't recognize a good behavioral plan if it kicked her in the ass, PLUS, she didn't much like ideas that weren't hers.

I know she wasn't MY biggest fan and Steve Lipinski was a lot like me, in that he didn't follow the straight and narrow, strictly using 'by the book' instructions. Missy Cornelius must have thought he would fail miserably, with his court class which would result in HER being dragged onto the carpet for trying to defend such a 'terrible idea.'

Other teachers loved the idea, and were very cooperative, too. They sent referrals for the Student Court to handle.... sometimes sending too many nuisance referrals, many of which were NOT taken up in the Court. But, by and large, they sent some good, eye-witness-backed accounts of poor behavioral judgement errors by students, and Steve's court handled them well.

Cornelius was soon gone, and the school's new principals applauded Lipinski's court and all the good work they did.

The judges were always top students, and took pride in being selected for that class. Steve DID, however, have to constantly remind his judges about taking themselves too seriously outside of class. They were still, after all, students at DeWitt, and should act accordingly when they were outside of their Student Court classroom. Their behavior, too, was monitored like any other student's, and they could be subjected to hearings if they misbehaved. Most of the judges were well-liked outside of the classroom, so there was never any 'revenge' taken on them for judgments they made on offenders.

Before I leave this chapter, I have to tell you about one interesting incident that happened to the Student Court.

An egotistical 'gifted' student was written up by one of his teachers during the Court's first year of existence, as he was disrespectful in the classroom. Naturally, the offended teacher wrote the young 'entitled' student up with a Student Court referral. Steve's judges decided to hear the case in an attempt to get this kid straight on proper classroom etiquette.

While hestating, at first, to be led to Lipinski's class by the Court's student bailiff, the student, FINALLY, made an angry decision and have his day in court. I believe his intent was to make a mockery of the class. And, upon hearing that he would have to write a 'sincere,' and 'heart-felt' apology, the self-grandizing kid refused to comply, promptly telling the seven judges that he had a deep distain for THEM as well as the teacher who wrote him up.

The peer judges informed the arrogant student that if he DIDN'T comply with his 'punishment' that he would find himself deeper in trouble than he should be. After all, disrespect toward ANYONE is never a good thing, and it was explained to him that all he had to do was to 'remember where you are,' (in a school setting) and 'act civilly' to your classmates and teachers.

The student, once again, indicated he would do NO apology, and again expressed distain for the school's court system.

At this point Steve Lipinski went to Mary Finnegan, to feel her out about intervening if necessary. Mary, true to her word, indicated she would back the Court completely in its judgment on the matter.

This would prove somewhat difficult, however, since the snotty kid was the son of a Brighton District Board member, who coddled her two children to the point where it was easy to see why this bright kid was as spoiled as he was.

The meeting between Mary and the Board member went as poorly as expected, and the day after the fateful meeting, the brat's FATHER gave Steve a visit. The dad was so irate that he promised to 'Bring this kangaroo court down,' expressing HIS outrage at having his son being judged by other students. The dad even threatened Mr. Lipinski saying he would 'Take action' in some way, and finishing with, "This is no idle threat, either!" The father had a friend, who was a legitimate judge in one of Phoenix's municipal courts. Dear old Dad asked his 'friend' to sit in on one of Steve's classes, with the intent of finding any illegalities, or ANY flaws that could prove the DeWitt Student Court to be a sham. The hell-bent-for-leather dad was determined to have Steve's Student Court class eliminated from the curriculum.

When Lipinski's class finished their court session for the day, Steve awaited judgement from his 'guest.'

The verdict came in, and it was just fine. The judge not only DIDN'T deride the program, he indicated that, in his personal opinion, DeWitt's court system had GREAT merit, and was run beautifully (and I'm guessing legally, too) by Lipinski and his student judges. Furthermore, the visiting judge had PARTICULAR praise for the student judges he saw in action that day, AND the decorum in which the atmosphere existed. He heaped praise on Steve for his ideas, too, which was a great relief for Steve, the student judges, and Mary Finnegan, as well, as SHE had gone to bat for the program all the way.

Bottom line, the arrogant kid DID write an apology letter to the person he offended. It may not have been as 'heart-felt' as Steve and his kids wanted, but hey, a victory is a victory.

This case helped prove that DeWitt's court system worked. While it was developed to deal with the KNOWN boisterous and mischevious students, who had developed reputations as trouble makers, ANY student could end up in Student Court....even those who didn't think their shit stank.

Whether the arrogant kid was embarrassed, or just learned a good lesson by having to write an apology, I didn't observed him displaying his usual haughtiness around school....at least not verbally. Don't misunderstand me, he maintained his 1%, I'm one of the 'entitled' people in this school, attitude through actions, (nose in the air, talk to me only if I talk to you, attitude) he just didn't express his conceit verbally. And I feel certain his QUIET smugness was appreciated by everyone at DeWitt.

That boy remained a top student academically, and I hope he DID become successful in his lifetime. But, for one brief, shining moment, he was made to 'face the music,' thanks to Steve, his student judges, Mary Finnegan, and a forward-thinking REAL judge.

DeWitt's Student Court handled hundreds of cases, in the seven years Steve and I remained teachers there. Buoyed by its success, Lipinski even presented his working plan to other schools, in hopes any of them might be inspired to follow suit. And I believe I heard that one or two schools gave the Lipinski 'court system' a whirl. All I really DO know is that the DeWitt Student Court was a well-oiled system, and helped control MANY offensive acts in our school, and I want to say THANK-YOU, Steve, for your vision.

By the mid-1990's, chaos at DeWitt had begun to get tamed, and that allowed teachers to TRY to have some interaction with one another. There were breakfasts planned, and while there weren't many of them, they were ALL fun. Usually, those breakfasts were tied into the Christmas spirit, and Secret Santa was involved, too.

But fun events were few and far in between, and the faculty just WASN`T as close as they needed to be in order to help one another through each and every tough day.....and it is hard to remember a day when there WEREN`T some tough moments on campus. The problem, as I saw it, was the lack of a comfortable, private, teachers` lounge. Wilhelm had spoiled me, and several of the OTHER veteran teachers, as to how teachers can get together, relax, and have some fun while getting ready for the day. DeWitt never seemed to acquire that same atmosphere, so teachers went to the mailroom/lounge area, saw the starkness and emptiness of the room, and went to their rooms to contemplate how to do their best WITHOUT camaraderie being a useful tool to start the day. Each day was becoming more boring than the last, and that lowered morale immensely amongst staff members.

I found myself visiting with Steve Lipinski before each day. He and I had a bond that was borne at Wilhelm. We kept each other moving ahead with as positive vibes as we could, and for the most part, that was effective. We tried to keep things light around campus as well….joking with other teachers, and kidding around with some of the more affable students. By the mid-'90's neither of us was coaching, so that was a deterrent to fun. What we DID have, however, was one day when we decided to shake things up around DeWitt. I'm not quite sure of the year, but it was a classic April Fool's joke that made THAT year memorable….in a positive way.

Oh, both he and I were notorious for our April Fool's antics, and teachers steered clear of us on that particular day each year, ESPECIALLY those teachers with whom we taught at Wilhelm. The gags we pulled THERE were tame, but people were wary when they got onto the Wilhelm campus. Sometimes Steve and I worked as a team, sometimes we pulled individual acts of tomfoolery, but we LOVED April 1st.

One of my top pranks was done at Wilhelm, and two teachers were my targets. In the end, however, I got caught in the prank, too, and had to pay the consequences.

For the gag to work, I had to obtain a Master Key from the secretary, and when she heard what I had in mind, she gladly acquiesced.

I then, quickly, went to Ginger Geiger's room to ask her to join me in some fun. My request was simple enough....just let me use her empty classroom (her children were at specialty classes that hour) to have my students transport Sam Armstrong's fixed-wing desks (his students were, likewise engaged elsewhere) to her room. I convinced Ginger that I would have my students come retrieve the desks once Sam opened his door where he and his students would notice nothing but a bare room for science.

She thought that sounded funny, too, but asked again if I could not wait TOO long to get Sam's desks out of her room, as she had a lesson for that day that couldn't be altered. Hey, what day was it? I said 'sure,' and when Sam was out of his room and heading toward the lounge, my students went into action.

Thirty-nine, single unit desks (table and chair welded together) were moved from the 8th grade section of the campus, into Ms Geiger's room in the 7th grade section of the school. Her room was located behind the 8th grade wing, but Armstrong's and MY rooms were two rows away from her. I could, however, look out my classroom windows and see the door to her room.

My kids were quick and efficient. As the last desk was being put into her, suddenly, VERY crowded room, Ginger again reminded me, and quite sternly I might add, to remember and come get the desks just as SOON as Sam Armstrong saw his empty room. Again, she must have forgotten what day it was as she had NO idea SHE would be a target of the gag, too.

Toward the end of my class, however, it started to rain, and quite heavily, too. The bell rang, meaning it was time for students to begin reporting to their next hour's classrooms. I stood under the building's eave, staying dry, allowing my kids to enter my classroom quietly. Obviously, they were not aware of what my last class of students had done with Armstrong's desks. I watched, too, as Sam's kids lined up outside his door. They realized that they had to wait for him to get to his room and unlock it before they were allowed to enter.

Sam arrived a tad late, which I thought was a good thing for that day. But when he opened up his room and peered inside, he immediately closed the door, turned to his class, and said, "We'll have class in the library today." And they were gone in a flash. Sam knew what was happening, and rolled with the punches. The same can NOT be said of Ginger.

I began my class, and I could SEE Ginger opening her door, again and again, expecting MY students to be headed to her class in order to clear her over-crowded room of desks. There was NO way she could teach her many students, with a room filled with desks, and I saw the frustration on her face.....for SEVERAL minutes.

But, that girl was smart, and rain or no rain, (and it had begun to rain even more heavily) she held the door open while her students began flinging Sam's desks ONTO the amphitheater grass. Without a single glance at my room, she shut the door, and did her lesson plan for the day.

Naturally, when the rain slackened, I had my kids retrieve the desks, and replace them back to Sam's room. My students enjoyed hauling those desks around, and even getting a little wet. We still got work done in class, thankfully. However, word got around about my ATTEMPT at a classic April's Fool's joke on Ginger and Sam, only to have it backfire on me, too. That lightened the mood around Wilhelm for the rest of the day.

Getting the secretary's involvement in more serious April Fool's pranks is a must, and those gals never let us pranksters down. However, it was more than difficult to pull any serious pranks at DeWitt, without gaining the ire of administration, as THEY wanted to have complete control over EVERYTHING in their schools. Most of DeWitt's head honchos could be real sticks-in-the-mud, as far as I was concerned. On the other hand, Wilhelm principals usually chose to turn an eye when pranks were pulled....as long as nobody got hurt or complained.

One year, at DeWitt, a new teacher came aboard the 8th grade staff. He was an Alpha Team member, so we didn't see much of him during the day. However, outside of the class setting, the new young teacher, Steve Lipinski and I got along famously. He appreciated Steve and me being his friend, even acting as his mentors in several instances, and we two experienced teachers were more than happy to 'train' our new protégé into the art of surviving a tough environment.

But, on April 1st of his first year at DeWitt, Steve and I wanted to let him know he was vulnerable to pranks like everybody else. So, Lipinski and I devised a classic prank, especially suited for that young and impressionable newby.

William Tweed (he liked Willie) was his name, and Steve and I had asked him to join us when we went to play golf on occasion, as well as invite him to join us on most Fridays when the faculty would go to a happy hour someplace. Generally, he hung out with us whenever he could, kind of like a kid brother. Steve and I enjoyed his sense of humor, too, as it matched ours. And, as the year progressed, it was uncanny how much Willie reminded, both Steve and me, of US when we were young teachers at Wilhelm. But we felt he needed a little initiation to remind him that WE were still his elders.

Willie was married, and unfortunately for him, told Steve and me that his wife was due to deliver their first baby during the early part of April. Willie trusted us enough to tell us about how precise he and wife were in their preparations in packing hospital clothing, calling the doctor, getting to the CORRECT hospital, etc, etc. As late March approached, that kid was making himself a nervous wreck. To Lipinski and me, Willie had become the perfect pigeon for a prank on April Fool's Day.

We enlisted our secretary into the plot, as usual. Quite simply, on April 1st, at a certain hour of the day, she was to call him with the news that his wife had gone into labor, and was headed to the hospital. Here's how the scheme unfolded.

"Mr. Tweed," our cohort in crime said after calling into his room over the intercom, "your wife just called and wanted me to let you know that she thinks this is the time for the baby's arrival, and she wants you to hurry to the hospital. But she wants you to drive safely, telling me she will have the doctor wait for you before having the delivery procedure commence. Mr. Stein is on his way to your room right now, and will watch them so you can leave immediately."

"What hospital?" Willie shouted at the intercom. Apparently his wife was to call the doctor when she felt the 'time had come,' and their doctor would direct her to whichever hospital he was working that day, as he had privileges at a couple of hospitals.

The secretary was a bit flustered, but got her cool back while responding, "Your wife didn't say, but I'm sure you can figure it out."

At that point, she hung up and tied up ALL the school phone lines so Willie COULDN'T call outside the school to verify the hospital his wife was headed.

When I arrived at his room, he was frantically packing his briefcase. Papers were flying EVERYWHERE! "What's up, Mr. Tweed? The secretary just called me and asked me to get here to take over your class. She said you had an emergency or something."

"My wife is headed to the hospital to have our baby, but I'm not sure what hospital she went to. We have two that we told out doctor is fine for the birth. But the secretary couldn't tell me which one to go to, AND all the lines are busy so I can't call out! I have to just go to one, and if she isn't there, go to the other one. What a MESS!"

And with that, young Mr. Tweed was flying out the door, papers STILL appearing to fall out of his briefcase.

"Kids," I asked, "What is today's date?"

"April 1st," one student said, and then ALL of them started to laugh.

"His wife ISN'T having the baby is she, Mr. Stein?" another student chimed in. "You're just pulling a joke on him, huh?"

"That's right. Mr. Lipinski is waiting by his car, and will get the opportunity to say 'April Fools' to him. But, he will be coming back here, and YOU have the chance to say 'April Fools to him, too. Just be nice. Having a baby is a very serious thing, and he may be upset, or embarrassed, so just say it and don't rub it in. He's a good guy, right? So, you being kind to him may be important to some of you, as Mr. Lipinski and I will be asking a lot of you to join us on the California Trip. Mr. Tweed needs to tell us who HE thinks would be fine to go. You upset him, and, well, he may remember those of you who went beyond a simple statement of 'April Fool's' and tortured him about the prank."

They nodded in the affirmative, and Willie entered the door shortly thereafter. He stood in the doorway, with a sheepish grin on his face. The class yelled 'April Fools,' and Tweed explained what happened in the parking lot. "I was racing to get to my car," he started, "And when I saw my car, Mr. Lipinski was standing by it. He asked what happened, and I told him about the 'call,' and the confusion I was having. AND I was fumbling to get the key into the lock. But I was so nervous I couldn't do it."

"Do you know what today's date is, Mr. Tweed?" Mr. Lipinski asked, I told him it was April 1st." Mr. Lipinski then asked if I knew what happened on April 1st. All of a sudden I realized he was pulling a joke on me, so I hit him in the shoulder with my bag. He says you are in this, too, Mr. Stein"

"Welcome to the staff, Mr. Tweed," I said before slipping around him to head out the door. There was still a little laughter to be heard when I did leave, but Willie was smiling and even laughing at himself for falling for the gag.

Ironically, his wife gave birth to a son the very next Saturday, and Willie Tweed was with her....at the correct hospital. Willie only stayed at DeWitt one more year, as he decided that he couldn't provide for his wife and child, financially, the way he wanted to provide for them...not with a starting teacher's salary, at least. He was gone from Brighton District after just two years, and Steve and I missed him.

In order for a job to be fun, there has to be SOME release of stress. I enjoyed many of the students I taught, throughout the years, but I needed interaction with teachers, too. DeWitt didn't provide enough inter-teacher interaction, AND the students attending were MUCH more aloof than were those at Wilhelm. Suddenly, my job wasn't fun anymore, and I found myself begging for an opportunity to early retire. I was just plain unhappy during my waning years at DeWitt.

12

First it Drags, Then It's Over

Pᴇᴏᴘʟᴇ ɪɴᴛᴇʀᴘʀᴇᴛ ᴍᴇᴍᴏʀɪᴇs in different ways. There are those negative souls who wish to remember only the tough times in their lives. Not only does that give them the 'woe is me' attention they crave, but the 'see how tough things were, but I survived' persona through which folk lore thrives. Polyanna-types ONLY want to remember the good times....the 'life is just a bowl of cherries' thoughts, which serve to help THEM mask the tradegies of their pasts. Though remembering the good is preferable, re-telling the tough times, however, has always served as a cathartic release for me. Life is full of the good and the bad, and nobody can go back and change them. But regaling both in combination can make for interesting stories. Graduations were ALWAYS supposed to be fun....but not every time, and not for everyone.

Growing up in Iowa City, I only experienced one grade school graduation, my high school graduation. In Phoenix, it seemed like graduations were happening at all ages. There were even kindergarten graduations at certain schools, which was beyond my scope of understanding. For Brighton District, the 8th grade graduation was a big deal.

In my early days teaching at Wilhelm, graduations always seemed rife with emotions. Our school's 8th grade teachers seemed to build a special report with many individual students every year. Therefore, graduations found students happy to be moving into high school, but sad to be leaving the teachers, with whom they had grown fond.

Our little neighborhood school was so special for some students, that it was not unusual for several of them to come back for a visit at least once or twice during their freshmen year. I'm not sure if visiting junior high teachers has always been common with other grade schools in the Phoenix area, but with Wilhelm students it was usual. I remember NEVER wanting to visit my junior high teachers after I left, but maybe that was just me.

Even as I write this book, students from the 1975-'76 8th grade class are looking to have a reunion, with both students AND teachers, next month. Yep, Wilhelm developed some VERY special bonds.

That school had some very entertaining graduation nights, too. I remember one of our two state senators coming back from Washington D.C. and giving a keynote speech for the out-going 8th graders. In the middle of his speech, however, a student who had been assigned to attend summer school, streaked right in front of our surprised guest speaker. Everybody laughed, and that kid became the 'butt' of jokes for the rest of the evening....especially soliciting comments about his 'short-comings.' But, in the end, that student DID get the attention he sought.

We had a Tony-winning Broadway star, a former Wilhelm student, give a heart-warming speech, and I enjoyed watching Sam Armstrong beaming with pride, as she had been a student in his homeroom.

Here, however, is where I have to mention a flaw with BOTH Sam Armstrong and Alex Fenstemaker during Wilhelm graduations. It was tradition, in Brighton District, that homeroom teachers call their own students to the podium as diplomas were handed out. At every single one of our graduations, though, it was almost a sure bet that either Sam or Alex (more likely BOTH) would have trouble remembering the names of all of their students. Neither had trouble covering up their faux paxs, however, so nobody complained.

One year, as an example, Sam had a VERY popular kid, of Native American decent, lined up and ready to come forward to receive his diploma. Armstrong froze for a second, then said, "Come on, Chief, you're next." In today's 'politically correct' frame of mind, that might cause a major incident. But, at THAT graduation, the young man just smiled, and walked forward to shake hands while getting his diploma. Then HE hesitated, briefly, just before moving toward his teacher and giving his mentor a big hug. In the '70's and early '80's, many teachers, students AND parents came to expect Wilhelm to be an extension of the family. I believed the 'hug' exemplified that concept.

From the mid-eighties forward, however, Wilhelm was going through a major socio-economic change. Dress codes in school, itself, began changing.

During my first several years as a Wilhelm teacher, I witnessed the school's more affluent families dressing their sons and daughters in expensive clothing for graduations.

However, as the wealthier families began leaving our district, the graduation dress code changed, too. Oh, the families of girl graduates still found ways to to make their daughters look like princesses, but the boys were becoming more casual in dress....a nice shirt and a good pair of pants became quite acceptable.

As dress changed, so it seemed that educational values were changing, too. For many of my students, graduation from high school had become THE dream, which made getting through 8th grade an even bigger deal then I ever imagined.

Let me state here that during MY up-bringing, getting through high school was expected, and successfully getting through the University of Iowa was most students' dream. While college graduation was the goal of every Iowa City kid in the '60's and '70's, sadly, graduation from HIGH SCHOOL seemed to be the primary goal of Phoenix's Inner City children from the 1980's until I retired.

It was easy to see that money had become a problem for several Wilhelm families, even in the later 1970's, but I STILL wanted to believe that the kids I taught should continue the dream of going to college. I had paid my own way through college, and my family didn't have ANY 'college money,' couldn't Brighton's college-bound kids chip in a little?

However, money was so much of a problem by the early '90's, more than half my students were on free or reduced lunches. MY goals changed with the times, too. If my students couldn't dream past a high school doploma, then my PRIME goal became teaching English skills well enough, not only to get my kids INTO high school, but through their 12th grade graduation.

Reality, about money being a MAJOR concern for Brighton families, first struck me during the graduation of 1984. (might have been 1985, I can't really remember which year) During the morning of the graduation, all the Wilhelm 8th grade homerooms had their students practice receiving diplomas. Everyone in MY homeroom seemed happy and excited about the ceremony scheduled for that evening.

However, when night DID come, and the school's graduation was about to commence, I became aware that one of my homeroom kids hadn't shown up for the ceremony. When he came to school the next day, to sign year books, etc., I asked him why he didn't walk across the stage and get his diploma. He said, "I wanted to come, but I didn't have proper clothes to wear for graduation. I would have been embarrassed. I want to go to high school and graduate, too, but I also have to try and get a job so I can help my mom pay the bills. I'm sorry I wasn't with our class last night, Mr. Stein."

I was stunned with his frankness, and my eyes welled up. I just hugged that young man, and all I could say was, "You should have come to me yesterday afternoon. I would have found you clothes to wear."

Later that day, I approached Alex Fenstemaker and explained how sad I was about what happened to my student. He told me that he had been talking to his graduating students about graduation clothing for the past several years. He even claimed to have given some of his OWN clothes to a couple of needy boys for past graduations. (Alex was a smallish man in stature)

After that year, it was the school nurse who got help for students needing graduation clothing, so no Wilhelm graduate ever missed the important ceremony again, while I was there. I believe DeWitt's nurses took care of graduation students, too, as I don't remember EVER having a student miss that school's ceremonies for lack of clothing.

DeWitt had one interesting difference at graduation from Wilhelm, which caused MAJOR problems for our district. Since there were three times more graduates at DeWitt than the neighborhood school, finding a venue, capable of holding all students and their families, was a constant challenge. Wilhelm only needed seating for approximately 300-350 people. The school's amphitheater, which created a beautiful setting, was pushed to its capacity limit EVERY year....but it DID work.

To have ITS graduates and families witness graduations, DeWitt always needed room for MORE than 1000 people. After the initial graduation, Brighton found itself having to compete with high schools for arenas large enough to hold a small city.

DeWitt had a natural amphitheater, like Wilhelm, which is where the 1991 graduation took place. But that natural setting was no match for the estimated 1400 people that came to witness the school's first graduation. The school had even thought of giving a certain amount of tickets to students, trying to limit the size of the crowd. But THAT was a disaster, too.

The amphitheater ended up being MORE than packed, as many extra family members AND friends attended simply by walking through the open gates. There weren't NEARLY enough chairs.... not even for the amount of tickets that were handed out, so people had to stand where they could find room. Seeing the stage became a bit of a problem for a lot of people, for sure, and the background noise created by all those people, standing EVERYWHERE, began drowning out the guest speakers.

To make things even more miserable, I remember it being particularly hot that evening. So hot, in fact, that I sweated right through my suit, and was drenched by the time the ceremony ended. I guessed I lost five pounds in water weight that night. At DeWitt, teachers did NOT call their homerooms forward to receive diplomas, and that was good. I had HUGE sweat stains under both arms, AND in the crotch area, and I most certainly didn't want to display them in front of....well, ANYONE!

I was in on ONE interesting event, however, that occurred midway through the program. I ended up having a seat by the amphitheater stage wall. The back entrance to the school, which came directly into the amphitheater, was less than fifty feet to my rear. We were having a major speech being given, when a fellow comes walking onto the grounds via that back entrance. He was dressed in old tattered clothing, and seemed DEFINITELY inebriated. Many homeless people wandered the busy streets near our urban school, so I just assumed that fella to be one of them.

"Whash goin' on here?" the elderly man inquired in a garbled, NOT-so-low voice.

I quickly got to my feet, and got to the man before he could walk onto the stage. Grabbing his arm, and gently turning him away from the crowd, I said quietly, "Come with me, and I will tell you." I led him back OUT the gated entrance, closed the gate, and he was sent merrily on his way, and he seemed COMPLETELY satisfied when I told him it was a private party for invited guests only.

There were NO more year-end ceremonies held at the DeWitt amphitheater, But every graduation, from that point forward, was usually a mess, too. The second year was a doozy, as we found ourselves having to compete with OTHER large schools, especially high schools, for venues to hold graduations.

For the 2nd year of DeWitt's graduation, Brighton got fortunate and reserved the theater building at the community college bordering our school district's boundary. But since that college was ALSO in the Inner City, there arose a different problem for us to face.

First, the theater's auditorium could only allow, at any one time, a limited amount of people inside to witness the ceremonies....its fire code would be strictly enforced. So, BOTH the Beta Team and the Alpha Team wouldn't be able to graduate at the same time. It was decided, and I am guessing by the administration, that Beta would graduate second. That meant my team, with its students, teachers and families, had to stand around outside.... again in extreme heat, and wait until the Alpha Team was finished receiving diplomas. (including ALL the speeches, too, I might add) However, there was more to worry about outside than just the heat and the waiting.

We're talking the early 1990's here, in a tough part of the city. While Beta Team was waiting outside, local gangs were seen entering the campus. Actually, some of OUR kids, who belonged to the various gangs, had invited their 'friends' to join them for a visit before the Beta ceremony. It should also be noted, however, that the rival gangs were just that, rivals, so things became tense almost immediately between them.

Add to that, the fact that the OLDER gang members, from BOTH gangs began 'checking out' the girls from our Beta Team. My fellow teachers and I asked for security to come to our area, as we were certain a major incedent was about to develop. Security personnel were just a couple of old rent-a-cops, and they knew they would be over-matched if trouble came. The police were then called, and JUST as they were arriving, Alpha was being dismissed from the auditorium and Beta was being asked to enter the building. EVERYBODY was gone by the time the Beta Team ceremony was finished....thankfully. However, the situation outside had become a bit scary just prior to us being allowed to enter the building, and THAT was for certain.

Yes, I remember both the good AND the bad during my teaching years in Brighton. For the most part, however, when it comes to remembering graduations, I tend to remember, mostly, happiness.

The mid-'90's turned into the late-'90's, and I remember the days seeming MUCH longer at DeWitt than what I remembered at Wilhelm. Facing the students was becoming a chore instead of a pleasure, and I started counting each and every day, WAITING until I had enough time in the classroom to qualify for an early retirement package. I could only pray that Brighton would offer one, soon, as I REALLY began feeling burned out.

It wasn't the student population, per se, that was dimishing my spirit. In fact, the problem children seemed to plateau. By the third year at DeWitt, both Alpha and Beta teams were getting closer and closer to having equal shares of troubled students and outstanding students in their respective classrooms.

I came to realize that 'higher' education WASN'T the priority for the majority of the families in our district. Learning the 'basics,' well enough to pass onto the next grade level, seemed to be the goal for our parents and kids. I saw very little motivation, by any district patron, to want to learn anything beyond the simplest of educational skills, and I was depressed with that notion.

Oh, there was still a small core of bright students, and it was a pleasure to have them in class. But, far and away, the majority of kids that I taught at DeWitt, during the later years of my career, seemed just content to survive the classroom, and move into a high school.

Certainly, parents expressed to me a DESIRE for their children to develop the necessary skills and impetus required to achieve higher educational goals. The fact was, however, that most of MY parents didn't have the experience or knowledge in education, themselves, which was ample enough to convince their kids that fighting for a top-notch educational goal was essential. Sadly, all I could see from many, MANY DeWitt families of Beta Team, was the constant struggle just to survive on a daily basis. By the latter part of the 1990's, lack of motivation by students was rampant, and I had a hard time seeing much help coming from the home front, either. It was depressing.

Teachers never gave up TRYING to impart a higher level of learning, but there were just so many students lacking the backgrounds needed for movement beyond junior high skills, that trying to get the majority of them TO grade level was a constant, daily struggle.

I really respected my Beta Team teaching partners in1995, and Ginger, Grace, Steve, Bill Teagarten, who had replaced Morton

Oleson during the early '90's, and I worked very well together. It just seemed, however, that the demands made on teachers by District administration, fueled by demands from the Brighton School Board AND from State legislation, (some came to us from the Feds, too, I believe) made the goals that EVERYBODY wanted, down-right impossible to attain.

When student achievement levels weren't even CLOSE to being met, it was the teacher who was the main target for harsh criticism. I had come into education thinking that true education was the result of efforts from four equal groups. Teachers were to present the material in learnable fashion. Students were to do the work NECESSARY to learn that material. Parents were to help monitor student behaviors, and stress getting school work finished before free time was given. And administration, who provided the material needed for teachers to teach, which included supplemental materials, so teachers didn't have to dig into their own pockets to get needed supplies.

What we had by 1995 were: kids with little or no motivation to do school work, many parents who had lost control of their kids, administrators who had budget constraints as well as demands from 'higher-up' to get better student test scores, and us teachers who received pressure being passed down from administrators to achieve those higher results while dealing WITH the non-motivated students, and frustrated parents. What a mess!

Suddenly, at the end of the 1995-'96 school year, Ginger Geiger had had enough of the problems at DeWitt and got a job at a private school. She just got tired of seeing the mundane efforts being put forth by so many students. AND she had grown weary of the day-in and day-out behavioral problems that had been plaguing

DeWitt from day 1. The Beta Team suffered with her loss, but trudged forward as best we could.

Then, just a couple of years later, Grace Armbruster decided to work through the '97-'98 school year and retire. She said that she would substitute teach, but she, too, was having trouble handling the day to day grind of stressful situations.

As it turns out, losing those two women was a great loss to the Beta Team. Taking their places would be teachers who had trouble making it in other school districts, so Steve, Bill and I found ourselves mentoring THEM while carrying our usual heavy loads.

The rest of the teams, Alpha 8th grade, as well as BOTH 7th grade teams, were experiencing great turnover, too. To the veterans amongst us, we were experiencing a morale drop that was palpable. It seemed like Brighton District was rapidly declining in prestige around the Phoenix area. I knew I didn't want to be in a classroom much longer, either.

Going to teachers meetings, during the late '90's, was a chore for me, too, as I was finding myself just trying to keep up with all the new and unfamiliar faces in the room. There didn't seem to be much camaraderie amongst the staff members, either. The fun I remember having, during the early days at Wilhelm, never made a strong appearance at DeWitt, and it seemed to get worse as the years passed. I was feeling miserable, feeling teaching had become a job....just work, and I needed to find a way out of my situation.

The influx of computers didn't help me, either. I wasn't good on them, and even though I took a class to learn the skills, I loathed having to get rid of my paper and pen for the computer. I knew I had become archaic, but I also knew I could get the work done with means OTHER than the computer.

Grudgingly I began going to my school where it seemed like I was facing new people in the teacher ranks and in the classroom most every day, as transiency was a menace.

The 21st century had quickly thrust computer science at me, and I felt uncomfortable with it. I, literally, needed technical support on MY computer, nearly every day. But, I ALSO knew that I needed to work in Brighton two more years before I could think about retirement, so working with computers wasn't an option for me, it was required. I REALLY had to work, each new day, to make myself come to school with a positive attitude. I knew I'd have to be positive to survive my final years.

During my first class, of the new 1998-1999 school year, I remember facing Homeroom class, with a little trepidation. I SO wanted this to be a good year, and I was bound and determined to show myself as a positive entity, not a down-in-the-mouth, discipline machine. I wanted, desperately, to present myself as, not only a teacher in charge of my class's learning environment, but one who displays a constant 'can't we all just get along' attitude, too.

To fight any negativism of doom that I might have had about returning for another year in a DeWitt classroom, I made sure that my opening day homeroom introduction was bright and cheerful. Lo and behold, my students responded with better than average attitudes, too. Oh sure, I was missing four or five students from my assigned roster. I chose to believe that THOSE students just hadn't come back from vacation yet. Or, perhaps, they overslept and would be coming to class a bit late. Sometimes leaving summer vacation hours and starting on school work hours CAN be a bit perplexing, right?

It really didn't matter why I didn't have a full homeroom, I was happy with what I saw from the students who DID make Homeroom. I would deal with my 'late to school' students with positivity whenever they actually showed up. All I remember was that my experience in Homeroom had gotten me off to a wonderful school year.... at least that was what my head was thinking. Then it was time for my 1st hour English class to come into the room.

I DID start my initial introduction with the same zest for learning and fun that I tried to infuse into my homeroom. I was positive, and nurturing, and it appeared as if ALL the students were looking at ME and not around the room. Several of them were even smiling. I felt like I had found the key to a wonderful year. Yep, with a little hard work, and a LOT of energy, I was going to make the 1998-`99 school year the best one I had at DeWitt. I was confident about that.

"All right, class," I said jubilantly as I finished my introductory welcome, "I need for everyone to get out a piece of paper, as I will need some information from you before we get into anything concrete in the world of English."

The students were doing as I asked, and soon everybody appeared ready to write down the information I wanted. Everyone seemed ready except for ONE student, sitting in the back row. He was just sitting there, staring straight ahead at....nothing, really.

Since I had collected a seating chart before I started my 'welcome,' message, it was quite clear that a student named Harry Tindall was occupying the desk. "Harry," I said, using my STILL positive tone of voice, "I will gladly loan you a piece of paper and a pencil, so that I may get my required information. But, starting tomorrow you will have to be responsible for bringing in your own work materials."

"Why?" responded the boy in a matter-of-factly manner. "I don't intend to do anything this year."

"What do you mean, by the statement that you 'don't intend to anything this year'?" I was still smiling, but my positive demeanor was suddenly beginning to wane.

"I didn't do anything last year, and they still passed me. I'm age appropriate."

And there it was, a student who knew that the Brighton District would not hold back any 8th grader who would be turning 15 years of age during a certain date of any current school year. I had known there was a common belief, expressed by 'the powers to be' that mixing older kids with younger ones in the same grade level, could cause a lot of physical intimidation. Armed with that knowledge, I was surprised that there weren't a lot more 'older' students, who didn't just coast through their formative years.

I once had a 16-year-old student in my 8th grade English class, who was, more or less, forced to attend school by the juvenile delinquency system. He was sent to us by a Phoenix juvenile correction facility. DeWitt just happened to be in this delinquent's educational neighborhood. As a juvenile, two-time, convicted car thief, the boy had been given a choice of early release, with mandatory school attendance being required, or of being incarcerated until he turned eighteen.

He wasn't a hard-nosed, trouble-maker as far as I could tell. The correctional system was, apparently, working to find ways of lightening their over-crowding situation. This kid must have been thought to be a good enough risk that receiving schooling was the viable choice to lock-up.

While he didn't want to be locked up, he didn't want to do any work in school, either. Then came my annual research paper/speech combination assignment. I was quite certain that I wouldn't be getting much of an effort from him, but I knew he was capable of, at LEAST, doing a short speech, AND a short paper on any subject he knew well.

This young man pooh-poohed every suggested topic I offered up. Then I FINALLY asked, "Why were you put into the reform center?"

"I got caught a couple of times stealing cars," the delinquent practically boasted.

"Could you explain, without really doing it, how to break into cars?" I asked, grasping at straws.

How to Break into Automobiles became the topic for his paper and speech, and he really did work on his assignement during class. All right, his paper didn't make the minimum requirement of 500 words or more, AND his speech didn't make the five-minute requirement I had asked my students to attain, but he DID make the effort, and would get a passing grade. It should be noted, however, that NONE of his information was new to his classmates, as many of them were quick to point out they already KNEW how to steal cars. But the kid did SOMETHING for a grade in English, and that satisfied me.

By the way, that would be the LAST year I assigned my paper/ speech project. The quality of work had diminished vastly, over the years, as MANY of my students chose to 'just get by.'

The point I'm making is that this boy was sixteen and put into the 8ᵗʰ grade. And I got him to do SOMETHING in my English. He was no threat to ANYONE. He just wanted to mind his own business, and not get into any more trouble than he already had. I actually think he was embarrassed to be in a class of 13 and 14-year-old kids. He certainly didn't seem to be a threat to them physically, and no other kid complained about him, either.

Sadly, two weeks before that young man was to turn seventeen…. that's right, he would be seventeen and in the 8ᵗʰ grade, he was arrested and thrown back into a detention center to finish out his time. He was attempting to steal a car when he got caught. I never said he was a smart 16-year-old, just no real danger to his classmates.

Harry Tindall, on the other hand, WAS smart. He knew the rules, rules that were, apparently, adopted by Brighton AFTER the car-thief kid. But Harry knew that if he could stay out of trouble, the school would NOT detain him.

Harry had delivered his 'non'work' message to another teacher on the Beta team, too, and on the very FIRST team meeting we had that new school year, we were discussing how to deal with the situation.

Grace Armbruster went on her research routine, and she was amazing. She had not only found an At Risk school, which was willing to enroll Harry, she convinced the Brighton administration that it would be in the best interest for both Harry AND DeWitt, if he would attend school outside the District. Grace convinced any administrator who would listen that IF the Tindall kid was allowed to float through 8ᵗʰ grade, other students might want to try the same scheme.

District personnel weren't certain THAT would happen, but told Ms Armbruster it had contingency money available for unforeseen conflicts, and Grace convinced them that THIS was an emergency. Bottom line, Harry's tuition would be covered. Beta Team was very happy with that outcome.

On the third day of school, Harry Tindall's dad was asked to come to our team meeting. When he was brought into the meeting room by a school aide, he looked disheveled, and sickly. He confessed to being a Vietnam veteran who caught 'something' in the jungles, and he was sure he was dying from it.

Hearing he was a vet, I immediately asked if I could run the meeting.

"Mr. Tindall," I started, "as a returning soldier from Vietnam, myself, I want to thank-you for your sevice, and welcome you home."

Tindall had the same far-off-in-the-distance stare his son had.

"We five teachers were assigned to teach Harry this year, but he has indicated that he isn't going to do anything in the way of classroom work. He apparently knows what being 'age appropriate' means, and with that knowledge he expects to be passed into high school no matter if he does or DOESN'T do any school work this school year." The continuous stare by dad let me know I had to get to the chase, and stop tip-toeing around the news we had.

"Naturally," I continued," that would slow down any progress teachers needed in order for them to move the REST of our students along academically. Therefore, we have found a solution that works for both Harry AND the other students of Beta Team." Again, no discernable reaction from our guest.

"Ms Armbruster, there," and she gave a little wave, "has done yeoman's work finding a school where Harry COULD find success. She found a school that specializes in student's with negative attitudes toward school, and will gladly accept Harry as soon as we can get him there. Sir, this is great news for your son. He would be enrolled in classes with much smaller student to teacher ratio, even get one-on-one instruction if needed. He would even be allowed to work at his own pace, meaning he wouldn't have to attend school EVERY day As bright as Harry appears to be, if he toed the line, and did the necessary work, he might well qualify to attend high school before the rest of DeWitt's eighth grade students."

The man sitting directly across from me was an absolute statue, I swear. "And, Mr. Tindall," I said trying to finish quickly, "even though this 'special school' is outside Brighton District, we have found funds to PAY for their services…meaning no cost to you for the privilege of Harry attending a specialized school."

Mr. Tindall FINALLY blinked then gave a slight twitch of his head, which indicated to me that he had heard the information I had presented, at least that was my hope.

I still had a bit of information to give, but it would NOT be positive information. "Mr. Tindall, there is ONE small situation that you and Harry would need to solve. The district does NOT have any way of transporting your son to and from his new school.

But there IS good news on that front, as well. The city of Phoenix has some tremendously good bus rates for students who need to go out of their neighborhoods for schooling. We're talking very little expense to you, Sir. Ms Armbruster can fill you in."

I looked for conformation from Grace, but she slightly shrugged her shoulders. "I'm not quite sure about the prices, but I DO know the cost is minimal and I would be glad to find out for you," Grace said enthusiastically.

I continued, wanting to finish and hope for SOME response from Dad, "Many students ride the bus, everyday. But, Mr. Tindall, we have gotten Harry a great deal, with a great school. I'm sure you will agree that a small bus fare is definitely worth paying in order to get this smart, young man the education he needs to compete at the high school level."

"You say I have to foot the bill for his bus, huh?" Mr. Tindall said in a drawl that sounded like he could have been fairly inebriated at the time. "I didn't want that kid in the first place. His mom ran out on us two years ago, and left me holding the bag. For him and me, it is live and let live. I don't mess into what he is doing, and he stays away from me. He don't have no job, so he can't pay for the busses. And I won't."

I interrupted, and with a bit more anger than should be shown toward parents, I said, "Mr. Tindall, I know life after Nam can't have been easy for you. It wasn't for ANY of us. I know what your situation is at home, and it's not wonderful. But you DO get full disability from the military. Ms Armbruster has worked hard to ensure that Harry gets placed in a proper environment....a place where he would be able to SUCCEED, poor attitude or not. And

I feel CERTAIN, the city will work with you on his transportation fees. I strongly feel that you, as Harry's parent, need to take SOME interest in your child's education. Paying a small bus fare is within your means, and you know it. Help your son, Sir."

"Now just a minute there, Hotshot," Daddy Tindall said, showing little patience for wanting to be lectured. "Even if I CAN afford his bus fares, I won't do it. He's got a perfectly good school right here. I don't care WHERE he goes to school, just as long as he stays out of my affairs at home. He's got to learn how to take care of hisself. So, if y'all ain't paying for his busses, too, then I guess you got him all year." And with that, he bolted out of his chair, and straight out the door.

Grace tried to look into having child welfare get involved, but nothing came of that. We had Harry Tindall for the entire year. He would often just put his head down on his desk, and try to sleep. But he didn't cause trouble for any teacher either. I would get another student to get his attention, (if Harry had his eyes closed) then ask the simplest of questions, and that stubborn kid would just stare at me, with vacant eyes, and say, "I just can't remember that now."

And so it went, in all his classes. He failed EVERY ONE, including P.E. Jerry Randolph had a 350-yard semi-oval track on the playground. Harry was asked to WALK around it once during each gym class....like ALL students taking P.E. Jerry told me that nobody failed in Physical Education if they just did THAT. Tindall refused and failed.

I found his lack of physical effort particularly galling since he claimed to be the next coming of Tony Hawk, the fabulously talented skateboarder of that era. Hell, I once saw Harry skating after school, with some of the other skaters from DeWitt. He not only wasn't the best skateboarder at DeWitt, he wasn't the best skater amongst Beta Team's group of 8th graders. Harry was just an angry kid, trying to prove the point that he didn't have to do ANYTHING in order to pass into high school.

He refused to go to Saturday school, after the first semester. And he told everyone who listened that he wasn't going to go to summer school, either. When the school principal came by our team meeting, at school year's end, and asked us to sign off on him so he could go to high school, we ALL said we wouldn't do it. Led by Grace, we declared that if the school wanted him to get out of the 8th grade, someone other than his teachers would have to sign him out. We declared him NOT ready for the next grade level. The principal was furious, but she couldn't get us to sign.

Three things here. One, news got to us that Harry ended up going to high school, but lasted exactly two weeks before being kicked out. Don't know what he did, but his education, apparently, was over.

Two, Grace Armbruster DID decide to make that her last year, so the Beta Team would get ANOTHER replacement teacher joining us the following year.

And third, I was even MORE anxious than ever to get out of the classroom. Harry Tindall didn't really infect the other students. Actually, they thought of him as an oddball, and nobody wanted to identify with him for that reason. But, the fact remained, students were getting tougher and tougher to reach, at least by me. And there were more and more Daddy Tindall-types out there, and I knew I had lost patience with pathetic parents. I dreaded coming back to school for the 1999-2000 school year. I HAD to find a way out of DeWitt.

It was at the start of the 1999-2000 school year that I realized how disillusioned I had REALLY become. DeWitt appeared to be stable, but it wasn't. First, finding money for supplemental supplies had become a main source of misery for teachers EVERY year. And, secondly, there always seemed to be a constant need to find quality teachers for our schools. The district's younger teachers were constantly leaving, being able to find more attractive salaries in newer, growing districts. There was certainly no doubt that Brighton District schools had become full-fledged Inner City schools, which brought with it the plethora of problems plaguing schools in OTHER tough neighborhoods.

It's not that 'bad' families were moving into the Brighton District, rather families that didn't seem to have any structure at home. Many just lost hope of a better life, too. Our families seemed willing to accept that they weren't going to have success. Welfare was a way of life. Unrest in the neighborhoods was rampant. Dreams were NOT of how to get ahead in this world, but of how to survive. Gangs were everywhere and were influencing our youth, and recruitment was heavy, even starting in the early elementary school years. Violence, sadly, had become a way of life, too, and was omnipresent for many of the district's families EVERY day. Even more sadly, for me, was the the fact that education had become, seemingly, less and less important for more and more kids in Brighton schools.

Administration WAS trying to do what they could to improve situations.

But, for reasons only THEY seemed to know, it was the legislators who just kept screaming for improvement in schools, but doing so without giving poor, ailing districts the necessary tools needed to win the education war. Teachers in Phoenix's Inner City school districts felt helpless.

Rumors were constantly being circulated that the problem of poor student achievement was due to poor TEACHING, and if teachers' salaries were directly tied to student standardized test scores, education would suddenly heal itself. Tying teacher salaries to student achievement on standardized test scores...THAT was an insult!

In March of the year 2000, the 'normal' standardized tests were to be issued. That was the tool used by administrators to evaluate how well the various school districts were doing. A chance for EVERYONE to see who was getting the job done, and who wasn't.

On the surface, that seemed fair. BUT, there was a huge disparity between students in charter schools, private schools, parochial schools and schools in the suburbs compared to students who were being educated in the Inner City. Call it a lack of motivation, having poorer educational backgrounds, or just plain being more interested in survival, the students, I taught in the late '90's, let it be known that doing well in school just wasn't their 'thing.'

Brighton families who DID have higher respect for education were fleeing to the 'burbs,' when they realized that our district's schools had so many problems. But moving took money, forcing SOME families, who didn't have 'moving' money, to stay in their deteriorating neighborhoods. And housing values just kept plummeting. The lowering home values had become enticing to foreigners, and THEIR going to Brighton schools began forcing ESL classrooms to teem beyond reasonable teacher/student ratios.

Since support systems, designed for students enrolled in English as a Second Language, were being overwhelmed; thus NOT allowing the specialists to be as efficient as THEY liked, we 'regular' classroom teachers realized that we needed to take more time on OUR objectives in order to allow ESL students the chance to grasp all the concepts presented.

I TRIED to maintain all my goals, but it wasn't easy, and not always as complete as I wanted them to be. As the years passed I realized I was losing not only many of the non-English speaking students, but more students who were EXPECTING to be fully prepared for high school challenges. I hated lowering my classroom standards and expectations, but I just couldn't reach everybody. Individualizing lessons was nearly impossible, as I had students, ranging from 2nd grade to 10th grade levels, in every class.

I, along with several of my contemporaries, were being frustrated by the slowness of progress being made in our classrooms, YET the 'higher ups' were making demands for even HIGHER achievement results. My colleagues and I....especially I.... felt like we could NOT compete with the academic results being put forth by more and more schools in Arizona and the nation, especially given our ever-changing neighborhood population.

I felt like my feet were being put to the fire to accomplish nearly impossible goals!

Brighton Schools HAD to teach all the kids who lived in our attendance area. Private schools, on the other hand, had the ability to decide who should and should not attend THEIR schools. Educational sluggards or known trouble-makers did not HAVE to be accepted if the private school didn't want to accept them. And students could be removed, if 'standards' weren't met. Public schools didn't have those options. We taught neighborhood students regardless of their personal situations.

With the suburban flight, and the 'we'll take who we want' attitude of the private schools, it didn't surprise me that standardized test scores at the 'choosy' schools were superior to the scores of our students at DeWitt. Yet, ALL schools, statewide, were being held to the same accountability of knowledge being measured by the use of standardized tests. And THEN, having the 'bright' people in legislature wanting teachers' salaries TIED to student results on achievement tests....that was down-right unfair.

Don't get me completely wrong, SOME accommodations were made for students who spoke NO English, but I found that I was testing more and more students who barely understood the English language, or had very limited backgrounds in learning the basics of English. How were foreign students expected to compete on tests where they couldn't even understand the questions, let alone try to figure out the answers.

When teachers complained about the predicament caused by the tests, the wailing only seemed to fall on deaf ears. Our Brighton administrators were just doing what they were told to do.....get the test results from all students. District teachers were expected to get great results no matter WHO took the tests. Toward the end of my classroom career, I felt like I was giving standardized tests as if I was playing a sporting event....an event where I had one hand tied behind my back. Our school results had NO chance of competing with high-faluting schools from other districts, pure and simple!

Then there were the students, like Harry Tindall, who could care less about getting a good education. The Tindall-type group included: students who didn't care about school, students coming to us with severely retarded educational skill levels, and those kids who didn't feel like doing standardized testing, whether they were smart enough to do well or not.

We were told to motivate our homeroom students to WANT to do well. Motivating students on standardized tests was never easy, and I often I felt like I was burrowing through hard ground with a teaspoon....something I once tried as a nine-year-old.

I have to admit, however, I DID have some success by motivating a (wannabe) street-tough student in my homeroom, and that, I remember, as a special and fulfilling event in my teaching career at DeWitt.

In the early-ninties, I had a big, tough gang member in my homeroom. He looked intimidating, and had a few followers, but I felt that he was really just trapped in his neighborhood situation. He wasn't menacing toward other students, but had a look that implied, 'stay away from me.' So, other students steered clear of him.

I had had a few conversations with him, without his 'vatos' in the area, and that kid seemed bright to me....VERY bright. He seemed to be absorbing the information I was teaching, (while NOT writing anything down on paper) as he constantly displayed disinterest in learning. To me it appeared like he was pretending to not care about school, just putting on a show for his posse which was meant to convince THEM that he had no interest in getting an education. My instincts told me I could reach that kid, and then the ITBS testing came along.

Javier Montalvo was his name, and I really wanted him to see how different he was from his followers. The Iowa Tests of Basic Skills was my opportunity, so I sought him out before he came into my homeroom that first testing day. "Mr. Montalvo," I started, "Can I have a word with you, please?"

He looked around, checking to see who was noticing him about to speak with a teacher. When he saw it was just him and me, I continued. "Today we start to take those dreaded standardized tests."

"Yeah, I know," Javier said quickly, while still looking around. "We take them every year, so what?"

"Have you ever done well?" I inquired.

"Maybe third or fourth grade, I don't remember which one. But, I don't like them, so I don't try too hard on them now. It's a time for me to relax, is all."

"Javier, are the questions every year too hard for you, so you have trouble answering them? Does your mom not care about how you do in school? I mean you are in school anyway, why not see if you know the answers?"

"My moms cares, but she knows that me and my boys don't DO tests. Don't need them where we live."

"Ever expect to get away from where you live someday, maybe move out of your tough neighborhood? Maybe help your family move away from there?" I queried, seeing him getting a little bit squirmy by talking to me.

"I don't know no other place but my 'hood, so I got nowhere to go. I never worried 'bout doing them tests before. OK, yeah, maybe I want something better in my life than what I got, but tests and good grades won't get anything for me....never have before."

"You talk a big game, Javier, and you do sound tough. But what if you actually TRIED to do as well as you could on these year-end tests just one year....THIS year? You're about to go into high school, and THAT is the place where important people can determine your potential and definitely help shape what happens in your future."

The big kid eyed me, and said with all seriousness, "My boys would make fun of me, then I would have trouble with them."

"Javi, your boys CAN'T do well on these tests....they don't have what it takes to do well. But, I think YOU do. Besides, nobody finds out about the scores except teachers and the individuals taking the tests....and their families. You wouldn't have to tell your buddies how well you did if you don't want to. But I bet your mom would be proud of you if you could do well. Of THAT I am certain. Now, if you don't think you ARE smart enough to get many correct answers, then you have nothing to worry about. You will get the low scores and make your buddies happy. But, like I have said, you seem VERY smart to me. I believe in you."

"I'm smart enough," Montalvo said rather defiantly, "I just don't want to cause any trouble with my guys by getting good scores on these dumb tests."

"It will be our little secret, IF you do well. I won't tell them, if you don't. All I'M asking is that you see how many of the answers you can get right....just this one year. That way I will KNOW if I was right, and you are smarter than you let other people think you are, or if you are just another dummy from the 'hood."

"Mr. Stein, I don't want nobody to know my score if I do try, OK?"

"You mean ANYONE to know."

"Yeah, I know....anyone. "I like you as a teacher, Mr. S., so if you promise not to tell people what I get, I will do the best I can on these tests.....but just this once."

"That's all I'm asking, Javier. I've enjoyed having you in my homeroom this year. Now, I'd like to see if you can be a POSITIVE representative of this class, and you can do that by trying to get as good a score as you can on the standardized tests. Focus on every question of every test, OK?"

Javier nodded affirmatively, put his head down, and moved quickly toward the amphitheater where he was going to meet up with his little friends.

I have to tell you, I got goose bumps when the test scores came in and I saw Javier Montalvo's English score. He had the SECOND highest, combined score, on the English portions of the ITBS tests….for the entire school….and that included ALL 8th grade students in DeWitt. Only one of the gifted students scored better. His other test scores were high, as well, and I called him in for a meeting as soon as I could.

"Mr. Montalvo," I began with some pride in my voice, "I got back your test scores, and you did better than average on the English portions of the test. Actually, you did better than average on ALL of your tests. In fact, on the tests related to English, you had the second highest score in the entire school. That's right, better than every student, but one, in DeWitt's 8th grade. I am very proud of you!"

"I did what?" Javier asked with a little disbelief in his voice.

"You had amazing scores in ALL your tests, and the SECOND highest score in English. You know what this means, don't you? When the high school counselors come in a couple of weeks, to sign our students up for their freshman classes, you need to sign up for the Advanced Placement classes."

"No way, Mr. Stein, I'm not going to do that. Uh uh!"

"Look, Javi, when you get to high school, things change. People there are trying to better themselves, and many of them are trying to get out of their impoverished neighborhoods by doing well enough to go to college. I know YOU have the smarts to be one of them. And for you to get into college, you will need to be taking great classes. NOBODY gets into college with average English, math and science classes. ALL the kids from private schools and suburban schools try to get into college. Their counselors tell THEM, that the best way to get to a university is to take the tougher classes in high school. So those who qualify WILL have taken advanced classes."

"Javier, college is where you get the chance to get a better life. You and your mom and sisters are living on welfare now. Wouldn't it be great if you could get a GOOD job, and help your family move away from their situation? Inner City kids don't always get the opportunity to move up and out of their tough environment. Your ITBS scores tell me that you CAN succeed anywhere you go. But you have to try to get ahead, and you can do that by your efforts in high school. Plus, being FROM an impoverished area, colleges are willing to give scholarships to poorer kids, and help them get a better life. Makes them feel like they are helping improve society.... which they are."

"You have EVERYTHING to gain, Javier, by going for the gusto. If you can't make it, you just slide back to your local ghetto where you will be continually bombarded with crime and drugs until you fall through the cracks and become a statistic. You have a real chance here, and I believe you can make it in the real world, Javier." FINALLY, I was finished with my speech.

"I want to help my mom and sisters. That part is true. But a smart kid, where I come from, can have lots of trouble. My posse will look down on me, and I will not have my support system. Those guys mean a lot to me. AND, if I take higher classes, I will have to do a LOT of homework. I HATE homework! I don't do it now, and I think I am too lazy to do it in high school."

I stopped Javier right there. "Javi, there are VERY few opportunities that come along that allow ANYBODY to improve themselves. School is one of them. I think you have the brains to succeed. You won't know for yourself unless you try, and I mean give it a long, hard attempt, and NOT just see the amount of work required, which may make you WANT to quit. Quitting is easy....

succeeding is hard. IF you have what it takes, you will know it soon, even during your freshman year. What you WILL find, however, is that your current 'friends' won't be around very long, that part is true. You will find NEW friends, though, likely ones without street cred. But THOSE friends will be interested in being successful in life, and those are the people you have to hitch your wagon to. THEY will help you get to a better place, not the guys you hang with THESE days."

"Yes, there will be more work than you can imagine. But the good life isn't just handed to you, it is worked for. Maybe you have what it takes to compete with other bright kids, or maybe you don't. What I DO know is that you won't know unless you give yourself a chance to find out. And I mean a REAL chance."

"One thing I know about you, Javier Montalvo, is that you are stubborn, and you don't like to be embarrassed. Fight to keep up with the other smarter kids. Don't give up. Do what is necessary to get that college scholarship. Make me proud. Make your family proud. Make yourSELF proud!" And with that, I asked him to go home, think about it, and when the high school counselors come to sign freshmen up, he would need to let me know what he's decided.

It didn't take long for Javier's buddies to find out his scores, and he tried to pooh-pooh them off. But, when it came time to register for high school, Javier Montalvo, with me beside him to assure the counselors that he could succeed, signed up for the Advanced Placement classes.

Oddly, I didn't hear from Javier until his senior year. He came by DeWitt, told me he had stuck with his advanced class load, finished well up on the graduation list, grade-wise, and had gotten financial help to attend a junior college. My heart was filled with happiness as I heard his report. He wasn't running with any gang. He was anxious to help his mom. And he told me he was 'bound and determined' to get a four-year degree from SOME university. We hugged, and he left. Never heard from him since, either. But that was NOT unusual behavior from kids who grew up in the tough Brighton neighborhoods, during the 1990's and beyond.

Javier's case was a rare case. He was a kid, having little to look forward to, willing to trust a teacher and take a chance on a battery of tests NOT designed for Inner City boys and girls. Most of the students I encountered, after Javier, could care less if they did well on those tests....even if they COULD do better. Take Miguel Cornejo as an example.

Miguel was a student in my homeroom and in one of my English classes. I would call him an average student, grade-wise. He did the minimum, but got 'C' grades across the board. He was fairly typical of the students attending DeWitt during the late 90's. He thought school was a necessary evil, but he had no illusions about going any further, educationally, than high school. He had manners, stayed out of trouble, and continually fought the angst of growing up that most junior high kids have had throughout time.

The Iowa Tests of Basic Skills were being administered, not only in a huge number of Arizona schools, but in many, many schools across the nation. Their intent was to measure the individual student's skills in a variety of academic areas, and it didn't seem to matter what part of the country kids came from, or the educational background of the students, test makers had a 'standard' level which measured competence of the 'normal' child at several grade levels.

I won't get back to being political here, but let's face it, SOME schools, in SOME parts of America, had better preparation for success on the ITBS then did other schools.

NOT taken in account, as far as I was concerned, were the kids who weren't blessed with 'normal' circumstances. These included transient children constantly moving when parents couldn't pay the rent, students attending schools lacking in sufficient teaching materials, and students with either mental deficiencies or new to the English language. These kids had very little chance of doing well on standardized tests....at least that is what I came to believe through my experiences.

Also, from what I remember during my day, MOST students in Brighton District were required to take the test REGARDLESS of handicap, and we had a LOT of students with one handicap or another. The 'bright' academic students were few and far in between at DeWitt. Oh, we had PLENTY of street-wise kids, and kids with common sense. But due to weak learning backgrounds, poor or unusual family situations, and strong peer pressure, many, MANY of the students I taught were void of the solid academic skills and motivation needed to be highly successful on tests like the Iowa Tests of Basic Skills.

Miguel Cornejo was a typical, middle-of-the-road student at DeWitt....as average as any student I taught in the 1999-2000 school year. He was the son of a mom and dad who were born in Mexico, and got to the United States for a better life. His dad was a laborer, and his mom stayed home to take care of the younger brothers and sisters. Neither parent had much education, but both wanted Miguel to graduate high school and get a job better than just being a common laborer. It was the PASSING of his classes that was important to them, not how WELL he did in his studies. DeWitt was filled with families having similar school expectations.

Every year, teachers were asked to motivate their students.... to have them as prepared as possible in order to score well on the year-end, standardized tests. However, with the heavy transiency in the District and a student population ill-equipped to handle anything past the rudimentary skills in basic classes like English and math, it seemed to me like I was asked to make a silk purse out of a sow's ear. I could just look at the vacant stares on the students' faces at test time and felt very sure that my desired outcomes and actual student results had VERY little chance of matching up.

Being competitive my whole life, I thrived on being better than the next guy....especially in sports. So, during each year my kids took the standardized tests, I tried to use a motivational speech that would have made ANY coach proud to have given. I highlighted my delivery with statements like 'it's us against them,' and 'no one can ask for you to do better than giving 100%." I challenged EACH of my homerooms to, not only 'be the top homeroom at DeWitt,' but to 'beat every homeroom of every school in Phoenix.'

I was fired up to compete EVERY year! I felt positive I could reach the majority of my students and have them give the maximum effort....well, maybe when I STARTED my encouragement speeches in the '90's. But then I would see blank faces looking back at me and realize, deep down inside, that I was going to be in for a lot of disappointment when the scores came back.

I remember, during Miguel Cornejo's year, saying, "All right, class, it's time. Make me, your family, this school, and especially yourself, proud with the results of your efforts on these tests." That was my standard rah-rah speech for ALL situations where I wanted someone to do his/her best.

I had them turn to the instructions page for the first test, and I read them very carefully. "All right," I continued, "pick up your pencils, and find the correct answer area for this test."

Students closed their instructional booklets, found the correct answer section, and grabbed their #2 lead pencils, which were the implements used to bubble in the answers. They were eagerly awaiting my signal to 'go,' when I spotted a student, toward the side and back of the room. That student was Miguel Cornejo, and he was putting his writing utensil DOWN on his desk. "Miguel, what are you doing?" I asked quizzically.

"I'm finished, Mr. Stein," he said with very little emotion.

"You finished bubbling in the answers for the first test? We haven't even STARTED yet. How can you be finished?"

"Does doing well on this test mean we pass or fail the 8th grade?" Cornejo asked in a, surprising, devil-may-care tone in his voice.

I was flabbergasted. I, AGAIN, used all the Jewish guilt I could in RE-explaining the 'pride' reasons for taking the tests, even making it sound like he was hurting MY feelings by not wanting to do his best. But I told him the truth, which was that the ITBS tests did NOT determine passing and failing the 8th grade.

"I had a terrible night last night, Mr. Stein, and I really need to sleep more than I need to take these tests."

I really didn't know what to do. I was required to have all my homeroom students take the tests....EVERY SINGLE ONE....so I couldn't send him to the office for counseling and possible re-testing. I could see me getting all the blame for his not wanting to do the ITBS requirement, but I also believed he wouldn't do them for anybody else, either. In fact, Miguel and I actually had a fairly good rapport with one another throughout the year.

But, I saw the kid resting his head on his two hands, and the time for the entire school to start the first test had already begun, so I gave a quick, 'Do your best, class," and got the test going.

Between the first and second tests, I talked to Miguel, who apologized for not doing the tests, and, basically, told me that he didn't intend to take any of the tests no matter WHO gave them, which STILL didn't make me feel any better. He mentioned something about wanting to take the tests when all the absent kids, from that day, had to take them. That way he could get out of class, too. He knew he was going to pass 8th grade, and that was the ONLY thing that mattered to him.

But I kept prodding him to try and understand how important it was for him to do his best....school pride, family pride, self pride, that kid just wasn't interested in doing those damn tests. From that point onward, it became a game for him....seeing if he could get through with all the answers before I could get finished with the instructions.

I talked to several people about what was happening, including the vice principal. I was told by EVERYONE, 'Just do the best you can.' I even heard 'glad he is not in my homeroom,' from one teacher.

Turns out Miguel didn't have a good 'guessing' system, either. If I remember correctly, he scored in the less than 5% range of all students EVERYWHERE who were taking the tests, one of the lowest scores in OUR school, and we're talking about kids who had to take the test who didn't really understand or speak English very well. Marking the 'A' answer for every question would have gotten him a better score. But he decided to make interesting patterns with his bubbling....less than 5%!

The rest of my homeroom did as well as expected, which wasn't as high as they should have scored without totally embarrassing themselves. I had very average kids, who received very average scores. But, the administration was NOT happy with the results, so the teachers got chewed out AGAIN for not getting their students to perform at a rate higher than their capabilities. I was totally dejected from the experience, AND the way teachers were made scapegoats.

THEN, one fine day in April, I was passing through the school office, when the secretary called me to her desk. "Mr. Stein," she said, "it seems like the District is offering an early retirement package for this year. Teachers who qualify have two weeks to decide if they want to take it."

It had been a while since an early retirement package, worth anything, was dangled in front of weary, veteran teachers, but I grabbed the paper eagerly. Not only was this an early retirement offer, it was a GREAT one. My guess is that the District wanted to get older teachers out, and use each of THEIR individual salaries to entice TWO new teachers for the exact same money. It didn't matter what their reasoning was, all I said was, "Do you have a pen?"

The secretary looked at me, "Why don't you take the offer home and let your wife look it over with you?"

"Do you have a pen I may use?" I said with some eagerness and impatience.

She handed me a pen, I signed where I needed to, and said jubilantly, "When this school year ends, I will be an early retiree." And I had the biggest grin on my face that I HADN`T had at DeWitt in.....well, FOREVER!

13

Success Gets No Respect

K NOWING THAT I was taking an early retirement package lifted a lot of stress off me. While I still loved kids, I knew that I had lost the love of the classroom. I had enjoyed 27 years, and all the hats that teachers wear. It WASN'T just go to class, teach a lesson, and go home. The reality, for me, was that teachers have to be surrogate parents, guidance counselors, LIFE counselors, even friends to their students. Being able to balance the many responsibilities is the key.There is just no way to stop the progression of time, and with the progression came the realization that I was becoming a relic….not as relevant to the modern day circumstances. It was time to move on.

Steve Lipinski, Jerry Hamilton, and I wondered what we would be doing for the District, as the retirement package meant we STILL had to give five years of responsible service to Brighton. I was the junior member of the trio, and MY responsibility would be working in the District 30 days a year for the next five years. Steve, too, had to serve thirty days. Jerry, having been in the district several years longer than either Steve or I, only needed to give 25 days a year.

Our problem was that NONE of us wanted to substitute in the classroom. That seemed more like babysitting than teaching. We talked about alternatives and came up with a way to do help students without the stagnation of us being cooped up in classrooms. We found a way to incorporate sports as our solution.

All three of us had had extensive careers in coaching, while in Brighton. At Wilhelm, Steve and I were part of a network of coaches who saw the benefits of getting our young students involved in athletics. We had after-school sports programs available for our 5th-8th graders the entire time I was at Wilhelm. Jerry had a similar network at Cahill, too. The athletes at both those schools learned some very valuable life skills through sports because we three 'coaches' emphasized sportsmanship, teamwork, discipline, and responsibility. We knew that by teaching those qualities at an early age, our athletes were learning important building blocks geared to help them become good citizens as adults.

Sadly, when Jerry, Steve and I moved through our careers at DeWitt, we began seeing less and less of those positive attributes being developed in our 'feeder' schools. After-school programs of ANY kind could be classified as scarce to non-existant.

The lack of good elementary sports programs was evident, too, when the new 7th grade athletes arrived at DeWitt each successive school year. They displayed poorer and poorer athletic skills and ATROCIOUS team interaction skills. Lipinski, Randolph and I believed that a lot of ANY school's success had to be credited to solid sports team achievement. We felt that good sports programs actually became the basis for most EVERY school's POSITIVE spirit and pride on campus.

Don't get me wrong. Students getting onto the school's honor roll was a positive and prideful achievement. Being involved with the school's student council, was a good thing, as well. Having an outstanding music program was also a wonderful way of developing pride. And schools, volunteering to help others in need, ALWAYS lifted people's spirits.

But at Wilhelm and Cahill, it was the after-school sports teams that brought the feeling of EXTREME pride to OUR schools. It seemed imperitive to us old coaches that raising morale at the feeder schools was something we needed to do, and we felt we could do it well. So we came up with a plan.

Jerry, Steve and I decided to present a plan, to both the Brighton School Board and District administrators, which would allow us to develop a solid after-school sports program for ALL 4th-6th grade boys and girls in the District.

We understood that we were expected to be substitute teachers at least SOME, but we also knew that being effective OUTSIDE the classroom would be a positive for everybody, too. NOT subbing in the classroom wasn't a foreign concept in Brighton.

There was at least one Brighton early-retiree who did nothing but give tests to students. He would go to schools and take students out of their classes in order to give them tests required by the district. Don't ask me how he got THAT job, and I don't even know what he tested. But he tested the kids one-on-one, and NEVER had to step foot into the classroom as a substitute, during his five-year early retirement....as far as I knew.

Another early-retiree had the job of verifying school attendances. He would go to homes in the District to see if there were children living in those homes who were indeed attending our various schools. This would have been a GOOD thing for Brighton in the '70's and '80's. When I got my job, I remember Wilhelm being a refuge for families desperate to get their kids out of the impoverished school districts. And many of them did so by giving addresses of people they knew, living in Brighton District. This, then, allowed their kids to get into schools like Wilhelm, which had stronger academic programs than did the Inner-City schools where they actually had 'full-time' residence.

I don't remember having an early retiree checking home addresses back then. So, having someone checking in the mid to late '90's, was strange. If anything OUR students were fleeing elsewhere to find stronger academic programs. Still, there he was, an early-retiree, checking attendance instead of substituting in the classroom. With knowledge of 'exceptions to subbing' like those, the three of us thought we had a chance of selling our plan to District big wigs.

We had worked out, before going into our district meeting, all the logistics we needed to run such a program, and we absolutely wanted to explain all the benefits that sports offered to youngsters, from our perspective. But we ALSO had a VERY compelling reason for wanting to develop our program for Brighton's younger kids. We knew we would be competing with local gangs for those very same youngsters.

Gangs in our school district were getting bigger and stronger as the years progressed. In fact, the rival gangs were actively pursuing kids as young as ten years of age to join them....trying to show the young ones how easy it was to control, even terrorize many of the people living in Brighton neighborhoods.We three sincerely believed that if we gave our younger people a viable alternative to getting involved in gang life, a more positive, and constructive alternative to gangs, we might just help increase the morale and well-being of our various neighborhoods, as WELL as increase pride in local schools.

Steve Lipinski, being the most political of us three, presented our program. He explained how we would arrange for getting coaches and athletes from each school to participate. We would set up schedules of games and tournaments, readying the fields and gymnasiums for each new sporting season. We would arrange for referees and hold coaching clinics. All of us would be on call to help with coaching instruction aid for any coach at any of our school when needed. We'd even referee when needed, too.

Steve explained that our program would need help from the Brighton District Board and its administrators in two ways. One, we would need the District to provide transportation to all games. Getting to and from school practices, and tournaments would be the responsibility of the athletes, themselves, but we NEEDED to have the transportation department help us out on game days as athletes would be leaving directly from schools. Some parents worked and couldn't get off early. Others had NO way to transport their kids. PLUS, our referees were on tight schedules, too. So, getting games started on time was a necessity. This was directly in line with our second 'need,' funding the venture to ensure success.

Bus drivers would need to be paid extra. Coaches would need to be paid, though they would get paid very little. Our recruited coaches would be told that they would basically be coaching for the 'love of it.' but we believed in the need of a small stipend to help entice many of them. When I recruited coaches, which was one of MY main responsibilities to the program, I had to make sure that the recruits understood that the money would just be a bonus, and that coaching young people was the real reason for getting on board.

I do remember, on occasion, telling potential coaches that when I started in Brighton District, I coached four sports a year, for the first FOUR years, but received NO coaching pay for any of those sports. I did it for the kids and the love of sports. It wasn't until my 5th year coaching, that our school board was convinced that coaching time was valuable. We received $100 per sport, per season….ONE HUNDRED DOLLARS! We DID take the money, however, pitiful as it was.

I mentioned again and again, to my coaching prospects, all the benefits that sports were giving the students of our schools. I told them all again and again, while the pay wasn't much, the rewards of coaching were priceless. I had little trouble finding capable adults wanting to work with the kids in our feeder schools.

Steve explained that we would need money to buy equipment for each program, as he let the Board and administrators know how important it would be for athletes to get ribbons medals and trophies for achievement INSTEAD of just participation at the various tournaments.

Lipinski knew that Brighton already had insurance for athletes involved with after-school sports, as DeWitt fielded several athletic teams. That meant the younger kids, involved in sporting teams, would simply need to be included in the coverage, as well.

We figured that Brighton already had in its budget between $45-$50 thousand a year to be used for after-school sports, (Steve found out somehow) and we ALSO knew our program would need some of that money. But Lipinski explained that we could help with expenses by bringing in SOME money when we charged patrons admission to attend our tournaments. Getting enough money for the success of our elementary school sports programs was necessary, BUT we believed it was NOT impossible to get what was needed.

When the presentation was finished, and we had made it perfectly clear that the positives WAY out-weighed the negatives, we awaited the decision. The Board loved the idea, but Distict administration....not so much.

Alberta Logia was the District administrator in charge of academics, who ALSO happened to be in charge of over-seeing our early-retirement program. While she expressed being not at all pleased with losing District baby-sitters, she DID finally accept our plan, but with one stipulation....Jerry, Steve and I would EACH have to agree to work five of our retirement days as substitute teachers. She made it perfectly clear that THAT would be non-negotiable.

And so it came to pass, Hamilton, Lipinski, and Stein were going to be allowed to develop a brand new program in Brighton. We knew it was going to be hard work, which it was, but we LOVED that we were being given the opportunity to take our vision to the schools.

Even though Steve had been a P.E. teacher for several years at Wilhelm, Jerry set up the game and tournament schedules, which he was a master at doing, and he also arranged for having referees at the various games, too.

Steve was the administrative liaison, and was in charge of getting soccer fields prepared, making sure that all the equipment needed was gotten for the schools, and he arranged for the transportation.

Both Jerry and Steve set up coaching clinics, too, so all the logistics were taken care of, and that was fine by me.

My job was recruitment. I went to all the schools, 'convinced' teachers, most of whom I didn't know, that we NEEDED their participation in order to make our after-school vision successful. There were, also, some former students of mine that I recruited as well, especially for the wrestling program, since finding teachers with a wrestling background was pretty much impossible.

I was delighted when I got such a robust response, from older and younger teachers alike, who saw this program as being a positive entity for Brighton's younger children. However, many of my recruits were NOT skilled coaches, just eager to 'lead' their schools' kids in such an ambitious endeavor.

Getting kids to join up was pretty easy, too. I knew I could convince the kids to 'defend' their schools' honors by competing against the other schools on the fields of athletic combat. After all, Brighton was a district with a lot of youngsters who were used to rough and tumble ways in their daily lives. They had LOTS of energy, too. So, convincing them that transferring BOTH natural occurrences to sports activities instead of using them on the 'streets,' would be fun AND keep them out of trouble. Since we had different teams for 4th, 5th, and 6th graders, I went to each school as much as necessary, in order to 'sell' our program.

When all the schools had kids out for teams and coaches to coach them, AND after clinics and strategies were given, the three of us made sure we went to the various schools' practices, each and every day, to help any way we could. On a few occasions, we asked if we could demonstrate certain techniques and basics that WE had used in our days of coaching. We only did that IF the 'new' coaches asked for some help. We would also help them outline their strategies for the next several practices, too.

I worried, somewhat, that several coaches might be 'put off' if we three older guys took charge of coaching at certain times of practices. Just the opposite happened. We were always introduced as 'guest coaches,' who were on campus to show some 'technique' approaches that we had used throughout our vast years of experience. The athletes, too, understood why we were there and seemed to appreciate our helping them. Turns out that the coaches not only kept the respect of their athletes, but didn't lose a bit of being the authority figures. I liked to think that everybody had a win/win situation.

The enthusiasm exhibited by both coaches and athletes during that first year was tremendous. Jerry, Steve and I went to the different schools for every game, and noticed that school spirit and pride was becoming stronger and stronger for each team. We arranged for our tournaments to be on Saturdays, and I was very happy to see how many parents and fans went to see them. I was especially pleased when the athletes' families came to us after the events were finished and thanked us for developing our program and giving their children a venue for releasing a lot of pent-up energy. We KNEW we had started something positive, and most everyone seemed genuinely grateful.

One of my responsibilities was to keep statistics for each sport. I collected sign-up rosters from the individual school's boys' and girls' teams when tournaments were finished. And I wasn't shocked when I saw that nearly 1200 kids, in total, had signed on to represent their respective schools in the five sports....TWELVE HUNDRED! The total included both boys and girls. However, I have to admit that we DID have some kids who didn't last too long on their respective teams. There were students who, when they found out they had to sweat and run, quit the teams fairly early on. And, certainly, we had athletes sign up for all five sports being offered, so in reality, we didn't have 1200 DIFFERENT kids sign up. Bottom line, though, we had around 1200 athletes showing interest in our after-school program that first year, and Jerry, Steve and I were thrilled!

It is also important to tell you that NONE of these four schools had huge student populations. Therefore, getting so many children interested in trying sports made the three of us 'old' coaches very proud of what we did, and we were VERY excited about, possibly, expanding our efforts for the second year.

Alberta Logia, however, wasn't as exuberant about the program as Brighton's students, coaches, families, and we organizers were. In fact, Jerry, Steve and I were informed that, while we could 'keep' the program for a second year, we would be required to give the District TEN days of substituting in classrooms in addition to running our project.

Steve, being our liaison, set up a separate meeting with Alberta, where he tried persuading the administrator to reconsider us as substitutes all together. He explained that the time we worked to make our program successful, added to the five extra days of subbing, put us retirees EACH well over three times the amount of hours we would have put in if we just substituted our contractual days.

Lipinski then produced timesheets, which Jerry, he and I kept of the hours we worked each day. Alberta was impressed, ESPECIALLY when Lipinski explained how we worked almost every day of the week on our project, even on the days we subbed. He explained how we worked on Saturdays, as well. Those were the days we held our tournaments, gave sports clinics to coaches, lined soccer fields, etc.

Steve finished his spiel by saying, "Our first year was busy, VERY busy. But Jerry, Abe, and I feel we did something important for the young kids of Brighton District. We, reluctantly, accepted the fact that we had to do five days of substituting, too. As I have explained, we put in MORE than the hours required by the district, according to our contracts, just working the after-school program. Those five days subbing in the class put EXTRA stress on us. We will be working in a lot of hours again THIS year in order to keep our program running smoothly....MUCH more than what we would have to do if we subbed ALL our days. In fact, we were hoping we wouldn't even have to do FIVE days of substituting during our second year. Telling us we have ten days....that just doesn't seem fair."

Alberta listened to Steve while nodding knowingly at everything he said. Then she said, "Steve, you and the other retirees did a wonderful job." How she knew that, I have no idea. She never once made a PRACTICE at any school, let alone attend a game or any of the tournaments. "But we already are paying you fellas a LOT more money than we have ever paid other early-retirees. Quite frankly, the District is spending much more money than we anticipated on your program, and that is putting a tremendous strain on our entire sports budget."

"In addition," Logia continued, "if we are still hemorrhaging money at the end of this coming year, we may have to make some DRASTIC decisions."

"Like what?" Steve retorted, as he was getting MORE than a bit agitated.

"Let's just see where things are going this year, then we will discuss what needs to be done. However, you all WILL be required to work in the classrooms for ten days this coming season. That should help relieve some of the financial strain on our sports budge simply by us saving money on paying 'ouside' substitutes. We'll have you three subbing."

The meeting ended and Lipinski broke the tough news to Jerry and me, and none of us was happy. It needs to be noted, however, that we DID consider going right to the District Superintendent AND School Board with our uneasiness of being substitutes in addition to running our successful after-school sports program. But we also knew that the Board usually did what the Superintendent asked, and SHE listened seriously to Alberta Logia. We would just have to sub for the mandatory ten days, or risk losing the sports endeavor and doing nothing BUT substitute through the rest of our contracts.

We had nowhere else to turn. We heard that Alberta was the ONLY administrator in the District office who had ever been involved in any sporting activity. Apparently, she had once been a school cheerleader, though none of us were certain where or when that happened. Sadly, this particular administrator was the only administrator to CLAIM having any athletic background, so we basically had NO support from anyone. It was Alberta's way or the highway.

Here's another sad circumstance. Talk about lack of administrative support for our after-school sports program….with ALL the games we had during our first year of existence, and with all the tournaments, too, we only had ONE administrator even come to ONE of our sporting events on purpose. We DID have a fluke visit from a school principal one day. Yep, a female principal, from one of our feeder schools, just happened to be on campus during a Saturday tournament. When she came up to me, she explained that she had heard a lot of noise outside, and came to see what was going on. I explained that her school was sponsoring the boys' soccer tournament, and there would be three games that day.

She smiled, looked at the action for a few seconds, then she disappeared. One principal, of one school, one time….and that is the ONLY time any of us remember seeing top brass enjoying what the young athletes were doing.

Turns out that the second year of our after-school program was more successful than the first, and that was good.

We had more students going out for their respective school's athletic teams, which meant getting more kids into trying sports. I didn't have to 'beat the bushes' to find all new coaches, either, as several established coaches, from the various schools, started recruiting some of their school peers into getting involved. These two situations created even MORE esprit de corps at all the schools, which was a VERY good thing….or so WE thought, anyway.

Also, DeWitt coaches got hold of Jerry, Steve and me to tell us that the in-coming 7th grade athletes had skills WELL above those of the previous several years, which was a tribute to the our new program, too.

I got VERY excited when that year's wrestling tournament came around, as two high school wrestling coaches from the area came by to offer assistance. They both told me that they had heard of our venture and wanted to see what kind of talent we were turning out in our lower grades.

When that tournament was over I had a father come to me and declare that his son, a NATIONALLY-ranked, age-group dirt bike rider had become interested in becoming a champion wrestler, and his family's focus was squarely on having the boy succeed in his new-found sport. Two sidelights here… the young 6th grader was asked to join a high school summer wrestling camp, (from one of the visiting coaches) and that same kid became a high school champion his senior year of high school.

We loved hearing parents singing praises about what we were doing, and attendance at both the games and tournaments tripled from the first year. Our program had a GREAT second year!

Unfortunately, the three of us had to each sub for ten days, and that made OUR days longer and even more stressful. We didn't put in as many hours on the after-school program, that is for sure, but we still put in MANY more hours than just being substitutes would have required.

As our third year approached, Ms Logia called the three of us to her office for a meeting. According to Alberta, money was STILL a major concern, and we three would be required to substitute FIFTEEN days, which would be a necessary stop-gap measure

'Helping to keep the after-school sports around for one more year,' according to the administrator.

Then Logia dropped some VERY disturbing news. "Starting in the fourth year, Brighton District will require us three retirees to be classroom substitutes ONLY. The sports program would be turned over to the respective schools' P.E. personnel. Those folks were to be paid $1000 a year, "BUT," Alberta told us, "The $1000 is just to do the after-school activity. There won't be tournaments, as the District would have to pay them more to work on Saturdays." Then she sort of laughed. "You guys could volunteer to do the tournaments, if you want. But the only way I can see us affording to keep the after-school program is to have the gym teachers do it. It's become way too expensive."

We sat there dumb-founded....fifteen days as subs during our third year, ending with us losing our project the fourth and fifth years because money was a problem. I can tell you, Jerry, Steve and I left THAT meeting in very angry moods.

The third year was WAY harder than the first two. Substituting was getting harder and harder on me, I know that. We had less time working with our pet project, and relied on the gym teachers to help us out, especially by convincing their respective students to join teams. The three of us felt the program slipping away, as fewer kids got involved that year, and we couldn't make as many visits to schools to help coaches, either. The games went well enough, and the tournaments were every bit as successful as the first two years. But we three were getting more exhausted and seeing less success. We were worried we'd lose our project, COMPLETELY, before we were finished with our mandatory five year early-retirement program ended.

Steve Lipinski, however, was NOT willing to concede the demise of our wonderful program. He told Jerry and me that he
would be working on finding a way to GET the necessary money.

Steve had established a lot of connections, during our initial
year as retirees, with companies whose businesses were set up to
help school sports' programs be successful. After contacting a few
newer organizations, Lipinski finally talked with a well-known,
youth-oriented company. That company's spokesman said his
group would be more than willing to look into helping Brighton.

Lipinski and the spokesman had several meetings, which lasted
several months, but the two men eventually came up with a work-
able solution. The company agreed to take on most of the financial responsibility Alberta Logia had complained about. The only
exception was that Brighton District would need to pay the three
of us, as we weren't employees of the company.

Here's how the deal went down. The three of us retirees would
stay on in the capacity of program supervisors. This was to ensure
the continuity of a smooth-working program. We would also work
with the various schools toward shifting whatever leadership was
needed, in order to maintain the program once the three of us
were gone from the District.

The COMPANY would assume the purchase of uniforms for
all teams. They would find and pay for referees. They would
arrange for transportation to all games and tournaments. With
this arrangement, Steve and the company would be freeing up
Brighton District, so it could use its sports funds any way it wished
WITHOUT using anything extra for an elementary school after-
school sports program. Of course, Brighton would pay us three

retirees, and the only REAL responsibility for the P.E. people would be for them to continue to encourage their athletes to join the schools` sports teams AND be ready to take over after we retirees finished our contracts. AND the District could save four thousand dollars a year by NOT having to pay P.E. teachers....just us retirees.

While negotiating this fine arrangement, Steve DID ask the company spokesman how his business would be making money in the deal. Lipinski was told that the company would recoup its money by collecting tournament attendance fees, selling t-shirts and other souvenirs at tournaments, and luring our young athletes into joining the various sports programs, which were being presented by the company throughout the school year and during the summer. Getting athletes to participate in camps was NOT a problem, or so Steve was told.

Lipinski was even given a list of a few area high schools happily under contract for the up-coming year, which he or Logia could call if there was any concern. Bottom line was that this company could, and would, help Brighton with budget problems. All Brighton had to do was pay US for the allocated days of our respective contracts.

Naturally, when Steve told Jerry and me about what would be happening, we ALL were ecstatic. We would be doing what we loved, which was working with kids in sports and knowing the rewards FAR off-set the time we would be devoting to it. Brighton would benefit by having our wonderful creation in the district, while NOT struggling to find more and more money, each year, for the sports program. And I was hopeful of NEVER having to substitute in the classroom again.

When Lipinski had the sports company fully committed to the plan, he called for a meeting with Alberta Logia. Importantly, the meeting was to take place WELL before the start of the fourth year of school.

Logia told us point-blank, "No company will be allowed to use our athletes and families to make a profit for themselves. Not in Brighton District. Not on my watch!"

To say the meeting got heated is an understatement. Tempers flared, and discussion turned into argument. Steve asked her to research the company, and call high schools for verification that this group was helpful, not hurtful. Finally, Logia said she was done talking. Her mind was made up. Our program was going to undergo HER major overhaul, and it would start in its fourth year of existence. She did, however tell us, graciously, that we could 'volunteer' to run the weekend sports tournaments, but finished the statement by telling us, "The last two years on your contracts will be used exclusively as substitute teachers in the Brighton District." We, graciously, told her to kiss off.

Once out of that woman's office, we headed directly to our District Superintendent for a chat. We three complained profusely that we were being shunned EVEN after we found 'the money solution.' We knew she had little background in athletics, but maybe we could get her to listen to reason....ESPECIALLY since it involved a lot of children without the use of a lot of extra funds.

We were told that Alberta Logia was 'on top of matters' and she (Superintendent) 'would not intercede. Alberta's decision was final.'

Jerry Hamilton, in a calm voice, asked, "How many days are we required to work in order to receive our early-retirement benefits?"

"Technically, only one," the Superintendent answered. "But each day you work, you get paid handsomely. Therefore, it is to BOTH our benefits if you put in the entire quota stipulated in your contracts."

"But, we won't be penalized if we teach just ONE day, right?" Jerry questioned.

"No, but we expect you to comply with your contract, Mr. Hamilton," was her answer.

Jerry Hamilton worked JUST one day, for each of his last two years as an early-retiree. Steve Lipinski worked all thirty of his days, for that time, mainly subbing for the physical education teachers of all the schools. As for me, I worked thirty painful days my fourth year, but only nine days my last year.

None of us worked any more tournaments, and the elementary, after-school program started going downhill. After my 32nd and last year in Brighton, I never asked if that particular program survived, but if I was a betting man, well, you know.

My fourth year of early retirement was stressful, and unrewarding. I dreaded going to substitute in those classes where discipline was just a suggestion, or where lesson plans were a joke. I spent a great deal of my time writing referrals for misbehaving kids, and I was never allowed to teach....just do the best I could with the students, and try to survive those thirty days.

Behavior was usually rude and disrespectful, I thought, for the 2003-2005 school years, ESPECIALLY at DeWitt. I remember subbing in a 7th grade class, one day, when a girl asked to go to the library to return a book. That was in homeroom, and AFTER I took attendance. She never returned. A boy came to my desk after homeroom and told me an interesting story. He informed me that she and her two best friends planned to 'skip' school on that particular day, so they coordinated a 'book return' in their respective homerooms. They'd done it before. I asked him why he didn't mention that to me WHILE she was trying to sign out. He shrugged his shoulders and went on to his 1st hour class.

However, I found out later, the other two girls weren't allowed to leave, as THEIR 'regular' homeroom teachers were on to them. I reported the incident to the office, and that was that. Still, I was glad I wouldn't have to have that delinquent in my English class later in the day.

Frequent shenanigans like that were, supposedly, an every day occurrence in the junior high, or so I was told. I missed the 'good old days' of respect, and discipline at Wilhelm. In 2003-2004, and 2004-2005, however, I was just a lowly substitute, and substitutes got NO respect in Brighton District, as far as I was concerned.

I remember having to sub at Cahill School, one day during my fourth year....a day when I KNEW I wasn't cut out for subbing. I was to work a split day, working the morning in the fifth grade, as that grade level was having a half-day conference on campus, and the afternoon in the 6th grade, when it was the 6th grade teachers who were required to attend the school-mandated conference.

The morning was a bit hectic, as usual, but doable. I then walked my fifth grade students to lunch, and said good-bye. As I was leaving the lunchroom to go eat my lunch in peace SOMEWHERE, I noticed a 6th grader raising holy hell in the cafeteria. He was cussing rather loudly at other kids, and bullying smaller boys by stealing their food. He was run out of the cafeteria by the teacher on lunch duty in the cafeteria.

I proceded to ask the duty teacher who that kid was, and she informed me he was a 6th grader. When she told who his teacher was, I could feel my blood pressure rising until I thought I might explode. He was going to be in the class I was assigned for that afternoon.

I forgot about eating and headed directly to the room where 6th grade conferences were going to be held. All the afternoon participants were filing in, and it didn't take me long to find the teacher I needed to see. I asked to see her outside of that room, and when I told her what I witnessed, she said, "Yes, he is a little imp sometimes, but he isn't a bad kid."

Not good enough for me. I responded, "He was definitely MORE than an imp in the lunch room. When he sees he has a substitute teacher for the afternoon, he will be hell-on-wheels. I will NOT work in your classroom if that student shows up, and that is the simple fact. He is out of there, or I am out of there, you make the choice."

The teacher was a young woman, maybe in her first or second year, I didn't care. She looked at me with disbelief that I would say such a thing about her student, and tell her MY intentions. While still smiling, she said, "I'm sorry you feel that way, but I need you to work with my class today. He will not be there." She turned and walked away without any more discussion.

My blood pressure felt sky-high as the bell rang for the students to get to afternoon classes. I heard that she arranged for that kid to be in in-house detention all afternoon, as a result of his 'acting-out' at lunch. He was upset about it, but I was delighted. Still, the afternoon had its usual ups and downs, and I couldn't WAIT to get home that night….just another miserable day of subbing.

The entire 30 days DRAGGED by, even though I spent way less time subbing than working the after-school sports program. I just wasn't happy. It didn't matter WHAT grade level I worked, there were disturbances, and problems like I had NEVER experienced when I was a classroom teacher. I can't think of a single day when I went home, after subbing, with a smile on my face.

As the fifth year began, I ran into even MORE trouble with students and their behavior. After eight days of being miserable subbing in any class that came along, I made a decision to ONLY substitute for teachers that I remembered being good disciplinarians….teachers I had known when I was still in the classroom.

Time passed, but then I got a telephone call from a friend of mine, whom I knew to have been been a wonderful 5th grade teacher, at Wilhelm, for more than ten years. FINALLY, on the ninth day of my last year substituting, I was going to be in a friendly class-room….or so I imagined.

Emily Quinn had a good reputation, and I knew her to be loved by all her students, EVERY year. She swore her class that year was not only the best-behaving class at Wilhelm, but amongst the best-behaved she had ever taught. Emily let me know that she had made out specific and detailed lesson plans for the morning classes, AND that there were class projects assigned for the afternoon. "All my students know exactly what they have to do," she said boldly. "You might just bring a book to read, for the afternoon, you will get so bored."

We laughed about that last comment, but I said it would be my honor to work in her wonderful classroom.

And they were wonderful....well, ALMOST every child was wonderful.

There was a girl in that class, Abby was her name. She was a special-needs child, having Down's Syndrome. Generally, students afflicted with the disorder are sweet and friendly....and Abby was, too, except for two interesting situations. One, Wilhelm usually had an aide in the class with Abby, as the little girl had trouble keeping up with the speed the other kids had absorbing daily material. She needed special, one-on-one attention, as she desperately wanted to fit in with the rest of her classmates. Wilhelm had the foresight to do that for her, and it worked. However, on the day I was subbing, the aide was absent from school. According to the rest of the class, it was the first day the aide had missed all year.

The second situation involved a boy, Alberto Saenz, by name. He was a great kid. A leader in the room whom everyone liked, especially Abby. She claimed him as her boyfriend, but he told me he had NO girlfriend.

I proceded with the lesson plans for the first assignment, but Abby raised her hand to tell me she didn't know what to do. Fortunately, a girl sitting next to Abby helped her friend understand what was going on. However, when it came time to work on her OWN assignments, say, the daily math worksheet, the 'neighbor' got busy doing the work SHE needed to do, and couldn't help Abby. I would go right back to Abby each time it was independent work time, and help Abby get started. But when there were OTHER students needing guidance on certain things, I felt compelled to go to their aide.

However, when I needed to explain something, ANYTHING, to another student, or if I happened to have my back turned away from Abby for any reason, that girl would get out of her seat, and go to Alberto's desk. There she would stand just start staring at him....always with a HUGE smile on her face.

"Mr. Stein," Alberto would softly say each time, "Abby's at my desk again, and I can't work with her standing over me like this."

The first time that happened, I excused myself from the student I was helping, and walked Abby back to HER desk. She kept looking back at Alberto and continued smiling.

Another student needing help from me....another visit from Abby to Alberto....and another, me, walking Abby back to her desk. That had become my morning routine.

After several of these incidences, I decided to ask Abby to return to her desk, unaccompanied by me. For whatever reason, she yelled, "NO!" and ran out of the classroom, heading toward Wilhelm's big playground.

I yelled, "Abby, you can't be out there! You have to be in class!"

She ignored me. Fortunately, another girl in the class said, "She listens to me. I'll go get her back." And in five minutes both girls were in class again.

This scene played out, yet again, with my giving the last lesson of the morning. And AGAIN the little volunteer went to get Abby and return her to class.

Shortly after Abby was brought back to class, we were informed it was time for Emily's class to line up outside and walk to lunch. But Abby didn't WANT to go to lunch yet, so once again she took off running toward the field. "Abby, come back!" I yelled, definitely running out of patience. There are no teachers on lunch duty yet, so I have to take you, and this class, to the cafeteria!"

"NO!" she yelled back, defiantly, and she continued on her playground journey.

"Alberto," I sighed with total exasperation, "will you, please, walk the class to lunch? And tell the lunch monitor teacher, that I had to go get Abby from the field. I'll get back as soon as I can."

By the time I got Abby to the lunch line, the rest of my students had already entered the building and were eating. Then Abby spoke up, "My lunch is in my homeroom."

Back we went to get her lunch, and then returned to the cafeteria. "I don't want to eat. I want to go play," Abby announced.

By THAT time, a 'duty' teacher was at her station, so I said to Abby. "I'm required to take you INTO the cafeteria. I won't be sitting with you, so you do whatever you want. But, I am CERTAIN that your mom would want you to eat your lunch. With that I wheeled around, and ONLY turned around when I reached the door to see what Abby was doing. She had opened her lunch sack and was eating. I left the building feeling totally exhausted.

The afternoon was just as frustrating. Emily had told me that the entire afternoon was to be spent with her students working on their own individual class projects. She had told me they ALL knew exactly what to do. So, I mentioned to the kids, EXACTLY, what their teacher had told me. Once I finished I went to my desk.

Within seconds, I had FIVE students standing by me. One student told me he had been absent and didn't HAVE an assignment. One student told me she didn't WANT to work with her group, while another girl complained that her group didn't want to work with HER. Two students were reporting to me that their respective groups had no idea what they were supposed to be doing. And the topper, yes, the topper, I hear Alberto telling me that Abby was back at his desk again.

I struggled to make it through the afternoon, and when I went to the front office to sign out, the principal, a woman I had known for fifteen years, approached me. "Well, Abe, did you have a fabulous day?" she queried with a broad smile on her face.

"You know Abby, the little girl with Down's Syndrome?" I asked.

"Sure, EVERYBODY knows Abby. She is such a delight."

"Is she supposed to have an aide help her with the work when she has trouble?"

"Yeah, she does, normally, and I guess I could have sent someone there to work with her today, since her regular aide was absent today," the principal responded.

I looked at the administrator, and she was silent for a pregnant moment, then she continued. "But, I remembered that we had Abe Stein in there with her today, and he can handle it." She smiled a huge smile, proudly thinking she was complimenting me.

I stood there, trying to ascertain if her words were meant to flatter me. I felt certain that NO other substitute would have been left with such a difficult situation, so I stood there, calmly fuming, if there is such a thing.

That is when I decided a short soliloquy was in order. "You know," I began, "I did my student teaching here at Wilhelm. I started my TEACHING career here at Wilhelm. But today....I felt like I was thrown into a situation without being given all the facts. Abby pretty much needs constant attention, and I believe everybody knows that. I was given a lot of assignments to present this morning, and that little girl became lost, each time, because I could NOT be with her 100% of the time. She needed someone to help her, but no help was sent, and I was put into a failing position. So, I have decided that today will be the last day for me to work in the Brighton District. Wilhelm, I salute you." Without another word being spoken by either the principal or me, I whirled around and left the building.

Thirty-two years I worked for the Brighton District, and it seemed only right that I ended my career at the same school where I started.

I was fully retired when that school year ended. I had started as a bushy-tailed, eager to reach EVERY child, idealist, and I left as a frustrated, totally exhausted, babysitter. When the next school year began, and I DIDN'T have to report for an assignment, I was delighted. I swore I was done with the Brighton District, and I was done with kids, too….though, truth be known, those two statements aren't exactly true.

14

GIVING BACK

A FTER I LEFT Wilhelm that day, I never really thought about that school much, OR of the District where I spent thirty-two of my life being employed. Steve Lipinski and Jerry Hamilton remained my best friends, and we did lunch together, and went to Las Vegas, from time to time, for a show and to have a little fun. But, in the back of my mind, I knew I had some unfinished business in Brighton District before I could feel COMPLETELY free from guilt.....damn, Jewish guilt!

It's true, I certainly wasn't happy leaving Wilhelm and Brigthon under the circumstances of my last day. And it is true that I never felt I got much, if any, respect from administrators....which is only fair since I didn't respect them much, either. But, just walking away like I did, that bothered me for several years after my early-retirement years were over.

I had had a LOT of good years at Wilhelm, and there were many, MANY great students that I remembered fondly, from

BOTH Wilhelm and DeWitt. I didn't want to be remembered as a teacher who got frustrated and walked away from the kids.

ALSO true, is the fact that the district didn't waver from the 'deal' it made with me, when I early retired. They followed through with each 'perk' they offered me to retire early. So I DID have some respect for them on that matter.

My first thought was to leave a legacy for Wilhelm….maybe buying a bunch of new books for their library. But, I wanted the people in the DISTRICT to know I did something special, and leaving books for just one school would not have the effect I wished to leave.

I thought on the matter a great deal. One of my most enjoyable memories, year in and year out, was the night when 8th graders graduated. The kids looked nicely-dressed. Behavior was acceptable. There was a lot of smiling and all-around happiness with everyone.

One of the highlights, of each graduation, was announcing students who had earned a scholarship. Certain organizations would send announcements to the schools, offering the chance for SOMEONE in the class to win a scholarship. There were certain criteria that had to be met, and someone had to write a letter, good enough to win the free gift, in order for anyone to be considered for a scholarship.

Granted, most of the gifts were a mere $100, and that money was deposited into the winner's high school library or office, and could ONLY be used for school supplies, but I never missed an opportunity to have one of my students represented in the contest.

If one of our kids won a scholarship, there always seemed to be a sense of unashamed pride shown by the student who had his name called out for that special free gift. And, naturally, if one of my students won the prize, I would beam with pride, too, knowing I did my part to get him/her the scholarship. And I can tell you that several of the scholarship offers were sent to schools throughout the Phoenix area, so getting even one WAS a big deal. One year we had THREE winners, and I had entered a letter for all three of them. But, none of the winners, through the year, knew I had written letters on their behalf. No one told them how they got them, they just got them. And I certainly wasn't going to blow my own horn on THEIR special night. I wrote them, the students got them, and that was the end of that.

The year was 2011, and I was getting Medicare, so my health benefits were no longer being picked up by Brighton District. I felt strongly that I needed to give back to the district that honored its contract with me, so when I mentioned the scholarship idea to Katherine, my wife, she agreed whole-heartily that my idea was perfect. I knew I wanted to give $1000, but thought multiple scholarships would be better than one big scholarship. With that in mind I went to my former junior high.

I decided to meet with Greta Jamison, who was not only a former teacher at DeWitt, but had become the new principal for that school.

I remember the whole event like it was yesterday. One the first week, of the last quarter of school, I strolled into the DeWitt office. I didn't recognize a single person working there, but saw that Greta was in HER office, working on some paperwork. When she saw me at the front desk, she came rushing out. "Abe, it is great seeing you.

You look wonderful, and we miss you around here. What brings you here today?"

Greta and I had worked together for the eleven years I taught there, and she was ALWAYS a positive-thinking person, who just seemed to not let herself get down with any problems. I was certain that her bubbly personality was exactly what DeWitt needed, so I was happy to see she had become the 'boss.' "May I talk you in your office for a minute?" I said with a happy-to-see-you smile on my face. "I know you're busy, but I have a proposition that I hope you'll like."

After exchanging a few pleasantries, I told her of my scholarship idea. I decided to give FIVE individual scholarships, to deserving students, for the 2012 graduation. When I mentioned that each gift would be worth $200, Greta stared at me with a bewildered look on her face. "Abe, that is mighty generous of you, but why so many, and why so much for each scholarship?"

"Greta, I used to fight tooth-and-nail to win our 8th graders year-end scholarships, and when our kids got them, I was proud, the students were proud, the PARENTS were proud." Then I commenced to explain how nice the District was to honor my entire early-retirement package....including picking up the payments on my health insurance until I turned 65. "I don't know ANYONE in this year's graduation class. So I have an idea of how to get these awards to the right people," I said with assuredness.

"Well, Abe, whatever you have in mind should work just fine. What's your plan?"

"I want to call them Sylvia scholarships," I continued.

"Sylvia? Did I know a Sylvia?

"Sylvia Contreras came to DeWitt, straight from Mexico, in her 7th grade year, "I explained. She was ESL, but was highly motivated to learn English, and was VERY competent in the language when she came to my homeroom in the 8th grade."

"Sure, I remember Sylvia," Greta interjected. "A really nice girl, and a hard-worker."

"Exactly," I said with some excitement in my voice. "She was a true star in my homeroom....star athlete in intramurals, honor roll all four quarters, volunteered for anything I asked the class to do for community service. AND, all the other ESL students would seek her out if they needed help with schoolwork OR social life. She was just so nice and helpful. Quite simply, Sylvia Contreras was the person I considered the most outstanding representative of my homeroom. But, Sylvia never seemed to be considered for any scholarships, and I thought that to be a crime. We had several 'gifts' given out at her graduation, but they all went to popular students, kids with big personalities, who were known by everyone on campus. THOSE kids were certainly deserving of winning, as popular kids seem to be EVERY year.

Sylvia was MY class's popular personality, but she was so quiet, Alpha Team didn't know her at all, and Beta Team's, more visible kids, considered her 'just a nice girl on our team.' I really wanted to see how I could find her a scholarship, but there weren't any with HER criteria that surfaced.

"She was a great person, for sure." Greata chimed in. "But, Abe, we have had several nice people EVERY year, and most of them just aren't visible enough to be thought worthy of scholarships. What criteria are you going to use for YOUR scholarships?"

"It's true, Greta, when Sylvia was on campus, she kept a low-profile," I began. "While she was involved in everything she could be, when AT school, she had several responsibilities, away from DeWitt, that kept her out of school-sponsored activities.

For our homeroom intramurals, she was a tremendous soccer player, as well as a very good volleyball player AND softball player. She just couldn't get involved in any AFTER-SCHOOL activities, either in sports, OR any of the after-school clubs that were offered then. Her family duties came first."

"Greta, her mother was a maid for some hotel, somewhere, and had to leave for work BEFORE her kids even got up each day. There was no dad around. Sylvia, being the eldest, had to get her two younger siblings up, get them ready for school, and walk them to their school, before SHE was allowed get to DeWitt."

"Her brother and sister, also, were OUT of school before Sylvia was, and they were told to wait in their school office until Sylvia could get there and walk them home. Every afternoon, when OUR tardy bell rang, Sylvia Contreras made a beeline to her little bother and sister's school."

"When she got them home, it was HER responsibility to have them do their homework, and she worked right along side of them to make sure all of them got finished. THEN, she would make dinner for the family, as her mother was putting in long, LONG hours. Mom had no transportation, either, so she was forced to walk to her job. Sylvia's mother couldn't afford bus fare, so she walked, EVEN if she was exhausted. Not having much money was a huge problem for Sylvia's family, but they chose NOT to be on welfare... too much pride, I'm guessing."

"In addition to everything else, Sylvia's family was VERY religious. They all volunteered for their church whenever they could, which was often. At least that is what Sylvia told me, and I DO believe giving was second-nature to the Contreras family."

"Greta, this kid deserved a MEDAL, let alone a scholarship. But she just couldn't get involved with all the clubs and sports popular kids were into, therefore, she was never considered for a scholarship....and I thought that a crime. So, I am going to honor her with, not one, but FIVE scholarships this year."

"And here's some irony, I have no idea how to find her, so she won't be at DeWitt's graduation to appreciate the honor she deserves. Sadly, I will be out of town when this year's graduation rolls around, too. We'll talk about who will give out the rewards later."

I saw the principal's eyes glaze over a bit, as I talked about the virtues of Sylvia. "Yep," she said, "Sylvia was a great kid, and now I wish, too, she could have gotten a scholarship. So, how do we go about getting five scholarships to five deserving students?"

"I have a plan that gets a lot of your students involved. In fact, my idea can be a help to teachers, as well," I responded, and feeling my heart pound with pride that I would, actually, be doing something good for the district.

"I propose that ALL students be told to be aware of the quiet, unassuming kid sitting in every class with them, or other 8th graders whom they know from around school." I continued, trying not to speak too rapidly. "Teachers can make this a GREAT assignment, incorporating some research with the writing of a wonderful essay."

"If I had given this lesson to MY students, I would have had each kid seek out a nice, yet QUIET kid, who isn't well-know, and find out everything about him or her….you know, what's the kid's life like outside of school, as well as what positive ventures he or she is into around DeWitt."

"Once information had been gathered, I would have had all my students write a MINIMUM 250-word essay, explaining why the researched student might be deserving of a scholarship. Students would NOT be allowed to write about anyone who is a good friend, OR anyone who is universally known as a star around DeWitt already."

"I want your teachers to emphasize finding students who are flying under the radar, but still doing wonderful things, both on AND off campus."

There were nearly nine more weeks left in school, the day I spoke with Greta, so I proposed that I meet with her teachers, sooner, rather than later, to explain to THEM my ideas, and answer any questions. I definitely wanted to emphasize how this writing could be used as a benefit to teachers, as well. "The assignment could be used as a creative writing exercise, where grades could be given for BOTH content and the correct use of established writing parameters in sentence structure, and paragraph formation," I said wanting to give concrete reasons for teachers to get involved.

"IF teachers already have a full schedule of work lined up for the rest of the year, they might use the writing as extra-credit work. No matter HOW DeWitt's 8th grade teachers incorporate my 'scholarship' writing, I believe EVERYBODY can benefit from getting on board with my idea. If I can get the teachers motivated, I know I won't have any trouble finding five, deserving 8th grade students, whom I could help financially during their freshman year in high school."

Greta seemed excited enough and she set a date one week, from that initial conversation, for me to meet with teachers working with 8th grade students. She told me the meeting would be held 'Before school begins,' and it 'Had to be fifteen minutes or less.' The principal apologized for the shortness of the meet, but explained that she wanted to make sure her teachers 'Have the necessary time needed to get their rooms ready for the day.'

The principal also ASSURED me that every teacher, who worked with an 8th grade student, would attend that meeting. I was grateful and left the school grounds with a huge smile on my face. I couldn't ever remember doing THAT when I taught there.

Greta Jamison was the FIRST administrator, who didn't try to belittle me, or pooh-pooh my ideas and achievements. She was a boss who let her teachers take the reigns of good plans, and run with them. I was grateful she was willing to let me 'pitch' my idea to her staff.

Katherine and I got to DeWitt early, on the appointed day, and talked to Greta for a couple of minutes. Then we headed to an Alpha Team 8th grade room for the meeting. The teacher of that room, a swarthy, young man, dressed in a baggy old shirt, a pair of old jeans, and a pair of sandals. He was at his desk, grading some papers, and when Greta introduced Katherine and me, he never glanced up from his stack of papers, nor said a word….just gave a curt nod of the head, while continuing to work.

This fella looked like he could have just gotten to school from a homeless shelter. Two thoughts came to mind when I saw him, either the pay scale in Brighton was unbearably low, or their dress standards were unbearably relaxed. Either way, I also thought about how my first principal, Mr. Charles Fletcher, would have re-acted to this fellow. The principal was upset that I didn't wear a white shirt and tie, for crying out loud. The sight of this guy might just have given the old man a heart attack.

For sure, this 'modern-day' teacher didn't seem the least bit interested in the fact he had two guests in his room. Actually, by his not uttering a word of welcome, or even glancing our way, I considered the lout extremely rude.

Ten minutes passed before all 14 teachers, who worked with 8th graders, arrived, and I was shocked at the way most of the OTHER new, young teachers were dressed, too. Many were just as dishev-eled as our 'host' teacher. But I didn't have time to gawk and complain, Greta let me know I would have to hurry with my pre-sentation, as the lateness of her staff, to the meeting, had limited my speaking time.

I recognized just one teacher from my past, and she was an ex-ception to the dress code that was, apparently, allowed at DeWitt. Her name was Allison Smithson, and she had been an aide for the 8th grade Beta Team when I was still in the classroom. She had, FINALLY, gotten her education degree and was an 8th grade teach-er, an 8th grade English teacher on the Beta Team. That made me happy. Her appearance was a throwback to the professional dress of teachers during my era....nice dress with shoes to match, and her hair looked well styled. I had noticed several of the young female teachers looking like they had just gotten in from a date, and didn't have time to fix their hair in a presentable manner.

I had sheets of paper with all the instructions on the scholarship idea available, and Katharine handed them out. With little time to get 'deep' with my inspirational speech, I decided to hit some of the MAIN areas of concern. "I DON'T want the writers just choosing a 'friend' to write about....but rather they need to write about students who don't run in the same social circles as the writers." I emphasized. "MOST importantly, I want to see students writing with flair. They need to explain generalized words and phrases like: 'good athlete,' 'smart student,' and 'friendly and helpful.' I need to read SPECIFIC examples when the scholarship candidate's traits were exhibited."

With the few moments I had to present my project, I was, 'Animated and full of encouragement,' according to Katharine when I asked for feedback) However my audience, except for Allison, and a couple of the older teachers who seemed to pay attention, the vast majority of my audience were either daydreaming, had their eyes fluttering while trying to stay awake, or were doing what the host teacher was doing....grading papers.

To me, it felt like the majority of them didn't give a rat's ass about trying to get scholarships for their students. I felt unwelcome and embarrassed to be wasting my time.

The bell rang, alerting students to report to homeroom. In the room where I was presenting, it was like a fire alarm had gone off. Teachers flew out of the room as Greta YELLED, "I want to thank Mr. Stein, for being here this morning..." She didn't bother to finish many words after those, as the room cleared instantly.....except for the host teacher, who kept grading papers....and Allison, who came up to greet me and tell me how happy she was that I was wanting to give back to the District.

Greta apologized about EVERYTHING, and assured me that she would gather those same teachers, after a school-wide meeting, being held later that day, and go over my handout. She and I DID set up a date when I would be allowed to collect the finished products, however. That date was set a GOOD five weeks after my presentation....plenty of time for the teachers to get the assignment to their respective classes.

I kept trying to convince myself that IF Greta would make sure the teachers understood the criteria, and IF she could 'push' them, a bit, until each teacher handed in several good papers, then I would be a happy camper as graduation got near.

I have to admit, though, I left DeWitt filled with consternation. I was worried that I wouldn't have even ONE good paper from any teacher except Allison Smithson. My reception at DeWitt had been horrible, but I wanted to trust in Greta, that she would come through for the 8th graders, and inspire her teachers to work at getting FIVE scholarship-worthy essays to me.

I thought about calling Greta many times, during the next five weeks. But I knew how busy she would be with year-end business, and making a pest of myself would NOT be in my best interest. I actually waited until two days prior to my 'collection' date before I did call.

The principal was friendly enough during our conversation, BUT, (and this was a big but) she asked if I could give her an additional two days, past the pick-up date, in order to, 'Collect ALL the papers,' as she put it. Sadly, I knew what that meant, and went to DeWitt expecting to be disappointed, which I was.

The principal was amiable enough, when I entered her office.... big smile, warm greeting, and all. Then she handed over a folder containing the 'finalists,' which were, supposedly, hand-picked by her stellar group of 8th grade teachers to be the best papers the entire 8th grade could come up with.

Sixteen papers....SIXTEEN PAPERS, were all that came in from the nearly 300 students. "To be fair," Greta said, as she saw the shocked look on my face, "While the assignment could be presented by any 8th grade teacher who works with 8th grade students, only those teachers who deal with the actual WRITING of the essays would make the determination of what was good and not so good. That group, then, would be only about five or six teachers.... which includes 'special classes' teachers as well as Language Arts teachers. Sorry about the lack of entries."

I stood in Greta's office just flabbergasted. Sure, I knew only the 'writing' teachers would be the ones requiring work from the students on this topic. But teachers of special classes were aware of 'lesser known' students in THEIR classes. I had hoped THEY would have given the 'writers' a few possible kids worthy enough to be considered scholarship material. To say I was more than a little disappointed in the DeWitt staff is an understatement.

I sat in Ms Jamison's office and read each paper....which didn't take long. Of the sixteen papers, twelve of them looked GREAT physically, but they all came from just one class….Allison Smithson's class, the woman who worked with me when I last taught school in the classroom at DeWitt. Her papers had been typed, or written in ink, and showed signs of editing and polishing. There were few grammar errors of any kind. Like I said, very impressive, and exactly what I was looking for.

The other four papers were in pencil, and there was NO sign of ANY kind of editing, or revision, let alone being polished. They looked like papers that had been written during the lunch break and turned in. I thought two of those papers to be just scribbling, but the second pair had some interesting, even poignant statements in them.

As I stood to stretch, I glanced out to the secretary's desk. I saw a teacher, Gary Rifkin, who was, yet, a second person I knew from the old days. He HADN'T attended my scholarship meeting. "Hey, there's Gary Rifkin," I mentioned to Greta, who was working at her desk. "I didn't know he was still here."

Jamison looked at me, rather sheepishly, then said, "He teaches our 'Gifted' program for both the 7th and 8th graders." Greta wanted to continue talking to me about him, but I excused myself to go talk to him myself.

"Gary," I said in my usual friendly manner, "I didn't know you had come back to DeWitt."

"Hey, Abe, how are you? Yeah, I've been back for two years now."

"Ms Jamison informs me that you teach gifted students…. English, right?"

"Yeah, we've been very busy, here lately...getting my students prepared to take the standardized tests. How's retirement?"

"Fine, Gary. But did you know I was here, five weeks ago, presenting an opportunity where DeWitt students could help OTHER DeWitt students get scholarships, which could be used for financial aid in high school?"

"Yeah, I heard about that."

You didn't make my meeting, but did you know what the parameters were in order for students to get scholarships?"

"Yeah," he responded with a wry smile, "I was running late that morning, so I wasn't really sure what the meeting was about. Another teacher mentioned something about it, but since my students are going to get a few scholarships this year anyway, and seeing how busy we were going to be, in order to do well on the standardized tests, I decided to let other teachers work at getting THEIR students scholarships."

First, I was annoyed that the cocky bastard started every sentence with the word 'Yeah,' but I was even more peeved that he didn't let his students get involved with my project. HIS students were the Honor kids, and with very little effort, they would have not only been able to write essays on deserving kids outside their social circles, they would have done a bang-up job. They were the school's elite academians, who weren't allowed to help get some lesser-known, yet deserving, fellow graduates scholarships because their lazy teacher wanted, apparently, to cruise into the final tests of the year and NOT have to grade another set of essays.

Instead of ripping into that conceited, anti-social schmuck, whom I remembered as a guy who was always trying get out of work by cutting corners, I whirled around and went back into Greta's office without another word. I was upset, and wanted to slap that ingrate, but causing a scene would have done nobody any good. Rifkin left the office, and I took the 16 papers home to mull them over.

Allison Smithson had done all of the right things required to have tournament-ready papers available for me to read. TWO papers were outstanding, and were particularly good at description, and not just 'listing' the topic student's attributes. Most of her students' other papers were only fair, mentioning things like: she's very athletic and plays on all the school's sports teams, he is a hard worker in school and makes good grades, or the less-than-stellar comment, she's funny. All right, good points of interest, but WAY too general in description. I NEEDED specifics. I had tried SO hard, both in our brief meeting and on my handout, to emphasize the use of details to back up generalizations. Getting just two 'detailed' papers was disappointing.

Allison was, however, sharp in her corrections of grammar, spelling, sentence structure, etc., but, her papers lacked detailed examples of character. I had figured a student's character to be the single-most important trait for me to know, when I initially decided to offer schoalships.

One of the 'pencil' entries was quite descriptive as well....VERY rife with descriptive incidences, but the paper was fraught with mistakes from a technical point.

When I went in to see the principal again, she could see I was a bit disturbed by what I read. "Yeah, Abe, I'm sorry about the poor turnout of papers," She said apologetically. She began to ramble on with excuse after excuse, defending her teachers. I kind of expected that. However, I was upset with her, AND myself. If I HAD called several times during the past five weeks, I feel she would, most likely, have goosed her teachers to get to work on the project. Who knows, perhaps she could have even gotten the egotistical Gary Rifkin involved in the scholarship project.

When Greta finished I said, rather forlornly, "I know I promised five $200 scholarships," Looking at the principal's face I believe she thought I may just tell her I won't be giving ANY scholarships. "But I only found three even CLOSE to being worthy."

"Sorry, Abe," she quietly uttered, head drooping somewhat.

"However, if it is all right with you, I would like to come in, maybe tomorrow, and interview all sixteen writers," If it is all right with you, I would STILL like to find five deserving students and help make their graduations a happier occasion.

Greta had this wide-eyed look of surprise on her face. "Of course you can come back tomorrow. I want to have happy graduates as well. We will have them come to the office, one at a time, and hopefully you WILL be able to find five deserving students to reward."

One by one, the next morning, my essay students came to Ms Jamison's office, and I asked all of them specific questions about their topic students. I started talking with the TOP eight writers, (whom I thought to be the best writers, anyway) hoping to settle on my five scholarship recipients sooner rather than later. Honestly, I really didn't want to interview all sixteen students.

I called the descriptive 'pencil' girl in first, and asked her, point-blank, how long she had to work on this assignment. "Two days ago, my teacher told the class that we might be able to get a friend of ours a scholarship. We were told to tell about some times when our friend did something good around school, or at home. So I told about things I remember about Charisse, and turned in my work yesterday." she said.

I was furious, but didn't want the student see me angry. "That is the way your teacher told you to approach this paper....write about a friend, and say 'nice things about them? And the first time she told your class was two days ago?"

"Yeah, but my CLOSE friends are all goof-balls. So I know this really nice girl, who is kind of a friend of mine. She is real quiet, and sometimes people pick on because of that. She is always so sweet, though, and doesn't want any trouble, so she just stays quiet. I just thought it would be nice is she got a scholarship, so I chose her to write about."

"So, the girl you wrote about is NOT one of your BEST friends?" I inquired.

"We ARE friendly to each other, but we don't hang out. Like I said in my paper, there were a few times when I needed to talk to someone, and she was there to talk to me, kind of like a friend. MY really good friends would have just made fun of me."

"Your really good friends would just laugh at you....nice friends," I said sarcastically, and the student just laughed nervously. "So you were told about this essay only two days ago?"

"Yeah."

Did your teacher want to collect the papers to read them, or have you exchange papers with other students to edit, revise, and re-write?" I asked, wishing the teacher had done that.

"No, I was the only kid who turned one in, and that was yesterday."

I finished questioning the girl about HER student, and was impressed with the maturity she exhibited in her answers. I knew, right then and there, that I was going to give THAT writer a scholarship, in SPITE of her teacher's lack of effort to help me with the project.

I had one other, 'pencil' student come in. "How long did you have to work on this paper?" I asked, already figuring out it wasn't long.

"Well, two days ago Ms ***** (forgot her name) told me and my friend that if we wanted extra credit, we should write about any student and tell why we think that person should get a scholarship. It had to be 200 words or more. Well, I don't LIKE Ms *****and am worried about passing her class, so I wrote the paper. My friend didn't. In fact, I wrote ABOUT my friend. I have to let Ms Jamison know that she has to get the paper back to my teacher so I can get the extra credit grade, OK?"

"Absolutely," I assured her. "Are all the things you wrote about your friend the truth? You make her seem like a girl who SHOULD get a scholarship. You used too many generic words, however, like: fun, smart, friendly, helpful, but you didn't explain times when she was any of these things."

"She's my friend, so I said as many good things as I could think of. She is SOME of those things, but I can't remember exactly when she was any of them right now. I just wanted it to sound good so I could get a good grade, and pass out of this school."

So much for pencil writer #2. I could NOT believe that, besides Allison Smithson, only three other 8th grade teachers even thought about getting involved in my scholarship essay, and NONE of them solicited much participation from their students. I was angry and disappointed. But, I knew Allison had some pretty good papers, so I focused on calling several of her students in for interviews.

When I was finished talking to the best eight student writers, (including those two students who wrote in pencil) I felt good about finding five deserving people for scholarships. Only three were written ABOUT, and I chose to honor two writers.

When I had my five winners, and was shaking hands with Greta before leaving, through the door walks the Brighton District Superintendent. Her name is insignificant to me, so she will remain nameless. I CAN tell you that she seemed mostly about the politics of education. I never saw her at any kid functions at either of my schools, and CERTAINLY she never attended one of Jerry, Steve or my after-school sporting events.

After saying 'Hello' to Greta's new visitor, I headed toward the door. "Just a minute, Abe, I want you to tell the Superintendent about what it is you are doing. Mr. Stein is doing just the most wonderful thing!" The school principal stated with obvious enthusiasm.

I gave a little two-minute dissertation extolling the scholarship happiness that I, and my former students, experienced in days of yore. I mentioned that giving scholarships was the way I chose to give back after the district followed through, completely, with my early-retirement package. I recognized that Brighton had been facing hard economic times, but showed strong character, by taking care of its teachers through all the adversity. I finished by explaining how I arrived at the decisions I made when determining the five scholarship winners.

The Superintendent stood there, quietly, for a minute of two. Since I had waited several years AFTER I was fully retired before offering my 'gifts,' I was kind of expecting a 'well done' or a 'thank-you, Mr. Stein, for being so thoughtful,' SOMETHING positive from the Superintendent.

Instead, she looked at me, and grimaced. THEN she started to bitterly complain about all the financial hardships Brighton had faced in the past decade. She rambled for a good five minutes, or more. I just stared at her, and waited until she was finished with her tirade. Then I bid both women adieu.

Before the Super had come in, however, I DID ask Greta for three things. First, since I wouldn't be in town to give the scholarship out myself, I asked her to ask Allison Jamison to hand them out. I, also, asked that Greta NOT let Allison know who the winners were....I wanted the teacher to be just as surprised as the students when the announcements were made.

Secondly, I asked if Greta could make sure that the winners got their scholarship money put into the correct school offices and libraries for each respective winner.

Finally, I asked Ms Jamison if she would be so kind as to call me, the Monday after graduation, so I could be home to answer the phone, and find out how the ceremonies went.

I left DeWitt, for the last time, but I WAS delighted that I had found five deserving kids, and hoped they would be appreciative of the scholarships given them at their 8th grade graduation.

Greta HAD promised to call the first Monday after graduation....but I never got the call. SO, on Thursday of that week, I called her.

The call lasted LESS than five minutes, and Greta apologized for NOT calling as she had planned. She said, "Everything went great. Allison gave out the scholarships, and both she and the kids were surprised and happy."

That was her report, so I had to inquire further. "How did Allison react when she saw that three of HER students won scholarships?"

"She was so proud, and hugged ALL the winners."

"Did Allison cry, of cheer, or what when she discoved she had three of her English kids win scholarships?" I inquired trying to get more description out of GRETA.

"Oh, she seemed very proud and hugged all the winners."

Again with the proud and hugging! I kept thinking, 'Come on, Jamison, tell me more,' but there seemed like an eternity of silence coming from the principal.

"How did the kids and parents react?" I implored.

"Oh, most of the parents were crying, and the kids seemed shocked to hear their names." Greta just didn't seem interested in telling me much about anything.

"Any reactions or words from other teachers or administrators about FIVE kids getting $200 scholarships from me?" I asked, now LOOKING to get a few pats on the back.

"No...uh uh....nothing."

And that was that! Greta didn't even mention if my name was spoken before the scholarships were given. I felt sad and somewhat disrespected. In the past, whenever a scholarship was given out, a 'big deal' was made about WHO gave the scholarships, AND how much money each gift was worth. Greta said nothing about me being connected with ANY of the $200 rewards, and yes, that hurt my feelings.

I may NOT have been mentioned or even remembered by anybody at that graduation, but I remember being happy for both Allison Smithson and the five students who received my scholarships. My final impressions of DeWitt, and even Brighton District left an awful taste in my mouth, and I wish to not be bothered by them again.

I will, however, never forget the accomplishments I, and my fellow teachers, made during my thirty-two years working for Brighton. And I will NEVER forget all the wonderful (even the not-so-wonderful) students, with whom I had the privilege to know during my tenure as an educator.

There is an epilogue to follow, but I want to say 'Thank-you' to EVERYONE I had the opportunity to meet throughout my lengthy amount of educational service….the good guys….the bad guys…. and everyone in between. I am a happy camper now, being retired, but ALL of you had input into what got me where I am today. With all my GOOD memories, I find myself smiling with fondness most every day….and what's this, I am smiling this very instant!

EPILOGUE

SINCE THAT GRADUATION there actually HAVE been times when I ventured back to Brighton District neighborhoods....Wilhelm reunions, and funerals come to mind. But those are rare moments.

I started by student teaching at Wilhelm, during the 1972-'73 school year, and finished with a five-year contract, as an early retiree, in 2005. Would I become a teacher again, if I was just starting out to find a permanent working livlihood? Good question.

Steve Lipinski, Jerry Hamilton and I are still very good friends, and I never would have met them without being in Brighton, so that was a definite 'positive' in my career.

It was economic change that FIRST brought about Brighton District's decay, as I remember it. From the mid-eighties onward, our district's money woes began multiplying. I was hearing more and more teachers complain about the lack of money available for 'required' materials, let alone available money to get supplemental materials. Several teachers, me included, began spending personal money to acquire extra items for the classroom. In my opinion, it absolutely was Brighton's financial struggle that dealt the FIRST devasting blow, causing the downword spiral of my beautiful district.

Discipline had ALSO become a definite problem by the mid-eighties'90's. Veteran teachers began feeling handicapped, by the new and refined rules, when trying to 'resolve' discipline problems. Students with poor attitudes, knowing that poor deportment had few severe consequences, began feeling emboldened to act out. According to some teachers I talked to, keeping control in the classroom was a REAL challenge, and TIME-consuming, too. Some of my colleagues felt like THEY were the ones being punished.

As for myself, I always felt comfortable in the classroom setting, and confident in my ability to control my students as well as depart the necessary information needed by students for them to be successful in an educated society. I was a paper and pencil guy, and that worked great for me. But, alas, modern technology was introduced and I felt technologically illiterate. KINDERGARTNERS, for crying out loud, could use computers better than I could. I knew my teaching days were numbered.

As if these challenges weren't daunting enough, rumors began spreading which threatened to tie student standardized test scores to teacher salaries. That was the last dagger to my spirit. People don't teach to become wealthy. What EVER were legislators, or whoever sponsored that ridiculous salary notion, thinking? Good teachers put in MORE than forty hours a week working with kids. Great teachers can put in 60-80 hours a week. For my first several years in the classroom, I remember dividing the salary I received by the hours I put into all aspects of my job, and MOST weeks I thought minimum wage looked good. Basing a teacher salary on student achievement was a terrible idea to me.

Each grade level has its own unique differences, but the fundamentals are the same....gain the respect of your students, teach what is necessary to be taught, and do what you know is right, and students on any grade level can be reached.

I taught 8th graders, one of the middle school years when a kid makes his/her transition from child to adult. Getting through that year may be the ultimate challenge any teacher has when trying to work with children. But, as each of MY teaching years ended, I was proud of the job I did, and absolutely confident in the fact that I helped mold caring, respectful, considerate, AND educated students....ready to undertake the rigors of high school. I wouldn't change THAT feeling for anything!